Archibald Constable

Bric-a-Brac Series

PERSONAL REMINISCENCES

BY

Archibald *Robert Pearse*
CONSTABLE AND GILLIES

EDITED BY

RICHARD HENRY STODDARD

NEW YORK
CHARLES SCRIBNER'S SONS
1887

Entered, according to Act of Congress, in the year 1875, by
SCRIBNER, ARMSTRONG, AND COMPANY,
In the Office of the Librarian of Congress, at Washington.

RIVERSIDE, CAMBRIDGE:
STEREOTYPED AND PRINTED BY
H. O. HOUGHTON AND COMPANY.

CONTENTS.

LIST OF PORTRAITS.

PREFACE.

IF cultivated readers are as much interested in authors as that special class of thinkers believe, the present volume will be welcomed, I am sure, as an addition to their literary enjoyment as well as literary knowledge. If my memory is not at fault, it deals more exclusively with men of letters than any in this series, particularly those of Scotland. With the exception of the greater names, they are not so widely known, I imagine, as their English brethren; at any rate the lesser ones are not. Perhaps they are underrated abroad, and overrated at home. This difference of valuation, if it exists, results, I suppose, from a sturdy belief in themselves, which is alike common to the English and Scotch. No great people was ever without it, perhaps no small one, for modesty in races is rather an acquired than inherited virtue. It is seldom practiced to excess; never, perhaps, where the English language is spoken. We, to be sure — but I must not digress. What I started to do was to indicate the kind of reading to be expected here, and to give a brief sketch of the two men from whose biographies it is taken. These are Archibald Constable and Robert Pearse Gillies. The memory of one was recently revived among English and Scotch readers by his son, Thomas Constable ("Archibald Constable and his Literary Correspondence," 3 vols. 8vo, Edinburgh, 1873); the memory of the other was freshened, perhaps, by his rambling autobiography ("Memoirs of a Literary Veteran," 3 vols. 12mo, London, 1851), but not for any time. The place of Constable is among great publishers; the place of Gillies is among obscure authors. They were contemporaries; they lived in the same city; they had the same friends, and they were unfortunate, — Constable the least so, in that he died when ruin overtook him, while Gillies lived in debt.

Archibald Constable was born at Carnbee, in Fifeshire, on the 24th of February, 1774. He received the ordinary education taught in the parochial school there, and though not more studious, perhaps, than his mates, was drawn to the profession which he afterwards adorned at an early age. A bookbinder removed from Edinburgh, and opened a shop as bookbinder, bookseller, stationer, etc., at Pittenweem. To this shop the boys from the neighboring country schools resorted on Saturday afternoons, for the purpose of supplying themselves with the stationery and the school-books required for their limited use, and suitable for their still more limited means. On returning home after one of these occasions, Archibald, a lad of twelve, expressed to his father his great anxiety to be employed by the Pittenweem bookseller, and to be bred a stationer. His father promised to consider the matter, and wrote to a correspondent in Edinburgh, an old apprentice of whom intended within a few months to open shop there, and who agreed to take Archibald as an apprentice, if, on seeing, he should approve of him. Seen and approved of, the boy was bound apprentice to this person, Mr. Peter Hill, in February, 1788. Mr. Hill's shop was soon frequented by the *literati*. Burns, when in town, was a constant visitor, as was also his fat friend the antiquary Grose. Archibald devoted his entire attention to learning the business he had chosen, attended book auctions, read catalogues, and embraced every opportunity of becoming acquainted with books. In the third or fourth year of his apprenticeship a collection of old books was offered to Mr. Hill in exchange for new publications, and Archibald obtained permission to catalogue them. The success of his catalogue induced Mr. Hill to allow him to collect books at auctions and elsewhere, a pursuit which he afterwards followed to his own advantage. His apprenticeship ended in 1794, and he soon afterwards married. His first step in business was a journey to London, where he informed himself concerning the state of business in the metropolis, and was introduced to the most eminent publishers of the time.

Returning to Edinburgh with the books that he had picked up in London, and in different parts of the country, the young stationer furnished a shop. To distinguish it from the circulating libraries by which it was surrounded, he inscribed over the door, " Scarce Old Books," which was quizzed by some of his neighbors into " Scarce o' Books," and published a sale catalogue, which made his name known to the buyers of old books. His business was confined to this department of trade, but it was not long before he determined to try his luck as a publisher. His earliest publications, which consisted of two or three pamphlets, involving but little outlay, were successful enough to justify him in embarking in larger ventures. His first book was an account of an insurrection in Grenada, written by one who had escaped from it, and it sold well. This was in 1795. The literary men of Edinburgh began to find their way to his shop, — among others, Francis Jeffrey and Walter Scott. The day of small beginnings was over in 1802, when he published the first number of the " Edinburgh Review," and put his name on the title-page of " The Minstrelsy of the Scottish Border," a share in the copyright of which he had purchased from the Longmans.

Constable's connection with Scott, which dates from this time, was a productive one, both in a literary and pecuniary sense. They may almost be said to have worked together, each was so active in the projection of new works. Scott was full of enterprises, which he executed rapidly, and for which Constable & Co. paid him royally, giving him for his next poem, " Marmion," the sum of one thousand guineas. It passed through eight editions in three years, the first being in quarto, at a guinea and a half a copy, and finally reached a sale of fifty thousand copies. Besides " Marmion," which came out in 1808, the house of Constable published for Scott in the same year, Autobiographic Memoirs of Captain George Carleton, and Memoirs of Robert Carey, Earl of Monmouth, and concluded an arrangement with him for the Life and Works of Jonathan Swift, for which they agreed to pay £1500. The fortunes of Scott and Constable were involved in the fortunes of the house of Ballantyne & Co., in which Scott had become a silent partner in 1805. The success of the firm was brilliant at first ; its typography was excellent, and the patronage secured for it by the influence of its unknown but unsleeping partner was extensive and commanding. Active and pushing as printers, the Ballantynes were not cautious as publishers, and the consequence was, that in a few years they were embarrassed, so much so that Scott determined to withdraw.

Negotiations were opened with Constable & Co., who consented to take a portion of the stock on hand, which consisted of the " Edinburgh Annual Register," Weber's " Beaumont and Fletcher," and an edition of De Foe's novels, besides the remainder of the edition of " Don Roderick," and a fourth of the remaining copyright of " Rokeby." Within a month after the arrangements had been completed with Constable, Scott was pressed for money to complete the purchase of an addition to his estate, and he offered him the copyright of an unwritten poem for £5000. The practical mind of Constable was of great assistance to Scott, for he not only gave him substantial aid, but opened negotiations in his behalf with certain London bankers, whereby the Ballantynes were enabled to tide over their difficulties, and keep afloat. It was a long story, but this was the substance of it. About this time, *i. e.* 1813, Scott looked into an old cabinet in scarch of some fishing-tackle, and his eye lighted upon a story which he had commenced at Ashestiel in 1805, and had thrown aside and forgotten. He read over the introductory chapters, thought they had been undervalued, and resolved to continue the story. It was a new departure, and the beginning of a new school of fiction, which has not yet ceased to delight the world. A portion of the first volume was shown to Constable, who at once detected the author, and offered £700 for the copyright. Scott declared that the sum was too great if the novel should prove unsuccessful, and too little in case it should succeed; so it was decided that author and publisher should equally divide the profits. The first edition of " Waverley " appeared anonymously on the 7th of July, 1814. It consisted of one thousand copies, which disappeared in five weeks after publication. It was followed by a second of two thousand copies ; a third and fourth, each of one thousand copies, appeared in October and November of the same year. "Waverley" was followed by "The Lord of the Isles," for which Scott received fifteen hundred guineas. The second novel by the author of "Waverley" (who could he be ?), "Guy Mannering," was published in London. Constable would willingly have published it, but there was a stumbling-block in his way in the shape of the dead stock of Ballantyne & Co., of which he had more than enough already. The battle of Waterloo, which was fought about this time, excited Scott so that he determined to visit the scene of that memorable conflict ; and, like the canny Scot that he was, he planned before leaving home a book that should not only pay the expenses of his journey, but add to his resources, which were as constantly diminishing as increasing. This was Paul's Letters to his Kinsfolk, of which Constable & Co. took one third of an edition of three thousand copies, the remainder being taken by Murray and the Longmans.

There was a mine of wealth in the Waverley novels, but Scott's connection with Ballantyne & Co., which still continued, and his passion for purchasing land, kept him in a state of embarrassment. He was perpetually discounting success. This unfortunate episode in his literary life is so well known through Lockhart's elaborate biography, that there is no occasion to dwell upon it here. Our business is with Constable, and his entanglement with the affairs of Scott. The next Waverley novel, "Tales of My Landlord," was published by Murray, and *not* as by "the author of 'Waverley.'" In the following year, 1817, Constable & Co. published the poem of "Harold, the Dauntless." Its success was not great, the unknown novelist having supplanted the known poet in public estimation. "Rob Roy" was published by Constable & Co. on the last day of 1817. Six months later came "The Heart of Mid-Lothian." In January, 1819, Constable made an arrangement by which all the copyrights of Scott's works then existing, with the exception of a fourth share of "Marmion," which was owned by Murray, were transferred to them at the price of £12,000. The list included "Waverley," "Guy Mannering," "The Antiquary," "Rob Roy," the three series of "Tales of My Landlord," "The Bridal of Triermain," "Harold the Dauntless," "Sir Tristram," "Paul's Letters," one edition of "The Lay of the Last Minstrel," and one half of "The Lady of the Lake," "Rokeby," and "The Lord of the Isles." These works must already have realized as much as the sum which Constable & Co. agreed to give for them. And yet Scott was in difficulties ! By his next four novels, "Ivanhoe," "The Abbot," "The Monastery," and "Kenilworth," the fruit of scarcely a twelve-month, he cleared at least £10,000, after which Constable & Co. purchased from him the remaining copyright for five thousand guineas. Nor was this all ; for, as Lockhart remarks, they had such faith in the prospective fertility of his imagination that they were by this time quite ready to sign bargains and grant bills for novels and romances to be produced hereafter, but of which the subjects and the names were alike unknown to them, and the man from whose pen they were to proceed. A year or two later Constable concluded another bargain for the purchase of Waverley copyrights acquiring the author's property in "The Pirate," "Nigel," "Peveril," and "Quentin Durward," out and out, at the price of five thousand guineas. He had thus paid, says Lockhart, for the copyright of novels (over and above the half profits of the early separate editions) the sum of £22,500; and his advances upon works of fiction still in embryo, amounted at this moment to £10,000 more. He began, in short, and the wonder is that he began so late, to suspect that the process of creation was moving too rapidly. There can be no doubt that such was the case, and that the process of publication also was moving too rapidly.

Constable's next enterprise was the publication of the Miscellany which bore his name, and which was to bring good reading within the reach of the poorer classes. The Waverley novels were published at a high price; could they not be circulated at a lower one, and without injury to the original editions? Constable was of the opinion that they could, but the London publishers, who had a large stock of unsold copies of the latter, — one house having £40,000 so invested, — were of the contrary opinion. The failure of Hunt, Robinson, & Co., the London agents of Constable & Co., precipitated the ruin of that house, and Scott was involved in it. How manfully and resolutely he set to work to extricate himself the readers of Lockhart's Life will remember; but for Constable there was no extrication, for though he continued his Miscellany, with reasonable hopes of success, the mine of wealth which had been opened by the magic pen of the author of Waverley, was now worked by his late partner Cadell for the benefit of himself and Scott's creditors. The end of Constable was at hand.

"The morning of the 21st of July, 1827," writes his son Thomas, "was spent by me in my father's sick-room. His interest in the welfare of his children was intense and unremitting; he had never spared expense in promoting our education, and was painfully anxious when any one of us suffered from illness that threatened serious consequences ; but it was only with the younger members of his family, or when an elder one was quite alone with him, that on ordinary occasions he allowed the deep tenderness of his feeling to find expression in words. I well remember that on this eventful day to him and to all of us, he was specially tender, and spoke to me from time to time in a more than usually loving manner.

"It happened that of all his family, on the morning in question, I was the only one at home. My younger brothers and sister had gone with their mother to seabathing quarters in the immediate neighborhood, and my elder sisters were also absent from Edinburgh. My brothers David and Henry had engaged to join us shortly after noon for an early dinner, but in the morning my father and I were for an hour or two alone together. As I sat reading near a window, he suddenly called me to him, and sent me to his private writing-table, minutely directing me where I should find a small box, which, when I brought to him, he opened with evident emotion, and took out a bunch of withered flowers. 'These,' he said after a time, 'are flowers I gathered at Polton for my beloved Catherine the morning that she left me ; Mary has told me that she had them beside her on her death-bed, and now they lie on mine.'

"After a time, when I had restored them to the drawer from which they had been taken, my father called me again to his bedside, and taking my hand, he said, 'Dear Tom, I leave you very poor ; had it pleased God to spare my life for a few years, it might have been otherwise ; but I trust that at least you will find the name you bear no disadvantage to you.' He spoke tenderly of rejoining

b

lost friends, and gave me many wise and loving counsels.

"The day wore on, my brothers joined us, and after
they and I had dined in an adjoining room, our father,
who had risen, and was seated in an easy chair, sent for
David, and had been conversing with him for some time
on subjects of interest to both, when Henry and I were
startled by a sound, which once heard can never be forgotten.

"We hastened to our father's room, and found him
supported in the arms of his son, with his head drooping
on his breast. Henry ran at once for medical assistance,
while, sinking on my knees, I looked up into the eyes
which to the last were fixed on mine. The summer sun
was shining brightly, but gloom fell suddenly upon my
spirit, and, for the first time in my life, I felt myself alone
in the world. My father had been far more to me than
until then I had realized."

Such, in brief, was the life of Archibald Constable,

"The great Napoleon of the realms of print,"

who died in the fifty-fourth year of his age.

Robert Pearse Gillies was born in 1788, where, he omits
to mention in his autobiography, but as his father died at
Arbooth, it is to be presumed that Arbooth was his birth-
place. He studied the classics with his tutor, Dr. Glennie,
and developed early a taste for reading and writing. His
first studies were devoted to magic and witchcraft, in
illustration of which he collected, when a boy, over one
hundred volumes in Latin, French, and Old English, em-
bracing the works of Baptista Porta, Cornelius Agrippa,
Kircher, and other authorities in the black art. Then
he turned his attention to theology, poring over musty

old folios and quartos, in which Protestant and Catholic divines set forth the merits of their respective faiths, each being convinced, as is the clerical fashion, of the perfection of his own. At the age of fifteen he began to write poetry, being led thereto by the perusal of Drake's "Literary Hours," an elegant but feeble volume of critical essays, of considerable repute seventy years ago. He translated into English verse Casimir Sobieski's "Ode to his Lyre," excelling, he believed, the version in Drake. Then he tried his hand at Horace's "Ode to Winter,"

> ("You see that now Soracte's height
> Is with the wintry snows grown white,")

and turned into heroic rhyme Virgil's first Eclogue, and the first book of the "Æneid." In his eighteenth year he went to Edinburgh in order to be matriculated at the University, and while there made the acquaintance of Dugald Stewart, Professor Playfair, and other notable men. His father dying in 1808, he was left his own master —

> "Lord of himself, that heritage of woe."

Gillies may be said to have commenced his literary career in 1809, when he contributed a series of sonnets to "The Poetical Register," and commenced a correspondence with Sir Egerton Brydges, which was printed in "The Ruminator." The subject of this correspondence was the advantages of retirement, and the disappointments of a fantastic hero as to his estimate of our wise and enlightened world. He was well known in Edinburgh, especially among the *literati* who frequented the publishing house of John Ballantyne & Co., where he used to have the first pick out of the fresh arrivals of old books, with the exception of those relating to witchcraft,

which were reserved for Scott. He contributed to the
poetical department of the " Edinburgh Annual Register," in the shape of an " Ode on the River Northesk."
It was followed by a copy of verses entitled " Glenfinlas,"
and a year later it suited the purposes of the publishers
that he should be credited as the author of Scott's " Bridal
of Triermain," which was published anonymously. He
met Scott daily at Ballantyne's and elsewhere, and received many invitations to dine with him, few of which
were accepted on account of ill health. In the summer
session of 1811 he prepared for examination before the
dean of faculty and his associates in the profound doctrines of the Corpus juris. It was a memorable year
for him, in that it affected his fates and fortunes ever afterwards. " One fine morning," he writes, " a near relative, in whose judgment I placed great confidence, addressed me in the following words : ' Money is wanted.
You are the only one now amongst us who has solid property to lean upon. The question is, will you now join in
a security for a few thousands, of which £500, if you require it, may be at your own command ? ' The question
seemed to me not to admit of doubt ; it was decided in
one instant. Not being in the least given to any speculation farther than that of purchasing old books and very
questionable old pictures, I rather wondered, it is true,
why so much hard cash was needed ; but my assent was
given instantly, after which no prudential arguments
would induce me to withdraw it. Every possible effort
for this purpose was made by a much nearer relation, who
pleaded that although I had never signed any bond, or
burdened the land with any debt, yet unluckily it was already burdened. I had in fact succeeded to an embarrassed property, and if this new debt were superadded to

the former, it would become next to impossible to borrow for my own purposes if I should ever have need to do so.

" Every such plea was parried by a home-thrust put in by a most amiable and kind-hearted lady. ' If relations won't help one another,' said she, ' who 's to help them ? ' So Messrs. Gibson, Christie, & Wardlaw received the requisite instructions on my part, the bonds were drawn, and next autumn I had the pleasure of a visit from a writer to his Majesty's signet, agent for the lenders, who was kind enough to take possession of my lands in their behalf ; a mere formality, as he observed, on which I then scarcely bestowed a second thought.

" The ground seemed as firm beneath my feet after the legal functionary went as before he came, but this firmness did not continue long. In 1815 the money was gone, the speculation had failed ; there was a sort of panic in the commercial world, and the lenders of course did most rigorously demand back their *argent comptant.* For their claim alone my poor acres were sold and sacrificed. No other claim was made or menaced, and the sacrifice therefore appeared to me both cruel and absurd. In equity and in truth, I was bound for only a third part of the sum ; but alas ! this plea availed me nothing. The aforesaid writer to the signet had done his duty ; the *entire* amount was charged on my property, the charge was publicly unregistered, consequently I was under the necessity to find an immediate customer for the whole security, or allow the tender mercy of the law to take its course. My joint cautioners had no lands to sacrifice ; the payments made by them did not take place before, but *after* the irrevocable break-up and downfall of my patrimonial rooftree ; and no sooner had I been dispossessed, than consolation was addressed to me in the shape of a long argumentative letter, showing how very beneficial and lucrative would be the investment of £10,000 out of my reversion money, in order to assist in another promising speculation upon a larger scale."

In 1813 Gillies assumed the gown and wig of an advocate, paying the sum of £360 for that honor, — an honor which he prized because it gave him access to an enormous store of books. His time when in town was principally spent in selecting rare volumes out of a large stock in the hands of Blackwood. His lodgings formed a convenient resting-place for Scott, during his daily walks from the Parliament House, and he often came to look at his acquisitions. He published at this period his poem of "Childe Alarique," an expansion of his correspondence with Sir Egerton Brydges, concerning which, and his literary patron, Byron wrote in his Diary, under the date of November 23, 1813 : "Redde the Ruminator, a collection of Essays, by a strange, but able, old man (Sir E. B.) and a half wild young one, author of a Poem on the Highlands, called 'Childe Alarique.' The word 'sensibility' (always my aversion) occurs a thousand times in these Essays ; and it seems to be an excuse for all kinds of discontent. The young man can know nothing of life ; and, if he cherishes the disposition which runs through his papers, will become useless, and, perhaps, not even a poet, which he seems determined to be. God help him ! No one should be a rhymer who could be anything else."

One of Gillies's correspondents was Wordsworth, to whom he sent some of his poems in manuscript, and who criticised them and his contemporaries with his accustomed independence. Among the poems so sent and criticised were "Egbert," "Exile," "The Visionary," and "Lucia Montalban." Wordsworth honored him with a

sonnet, in which he exhorted him to rise above his de-
jected moods, and which concluded with the following
couplet, —

> "A cheerful life is what the Muses love,
> A soaring spirit is their prime delight."

The loss of his property, which was sold at a sacrifice
in 1815, determined Gillies to settle in Edinburgh. His
means, had they been carefully husbanded, would still
have sufficed for his maintenance ; he had besides a
profession which would have yielded him something. It
was not to his taste, however, which is not to be wondered
at, seeing that three guineas was once his guerdon for ten
days' labor and much writing. He abandoned it, therefore, from the foolish notion that the same quantum of
time and thought which were needed to insure an income
of £400 or £500, would insure double that amount by
literature. He wrote many verses, he says, all bearing on
the favorite notion that there were two spheres, or worlds,
the influences of one being in fierce antagonism with
those of the other ; also, that the poet's happiness and
well-being depended mainly on the question, how much
time he could contrive to pass in the imaginary, to the
utter exclusion of the real, world. His productions may
have been vastly original, but they were queer and odd.
The best of them was a poem in four cantos, which was
entitled "Oswald," and was printed, though not published, in 1817. About this time Gillies began to grope
in the dark after foreign literature, having got the idea,
he knew not how, that the German language concealed an
inexhaustible mine of the richest ore. It was a novel
idea, for so little was then known of German literature,
both in England and Scotland, that it was thought it had
been well nigh exhausted by such prodigious efforts as

those of Holcroft, Monk Lewis, and Thompson. Vain at first was the quest of Gillies for German books and German professors. At last he discovered one author of the old school, Wieland, in twenty-five or thirty volumes, and two ancient professors, a Prussian Jew and a Frenchman, neither of whom understood the language he professed to teach. Finally there arrived at Edinburgh an impudent personage, who styled himself Baron Rabenstein of Rabenstein, dans le Carniolique (which might be freely translated Baron Gibbet, of Gibbet Manor), who, on the strength of having a mother who was a German, and being himself, as he said, a native of Spain, undertook to instruct him in Spanish and German, or any other European language that he might desire. Gillies had a copy of Schiller's " Glock," which the learned Baron could not translate intelligibly, on account of the wildness of German genius. He had also a copy of Calderon, who, according to the Baron, was a still wilder genius than Schiller. Ariosto was, if possible, wilder than either, for the professor could make nothing out of one of his stanzas, the purport of every syllable of which was plain to Gillies. Of course Baron Rabenstein soon disappeared from Edinburgh. A better teacher was at last found in the person of Dr. William Gardiner, who was a good French, German, and Italian scholar.

Gillies broke ground in foreign literature with a translation of Müller's " Schuld," which he entitled "Guilt, or the Anniversary," and which, as fast as it progressed, was printed in a small quarto by James Ballantyne. The success of this *brochure* was unexampled. Blackwood declared, before he saw it, that the idea of discovering an important novelty in German literature was a delusion. A review in " Blackwood's Magazine," of the translation (which was printed for private distribution only), with extracts and notes by Lockhart, changed his opinion, and put twenty guineas in the pocket of Gillies. Applications for the entire play came to Blackwood, and Mr. Harris, the manager of Covent Garden Theatre, asked the translator to adapt it to the English stage. Elliston, the manager of Drury Lane, made a similar request. The translation from Müller was followed by a series of miscellaneous translations, which were printed in " Blackwood " under the title of " Horæ Germanicæ," and " Horæ Danicæ," the series extending over seven or eight years. Complimentary letters flowed in upon Gillies as the series advanced ; chiefly, no doubt, because it was so new and unexpected. There were some clever bodies, however, who doubted the existence of the writers whom he professed to translate ; and when the name of Oehlenschlager first appeared, it was confidently decided that the Danish poet had merely the same sort of existence as Ensign and Adjutant Doherty, and that his excellent tragedies were original compositions by Prof. Wilson.

After a year's residence in Germany, where he met Müller, Tieck, and Goethe, Gillies returned and settled at Lasswade. His neighbors were William Tennant, orientalist and poet, author of " Anster Fair ; " Captain Hamilton, author of " Cyril Thornton ; " Patrick Fraser Tytler, the historian ; and, for a brief period, during his visit to Scotland, his corpulent Majesty George the Fourth. The panic of 1825, which affected all ranks and conditions, and was so disastrous to Constable and Scott, was not without effect upon his humble fortunes. He sought the advice of Scott, whom he found at the old house in Castle Street. The library, the scene of so many invocations to the Muses, was dismantled and abandoned. All that remained of its furniture was a cumbrous writing-table, at which the great magician sat and worked, under the shadow, so to speak, of a cast from the skull of Robert the Bruce, recently exhumed at Dunfermline. He was as kind and cordial to Gillies as in the days of his prosperity, giving him the best of advice, and, better still, offering him the use of Chiefswood. "The coal-cellar, I know, is well stocked for the winter ; the furniture will be enough for the wants of your family ; of the wine-cellar I need not boast, for you have your own bins of Hock and Rudisheimer. After arranging most of my year's accounts in advance, I have fifty pounds in my desk, ready to cover all your expenses of removal. One carrier's load, and your own carriage will, I suppose, do for all. My best advice, after matured reflection, is to retire with your books to Chiefswood, where, possibly, I shall not be the worst of neighbors ; and henceforward let us see what we can make of the world together." Gillies declined Scott's kind offer, unwisely it would seem, for he was constantly threatened both with loss of liberty and property ; he was again and again proclaimed a rebel, and Scott officially had occasion to sign the warrant for these proclamations. He had a wife and children to support, and it was certain that if the state of civil war between him and the law was kept up, that his means of providing for them would be annihilated. His income was consumed in law costs, his time was occupied in useless negotiations, and his property was by degrees frittered away. The fertile mind of Scott conceived the plan of a periodical, the specialty of which should be foreign literature. He suggested it to Gillies, who turned it over in his mind and resolved to attempt it. Scott gave him the use of his name as an intending contributor, along with the names of Sir William Hamilton,

De Quincey, and others. As there was no chance of such a periodical being successful in Edinburgh, Gillies went to London, where the project was favorably received. He removed his family thither, and without any money at his banker's, and without one remnant of property, assumed the editorship of a Quarterly Journal of Foreign Literature. Its success at the outset was greater than he could have anticipated. The publishers were bound to pay him by contract about £600 per annum, out of which he had to provide payments to authors. He never published an article, with the exception of the first, by Scott, for which the writer was not remunerated. By a special clause in the contract, the publishers and author were bound to renew it year after year so long as the work continued, so that he had it in his power, either by writing the whole himself, or obtaining gratuitous contributions from his friends, to pocket £600 per annum. He reckoned, however, that without such aid he might gain by it at least £200 yearly, and that by other work he might easily earn £800 more. He received compliments and congratulations from all quarters, and, if ready money failed, he had at all events complete credit.

The vague and unsatisfactory way in which Gillies writes of his London life does not enable us to trace his literary career in its details. On the whole, it was unsuccessful. He fell into difficulties, which were increased by the enormous cost of the proceedings against him. How he got into debt he does not tell us, — probably he did not know how, — enough that he *was* in debt, year after year, with no hope of extricating himself. A lover of peace and quiet, he gained the renown of being the most persevering and extravagant of spendthrifts, every attorney's bill being set down against him to the account of daily turtle, champagne, and a four-in-hand turn-out. Barring and bolting his hall-door, he intrusted his keys to a faithful old butler, who kept "watch and ward," and admitted no one that he did not reconnoitre and cross-question. Thus fortified, he stayed in-doors for months together, finishing some literary labor for which he was liberally paid. During these intervals, writs of execution collected and crowded together, and at last, after divers attempts, a bailiff obtained ingress (by means of a large hamper, duly ticketed, and borne by two porters), and he was taken to a spunging-house. During his absence on one of these occasions, his family, after having carefully guarded the gates of their castle on week days, thought they might be allowed to attend divine service, and did so. On their return they found that the walls and windows of the house had been crowded with placards of a sale, within a few days, of lease, furniture, books, and all other effects. Having obtained admittance to the apartments, where strangers were busied in making an inventory of goods and chattels, they were informed that if they offered any obstructions to such proceedings, the room doors would be locked against them.

After six years of this sort of life it seemed as if Gillies's personal embarrassments had been surmounted. His debt (exclusive of that to friends) had never risen in London to so much as £1000, and in 1833 the sum was reduced to a very trifling amount. He passed an entire year without being arrested. Then a dissolution of partnership of the house which published the "Foreign Quarterly Review," and the subsequent failure of the person who undertook to continue the business, and whose notes he had indorsed, was a signal for one of Gillies's creditors to come forward. Two other executions followed. His house was broken up and ransacked; the grates were torn out of the chimneys. The walls were almost pulled down. Books and manuscripts which had been exempted from the mortgage (on which, by the way, only £10 of interest were due) became objects of contention among the conflicting claimants. Bailiffs fought like demons, tearing the books and flinging them at one another's heads, trampling on them, and each party struggling to get them heaped and shoveled into carts like brickbats. Among the ruins, afterwards, the life of Werner, the poet, was discovered in the coal-cellar, and the only copy in existence of Gillies's "Winter Night's Dream" had been left in a back parlor, when the last vestige of it was a *fidibus* which had been used by a possession man! During the process of breaking up, the unfortunate master of the house could only visit it on Sunday, knowing that at any other time he would be liable to arrest. He wished to return to Brighton where his family were, but that was impracticable, as two bills of the insolvent firm had followed him, and were in the hands of a sheriff's officer, who kept strict watch for his arrest. The loan of £35 from an old friend enabled him to remove his family to London, where he subsided into the occupation of what he called a scrap-writer, which in those days was still profitable ; he produced divers stories, critical and miscellaneous essays, and wrote his recollections of Sir Walter Scott.

About Christmas Day, 1835, he was arrested for a balance still due to one of his old creditors, and the New Year dawned for him in the sheriff's prison, where he remained three months. It would be tedious to follow him through his many financial and legal misfortunes which at length stranded him and his family in the King's Bench. He found a fellow-sufferer there, an ex-magistrate, and the two resolved to make the most of their time in prison by exposing the system of abuses which confined them there, and which were a disgrace to the boasted civilization of England. They printed and circulated a series of pamphlets, which were not without weight, the last being an argumentative petition, which was presented in the House of Lords by the Marquis of Lansdown. Freed at last, Gillies lived eighteen months without molestation, though not without daily anxiety. In 1840, he removed with his family to Boulogne, where he devoted himself to literary pursuits, until the summer of 1847, when he returned to England, and was again thrown into prison. He migrated to the Queen's Bench, whence, in May, 1849, he was finally liberated. Of his subsequent life I know nothing. Indeed, it is with considerable difficulty that I have drawn the foregoing sketch of it, so rambling and evasive is his autobiography. His recollections of his contemporaries are clearer and more interesting than his recollections of himself. He had a strong inclination to literature, but was not, I conceive, a born author. His forte was translation, and not original writing.

Enough, however, by way of prologue. Shadows of Gillies and Constable, depart! Enter now, ye greater shadows, who called them — friends.   R. H. S.

ARCHIBALD CONSTABLE.

ARCHIBALD CONSTABLE.

THOMAS CAMPBELL.

ITH Thomas Campbell, who, before he had attained majority, had written his greatest poem, my father was for several years in close and familiar relation. Few of Campbell's letters to him appear to have been preserved, but some of these are of interest, and contain records of incidents and projects which have escaped the notice of his biographer. The earliest is dated November 3, 1802, and it runs thus : —

"DEAR SIR, — 'The rain it rains in Mirryland town,' as an old songster says, — and having caught a severe cold, I dare not expose myself to-day to bide the pelting of this pitiless storm — like old Lear — but propose to spend the day at home in fasting, meditation, and prayer. I trust that two refusals of a good dinner will not eject me from your dining-table to all eternity, for I live in hopes of another invitation, when I shall be able to venture abroad. With great sincerity, I am, etc. THOMAS CAMPBELL."

A week later Mr. Campbell writes as follows : —

"ALISON'S SQUARE, EDIN., *Nov.* 10, 1802.

"MY DEAR SIR, — The conversation between us this forenoon has led me to offer you the following proposal : —

"I should be willing to give you an account of my travels on the Continent for two or three years, provided my expenses were defrayed by Messrs. Longman and Rees, Manners and

3

Miller, and yourself; these expenses I estimate at the rate of £200 per annum. That I should execute such a work with all the industry which ought to be bestowed, I need hardly promise, as my name being affixed to the performance is a motive sufficient to deter me from negligence, and stimulate my efforts for obtaining applause. The public (were I so unprincipled as to furnish you with a useless book) would punish me with that contempt to which I hope I am hitherto a stranger.

"As to my ability for satisfying public curiosity, or supplying you with a splendid production, I cannot refer you to a certain test. I cannot promise that my *tour* will pass through so many editions as my poem, for nothing is more common than an author writing at one time a popular and at another time an unpopular work; but I will promise sincerely not to let the account of my travels be unworthy of public favor from any deficiency in materials that I can collect, or from carelessness in the style of its execution.

"My correspondents in Edinburgh and elsewhere can inform you how far my letters from Germany in 1800 and 1801 appeared to them the transcripts of a mind capable of observation and description.

"On my return from the Continent, and delivery of MSS., I should wish to stipulate for £200 besides my two years' salary.

"I have said I should propose to be absent two or three years. Now, I only mention the possibility of a three years' tour in the event of extending my travels to Turkey and Persia. You know my idea is to set out from Dantzic, and after traversing Poland, Hungary, Italy, and Spain, to return by way of France, Turkey, and Persia, not very practicable regions; and I must own, that until I get to the frontiers of Hungary, and reconnoitre the adjacent places, I shall not presume to think of treading on Mahometan ground; but I know your spirit of enterprise too well to suppose that you would recall me provided there were a probable chance of crossing the Black Sea and getting to Ispahan. Russia is a country which I detest, and I will not endeavor to get at Persia by trespassing on its boundaries. This proposal of the additional year being spent in such a glorious journey as one to the plains of Troy or to Ispahan, if it seem to you *outré*, need not interfere with our minor or more strictly rational scheme, although I confess that my heart beats high at the prospect, and I know that the strength of imagination excited by novelties so far from the beaten track would more than compensate the expense and hazard of such a journey.

"Be pleased to communicate with your friends upon the above subjects, and give me your ideas in return. I am, etc.,

"THOS. CAMPBELL."

Mr. Campbell's plan was favorably entertained by all the parties to whom it was now made known, for on February 9, 1803, he addressed them in the following terms : —

"EDINBURGH, *February 9th*, 1803

"To Messrs. Manners and Miller, and Mr. Archibald Constable, booksellers in Edinburgh, for themselves, and for Messrs. Longman and Rees, booksellers, London, jointly and severally : —

"GENTLEMEN, — Let it be understood as a bargain finally concluded between us, that I shall give you the perpetual copyright of my travels upon the Continent, upon which I am now to set out. The time which I mean to occupy in accomplishing these travels is two years, unless I extend them beyond the boundaries of Christian Europe, in which case I shall require three years upon the same terms as I shall just now mention to be made regarding the two years. That is, to be furnished with £200 sterling during each year of my absence, and a bonus of an additional £200 on my return home, and delivery of the entire manuscript.

"What countries I shall visit during my two years' absence you very properly have left to my own discretion. My own character as a literary man being staked in this adventure, I think it is needless for me to proffer any promise that the notes I am to take in the course of my peregrinations shall be

collected into a book as well written as it is in my power to
execute.

" With regard to the conditional third year, I shall be more
explicit in my promise, and shall give you my word of honor
that the countries I visit beyond the limits of civilized Europe
shall be as faithfully, carefully, and well described as my
powers of observation and description extend, and that my
most particular exertions shall be used to make up to you the
difference of an additional year's supply by the novelty of that
tract of country which I explore.

" The size of the book is to be two vols. 4to, or four 8vo.

" The procuring of landscapes or the few drawings necessary for the work is to be defrayed by you. I am, etc.,

" THOMAS CAMPBELL.

" P. S. — At the end of two years from my first draft upon
you, I promise to furnish you with materials for two vols. 8vo,
or one 4to, ready to go to press.

" I shall draw upon you in general pretty early from the
commencement of each year of my travels.

" THOS. CAMPBELL."

The only notice of this project in Dr. Beattie's memoir of
the poet is as follows : " Before leaving Edinburgh (February, 1803) he appears to have entered into some arrangement
with Mr. Constable, and agreed to furnish him with a book of
travels. On the faith of this, Campbell received an advance
of money, but as no travels were ever forthcoming, it was repaid with interest."

At page 331 of the first volume of Beattie's memoir, Campbell tells of an accusation against him in the public papers,
that he *falsely* claimed to be the author of the " Exile of Erin,"
one of the most exquisite of his minor poems. It was ascribed in a provincial Irish newspaper to a Mr. Nugent, whose
sister declared that she had seen it in her brother's handwriting at a date earlier than its possible composition by Campbell.

Ridiculous as this accusation must appear to those who appreciate the genius of Campbell, his own sensitive mind, we are told, was for a time deeply hurt by the impeachment. Were additional evidence required, however, I have been interested to find it in my possession. Among my father's relics of the poet is an 8vo scrap of writing-paper, with several stanzas upon it in his handwriting, which, from the corrections they bear, are evidently embryo of poems. The earliest of these is doubtless the first idea of the " Exile of Erin : " —

1   2   3   4   5   6
" There came | to the | beach a | poor ex | ile of | Erin,
    The dew on his thin robe was heavy and chill,
    For his country he sighed
    ~~As he wander'd along~~ ʌ when at twilight repairing
    To wander alone by the wind-beaten hill."

The second stanza is the following : —

2   3   4
" While wan | d'ring a | lone 'mid | thy ever | green hills
    And thy heath-covered mountains, old Scotia, I roam,
    Then sad recollection my bosom may thrill,
    And awake the sad thought of soon leaving my home."

The careful scansion of the first line in each of these stanzas is characteristic of the writer ; and we have in them perhaps the original suggestion of poems which, when elaborated, silenced alike the critic and the grammarian.

The filial loyalty of Campbell receives frequent illustration in his intercourse with my father, to whose ready help he evidently trusted, when needed, for the payment of his mother's allowance. On the 10th September, 1804, exactly a year after the marriage of the poet, correspondence was resumed in relation to " Specimens of the British Poets," a project he had laid verbally before his publisher. My father writes as follows : —

               " LONDON COFFEE-HOUSE, *Sept.* 10, 1804.

" MY DEAR SIR, — I write you a few lines to say that you shall have £500 for the Collection of Poetry you talked of the other morning : and I will trouble you to put the outline or sketch of the plan in writing before I have the pleasure of seeing you on Wednesday morning. With best wishes to Mrs. Campbell, I remain, etc.,   ARCHIBALD CONSTABLE."

On the same day Mr. Campbell wrote to my father : —

"*September* 10, 1804.

"MY DEAR SIR, — I have been recollecting since we parted that at the time you inform my mother respecting the addition to her annuity, you had better not direct her to apply to you in the first instance, but only in case of any demurrage on the part of Mr. Doig, which however I do not expect. Mr. Doig will have his MS. in a few weeks, and then I think there is no chance of the old lady being turned back. You will have the goodness therefore to say to her, that within two months she will receive £25 from Mundell's house. In case of disappointment she knows what to do ; but, as you observe, I think it more like justice to make that house pay for what is written, than you to advance money for what is in the womb. Wishing you all good luck, I am, etc.,   THOS. CAMPBELL."

I have pleasure in quoting the above letter, not only as showing Campbell's anxiety for his mother's comfort, but his confidence in my father's liberality, which, indeed, in spite of their subsequent literary separation, appears to have remained unshaken. Whether he had just cause to complain of Mr. Doig I shall not venture to decide, for if publishers are not always liberal, the reasonableness of authors may also occasionally be questioned ; certain it is, that while Campbell is always loud in commendation of Mr. Mundell, he never has a good word for his partner.

Two months later he writes to my father from Upper Eaton Street, Pimlico : —

"*November* 10, 1804.

"MY DEAR SIR, — I have again to let you know a little more of my private history, that by laying the state of things more clearly before you, I may have the better right to your advice and assistance.

"I have been engaged, since we parted, one half of the day canvassing for the Popular Compilation which we agreed upon, and the other at the business for Doig, of which you saw the unfinished MS.[1] You will think it a bad proof of my industry

---

[1] *History of England, a Sequel to Smollett.* See Beattie's *Memoir*, vol. ii. p. 18.

that I have not yet got through it ; but I have the testimony of my own conscience and my wearied back to witness that I have not been remiss, and yet this laborious operation is not yet concluded. Several unfortunate interruptions have indeed occurred. I am now within a few months of the Peace of Amiens, at which I think the narrative ought to close. When that unhappy peace is patched up, I must undergo the labor of overhauling the whole, and then I shall be at liberty to pursue a more congenial task.

"In these circumstances I find myself obliged to remove a few months sooner than I expected to a new house, of which I have taken a lease for twenty-one years. The trouble of this migration is very serious. I have spent as much time as might have served to build a house in superintending repairs, measuring fixtures, inspecting furniture, and covenanting with my attorney and landlord. The job is not yet over ; it will be three weeks before I can fairly settle myself.

"You will perceive from what I have stated that I am exposed to all the expenses of an unestablished and preparatory state, and still unable to draw upon Doig. Had I but a week or two longer, I should send him his MS. with a demand, but as the case stands, I can fasten to no industry till the moving be over and everything settled about me. The season will not admit of delay. I have seven miles to go (to Sydenham), and I should be afraid of travelling with my furniture in frost and snow. I have ventured, on the faith of your support, to purchase the fixtures of a very excellent house, and about £100 worth of furniture, which, being sold along with the fixtures, I get at broker's appraisement, *i. e.* half of prime cost. This furniture I should be obliged, one day or other, to get, and having an opportunity of getting it so cheap, I thought it would have been folly to have let the occasion pass. Now, finding by this establishment that I should incur an expense of about £200, I applied to Mr. Hood on the one side, and must now rely on your house on the other, for enabling me to bear the cost. It is a great demand to ask of you £100 by the lump, but Mr. Hood has arranged matters so that the mode of raising it will be as convenient as possible, and I trust the time of the year, inconvenient as it is for money payments, will not be a troublesome obstacle. I cannot describe to you how much comfort I should feel if I were fairly settled. I am at present extremely harassed in my mind, for the business of house-taking and furnishing is rather new to me, and I must confess the necessity of even availing myself of your liberal offers in the way of assistance gives me a good deal of pain. It is not the distrust of your friendship, but the fear of being unseasonable in this request at a time of the year when money is most difficult to be got.

" Of this, however, I can assure you, that both the necessity I describe is urgent, and the *absolute* necessity of being set down comfortably is such as I feel it more and more every day. As a friend, I think you will be rather pleased than surprised that I take the bold measure of launching to this amount for the purpose of domestic comfort. If you come to London and drink to the health of Auld Reekie over my new mahogany table — if you take a walk round my garden and see my braw house, my court-yard, hens, geese, and turkeys, or view the lovely country in my neighborhood, you will think this fixture and furniture money well bestowed. I shall indeed be nobly settled, and the devil is in it if I don't work as nobly for it.

" I think this is but a fair promise to you. As soon as Mr. Doig's MS. arrives, I shall hand over out of what he owes me all that I shall have drawn from you. And thus, when our Collection comes out, I shall have the old sonsy sum total to comfort me. This is the least thing I can do, and I have no doubt but the punctuality of Mundell's house will not leave the payment long unsettled. At all events, from the date of the MS. arriving, they become to the amount of whatever you please out of the £300, *your debtors and not mine.*

" I am extremely glad that Hood communicated to you and is to share with you the other business. I have a thousand times wished myself rather in Edinburgh than London, that we might have the benefit of confidentially talking over every project that seems feasible, just as it occurs to either of us. Without such confidential vicinity and speaking face to face, I assure you it is difficult to make any proposal of a literary nature. I felt it so in the case of the above affair. That disadvantage we must endeavor to obviate by correspondence. I shall always endeavor, therefore, to consider you as at my elbow, and without reserve open my mind to you on any project or subject that may promise to combine our mutual interests. I have one favor to ask, which, perhaps, none of your literary correspondents have presumed upon. You must regard me so much in the light of a friend as to be writing (although upon business) exclusively to yourself. I will take this as a very particular favor. A thousand things which I could say to you in the confidence of no one seeing my letter but yourself, would be checked by the embarrassment of conceiving that the forms of business require transcription even of a letter on business. I have drawn you thus through a long, miserable scroll, which comes from a brain oppressed and stupefied with fatigue of travelling, and communing with a pack of brokers, bricklayers, and attorneys. Before I close I must beg the favor of knowing from you (if you know yourself) how soon Mr. Doig is to be in London. I wish particularly to know. And now your most troublesome correspondent must wish you a good night, health, wealth (that of all things), and happiness. Yours, etc., THOMAS CAMPBELL."

Before the date of Mr. Campbell's next letter, March 10, 1805, he appears to have acquired a right to remuneration on account of his historical labors, but he found it necessary again to have recourse to my father : —

"SYDENHAM, *March* 10, 1805.

" MY DEAR SIR, — Having written to Mr. Doig for an advance of money now due to me, he says he will speak to you about discounting a draft for me. I hope you will do me the justice to believe that this application comes to you, not from my wish to burden your good-will, but from Mr. D.'s house being unfortunately unable to succor me, now that I have

certainly a fair claim to prefer for ready money. I do not wish
to say of that house anything that I should be unwilling to tell
them openly ; but I think it hard that after toiling eight
months I should be now obliged to solicit my friends to discount a bill. Really, when people become publishers they
should possess a better capital than this proceeding bespeaks.
It is a strange contrast to the offer which was made me when
I sealed the last agreement with two gentlemen in the Poultry,[1] — an instance of liberality which, if I had but ten facts
in the history of what I have met with in life to tell my biographer, I should leave on record as a proof that the best patrons of literature are the *enlightened part* of your profession.[2]

" I am brought by alluding to that agreement, of which the
recollection has always impressed me with a strong confidence
in your power to promote the cause of literature by undertakings at once sagacious and bold, to mention an occurrence
which it is necessary you should know, and respecting which,
if you have a leisure hour, I should like to have your observations.

" It was always an object with me to keep the Musa Britan-
nica a secret, in case our compilation should be anticipated.
It was a matter, however, of still more importance to attempt
the raising of the clans of literature in my favor. I spoke to
all the best literary men of my acquaintance ; told them my
plan, and was promised by one and all most cordial support
and assistance. Among these was the celebrated Sharpe,
who is the tongue of taste wherever he goes. I thought him
the most prudent of all my friends ; but owing to a wretched
misapprehension, viz. that Longman and Rees were the pat-

---

[1] Messrs. Vernor and Hood.

[2] " *Verbum sapienti* — they are the greatest ravens on earth with whom we have
to deal — liberal enough as booksellers go — but still, you know, ravens, croakers,
suckers of innocent blood and living men's brains. As to terms, it is of consequence
to the general cause of letters, that neither journeymen like myself, nor masters —
independent artists like you, should be overreached in their transactions. C. is a
deep draw-well. I was really duped by him. It is not two months since he made
me absolutely believe he had not been meant by nature for a bookseller. But, God
knows, he is not the worst of the bunch." — *Life of Campbell,* vol. ii. pp. 52, 54,
June 3, 1805.

rons of the collection, he blabbed it to them. It was the most unlike Sharpe of all men on earth to be so unguarded.

"Longman, Hurst, Orme, and Rees, accordingly, as soon as they had an opportunity, asked me, Was so-and-so the case ? I was so situated that evasion would have made the matter worse. I was a little vexed at the disclosure, but on recollecting that you had said you meant to give the trade an interest in the work, and conceiving the best way, if I spoke about it at all, was not to speak sneakingly, I burst on them at once with a full description of the great nature of the work and the assistance I had in view to call in. I saw that their idea of the probable success of the work was as sanguine as my own ; and when they expressed a feeling of impatience that they had not been consulted, I said that until I had secured certain literary aids and matured the plan of the work, the publishers and myself had not intended to speak to them ; but our delay was only owing to the immaturity of the design, and I added that I knew the gentlemen whose enterprise was likely to be the great support of the work had never intended otherwise than to offer them a share in it.

"Have I done wrong in so doing ? The moment I found the secret thus unfortunately blabbed by Sharpe, I thought mystery was to be avoided. I think the best way is to take them into the whole affair ; to give them a share with Mr. Hood's permission. What alarmed me a little was their hint at some work (I believe a prose work by Southey) which ours might interfere with. I believe, however, that our plan would be more agreeable to them, and would effectually neutralize them from anything of Southey's — a man whose taste they have found by experience and unsalableness to be unclassical. I see that they evidently desire an union with us, and I must own that little as I think of the literary fags whom they have in employ, yet, as booksellers, I should fear their hostility and court their alliance. It is the more desirable, as they are eager and enthusiastic in their idea of the success of a work of selection on this plan in prose as well as poetry. I shall not see you relinquish to them any share of this work without endeavoring to secure a counterpart relinquishment on theirs of something else.

"If you have a moment's leisure I shall be much obliged to you to give me your sentiments on this occurrence. I am, etc., THOS. CAMPBELL."

On 1st of May Mr. Campbell writes as follows : —

"DEAR SIR, — I shall be particularly obliged to you to advance my mother £15 for a quarter payment of her annuity. I am sorry to trouble you with this request, but I make it at present from unavoidable circumstances.

"My compilation is now so far advanced that I think you may advertise it when you think proper. I await your directions in concert with Mr. Hood respecting the place of printing it. I have spared neither pains nor consultation in bringing it this length, and I trust it will turn out a permanently valuable speculation. With compliments to all our common friends, I am, etc., THOS. CAMPBELL."

Mr. Lockhart, in his Life of Scott, quotes a letter from Sir Walter to James Ballantyne, dated April 12, 1805, in which occurs the following passage : "I have imagined a very superb work. What think you of a complete edition of British Poets, ancient and modern ? Johnson's is imperfect and out of print ; so is Bell's, which is a Liliputian thing ; and Anderson's, the most complete in point of number, is most contemptible in execution, both of the editor and printer. There is a scheme for you ! "

The biographer adds : "The design ultimately fell to the ground, in consequence of the booksellers refusing to admit certain works which both Scott and Campbell insisted upon. Such, and from analogous causes, has been the fate of various similar schemes both before and since. But the public had no trivial compensation upon the present occasion, since the failure of the original project led Mr. Campbell to prepare for the press those 'Specimens of English Poetry' which he illustrated with sketches of biography and critical essays, alike honorable to his learning and taste."

Mr. Lockhart was mistaken in attributing Mr. Campbell's project of the "Specimens of English Poetry" to this cause, seeing that it was proposed by him to my father in September, 1804, and intimated to Sir Walter in a letter dated March 27, 1805, a fortnight earlier than that from Scott to Ballantyne above quoted. The work was indeed already in progress, and in a letter of April 10 Campbell writes to Scott : " On Constable and Co. I am drawing and have drawn liberally for the compilation, on which I subsist at present with comfort. Constable's conduct to me has been very friendly." It would rather appear that the work contemplated by Walter Scott had been suggested by Mr. Campbell's letter.

On the 4th November, 1806, Campbell writes to Scott : " A very excellent and gentleman-like man — albeit a bookseller — Murray of Fleet Street — is willing to give for our joint Lives of the Poets, on the plan we proposed to the trade a twelvemonth ago, a thousand pounds." After mature consideration Scott decided to withhold his assistance.

On the 18th November, 1806, my father writes to Mr. Murray : " We have lately had a long conversation with Mr. Walter Scott on a variety of topics, but particularly about an edition of the British Poets, respecting which he has had a letter from Mr. Campbell, with whom he proposes being connected in the undertaking. The terms, £500 to each for writing Lives, etc., is certainly not too much ; but is there really room for such a work ? Twelve or thirteen volumes royal 8vo is a serious concern. In what size are the London booksellers printing Johnson's Collection ? Who are the people with whom you would propose to coöperate to hold shares ? We should like to hear from you very fully on this subject, and we shall turn it over in our own minds in the mean time, and be prepared by and by to say decisively what we would recommend to be done."

Mr. Murray's reply to the above, unfortunately, I do not find, but that its tenor was discouraging may be gathered from the following extract of a letter from my father : —

" *Dec. 9th*, 1806. —We were particularly obliged by your very full and interesting disclosure of the plan of the 'Corpus Poetarum,' which, though we are not remarkable for want of *spunk*, we confess alarmed us a little ; but we consider the plan as now at rest. Mr. Scott communicated to us his letter to Mr. Campbell, which you saw ; and since receiving Mr. Campbell's reply, and conversing with us more fully on the subject, he has sent him a letter declining the concern, but mentioning at the same time his intention, at some future period, to write the lives of certain of the English poets, — a task for which he is most admirably calculated. Mr. C. will no doubt show you Mr. Scott's letters ; and as to Mr. S.'s own plan, it will keep cool, and can be talked over next time you visit Edinburgh. Lives of poets as a separate publication would do well ; but we suspect Mr. S. would prefer editing the works of certain favorite authors. In the mean time he has enough on hand — Dryden, Strutt, and the Sadler Papers."

To this Mr. Murray replies on the 19th December: "We have managed well with the 'Corpus Poetarum.' I saw Campbell two days ago, and he told me that Mr. Scott had declined, and modestly asked if it would do by *himself* alone ; but this *I* declined in a way that did not leave us the less friends."

From one cause or other Mr. Campbell's compilation lay long upon the anvil. On January 13, 1809, he writes to Henry Cockburn : "I received from Constable the most warm assurances of the strongest personal regard ; and now that I only solicit justice, and a plain single answer to my repeated letters, he refuses all answer and all explanation. My single question is, Does he choose the work to proceed ? It is desperately hard that I cannot get this question answered." Of my father's silence I can offer no explanation, except that he had perhaps lost temper at the delay ; but he seems at once, on the intervention of Mr. Cockburn, to have offered to release the poet from his engagement.

Among the following letters of Mr. Campbell to my father are those which unhappily remained unanswered : —

"My dear Sir, — Having now arrived at the Index of our Collection, and feeling pretty well satisfied that we shall furnish the public with the best selection of poetry in the English language, I am anxious that you should settle where it is to be printed, as I think to have it out before winter. We must now be setting to work. I should be greatly obliged to you, therefore, to make that adjustment a part of your earliest correspondence with Mr. Hood.

"I have to solicit, what I hope you will admit from your usual friendship and respect for the purpose for which I am obliged again to trouble you — my mother's fourth quarter of the annuity, commencing from your first delivery to her. It is £15. This will amount to £60 which *she* has received from you, independent of the other remittance. I shall be extremely obliged to you if you can favor me in this request, and remain, my dear sir, with sincere esteem, yours,

"Thos. Campbell."

"Sydenham, *August* 20, 1808.

"My dear Friend, — Since our meeting in London I have kept in view the new position which I am much happier to think upon reflection our Poetical Collection is to assume. I am convinced that although a simple collection with occasional notes would have answered, that with regular notices of criticism and biography it will answer a great deal better. I have written a good many of those prefaces, and I am well pleased with the way they read. I have read them to several of my friends, and their opinion is also favorable.

"But to complete this new form of the work, I find that the books which would be sufficient for a compilation will not help me through the biographical notices. I have applied for access to several libraries, and as far as public libraries will do, I am at no loss. But I find it impossible, without having some book occasionally beside me, to make any progress, and those libraries (such as the British Museum, etc.) do not permit any book to be given away one day.

" In this emergency I must rely on your goodness to assist me. If you will only recommend me strongly to any bookseller, your correspondent in London, who will with a good will assist me occasionally to get access to a book, the work will prosper to our most sanguine wishes, and you shall have my thanks as well as, I trust, the remuneration of a respectable book. Depend on my word, that I shall not abuse any liberty you may give me of getting a book borrowed on your authority. I shall be answerable for the prompt return of every one of them in a safe *state*, which may be given me in consequence of this solicitation.

" Hood, you know, is not concerned in this affair ; at least I suppose he made that arrangement with you, so that I cannot apply to him. I assure you, my dear sir, it is no idle curiosity to look at new books, but a real zeal for my own reputation as connected with the work that prompts me to request this favor. An answer when you first find convenient will oblige in no ordinary degree, your sincere and affectionate friend, Thos. Campbell.

" Compts. to Ballantyne.

" P. S. — I expect to have the whole done next winter, and be among you to set B. at it like the devil."

" Sydenham, *November* 27, 1808.

" My dear Sir, — Knowing the variety and importance of your avocations, I forebore to trouble you again on the subject of our compilation, but now so much time has elapsed that I cannot but suppose my letter has escaped your memory.

" I hear reports of your being expected in town, and of your house in London being established, but having no distinct idea when either of these events is to take place, I think it better to request a few lines from you in the mean time, than to wait the indefinite time of your arrival. My request when I last wrote you was to have an introduction to some house in London who would supply me with a few books requisite for the biographical part of the compilation, — it is but a few I shall need, but those few are indispensable. If it be not convenient to grant me that advantage, I must redouble my efforts to obtain such aid from a different quarter ; but if that be the case, I should really take it kind to let me know it. I have made use of all the books I had access to in finishing the work according to our new arrangement, but I have still a good deal to do, and from my letter being unanswered, I am at a loss how to proceed.

" If anything new has occurred to you on the subject of the speculation, it would be better to communicate it now than to delay. The points with which I alone wish to trouble you, are merely to let me know whether it will be convenient for you to further my progress in the work in the way I have requested, and if so, when in the course of the winter I may expect the favor of that advantage.

"An answer, my dear sir, will be a most particular obligation to yours very sincerely and respectfully,

"THOS. CAMPBELL."

The following letter is undated : —

"DEAR SIR, — Apprehensive from your silence towards my two last letters that your time is too much engrossed to take notice of them, I have taken the liberty of troubling Mr. Jeffrey with the delivery of this, and at the same time must beg your excuse for requesting a verbal communication to him on the subject of the Poetical Compilation. I am really very anxious to know your sentiments on that subject. Previous to our meeting in summer, and long previous to it, I had spent a very considerable space of time in the sole employment of reading and selecting from every poet in the English language worth reading or selecting from. From Mr. Hood's wishing to resign the speculation, however, and from the consciousness that the announce of my readiness to set the press agoing was not given within the legal time, I left the affair to your own sound decision and choice, and at our parting interview was happy to find that along with the addition of biographical and critical sketches, the reading I had spent would not be lost, but the book go on. I exhausted all the books within my reach in

4

adding to my biographical notes, and have only waited for your further aid to get as soon as possible ready for press.

"If you wish me to go on it will particularly oblige me if you will attend to my request. If you do not like the speculation, still it will put an end to my suspense to know your wishes. In either case I shall be much obliged to you for a communication through our common friend Mr. Jeffrey. I remain, my dear sir, yours very sincerely,

"THOS. CAMPBELL."

Campbell, according to his biographer, now set to work in right earnest ; and although often interrupted in his task by other demands on his time and pen, made gradual progress in the "Selections" which bear his name. Slowly gradual the progress must have been, for on April 26, 1810, Mr. Murray writes to my father : "I shall send you in a few days a printed advertisement of Campbell's work, which is nearly ready for press : he has completed the Lives, and all is just finished. When you receive this I will beg the favor of your candid opinion, and whether or not — supposing it to be actually done, and if you please, actually *printed*, so that there can be no trouble with the editor — you will take half with me." Again, in November, 1811, Mr. Murray writes : "Miller, with Davies and Baldwin, are to join me in Campbell's 'Lives of the Poets,' which will form three volumes crown 8vo, printed uniformly with Ellis's 'Specimens.' Campbell has exerted all his talent, and a very great share of industry, and it will make an interesting work. The 'Life of Burns' is very beautiful. We go to press in the summer, and intend to publish in January, 1813. It is unnecessary to say that if you feel any disposition to join us, you may have a fifth, a tenth, or any share you like." The work did not appear till 1817, by which time the patience of author and publisher must have been alike exhausted.

JOHN LEYDEN.

The interesting account of Leyden in the "Edinburgh Annual Register" for 1811 is now accessible to all in the Miscellaneous Prose Works of Sir Walter Scott; and the Memoir by the Rev. James Morton, prefixed to the "Poetical Remains," may be known to many readers; but the life and character of such a man may with advantage be reconsidered, and I shall here recapitulate a few of the leading features in his brief and bright career.

He was born on the 8th September, 1775, in Teviotdale, whose charms he has made known and endeared as only a true poet can. It was there that his infancy and early youth were passed, in humblest outward circumstances, but with the inestimable advantage of judicious love and care, for his parents were pious and intelligent. In evidence of the unselfish nature of his father, it may here be mentioned, that in the year 1817, when informed by Sir John Malcolm that a selection from the writings of his son was about to be published for his benefit, he said, "The money you speak of would be a great comfort to me in my old age, but, thanks to the Almighty, I have good health, and can still earn my livelihood. I pray you, therefore, to publish nothing that is not for my son's good fame."

Leyden, the first-born of four sons and two daughters, was nine years of age before he was sent to school, where he began to learn writing, arithmetic, and the rudiments of Latin grammar. But the previous years had not been unemployed or barren. His grandmother, a willing and competent instructress, had taught him to read the Bible, which he held in life-long reverence, and whose historical passages first caught and fixed his attention. On the shelves of neighboring cottages he found some works of Scottish history, a translation of Homer, Sir David Lindsay's poetry, and Milton's "Paradise Lost."

Sir Walter tells us also of a copy of the "Arabian Nights" which Leyden discovered in the possession of a blacksmith's apprentice, and that, proud-spirited though he was, he pursued its owner from place to place in the severest winter weather, until, like the petitioner of the unjust judge, by continual coming he had so wearied him, that for the sake of peace the treasure was yielded up. The charm that Oriental literature had for Leyden in after life, and his love of the marvelous at home and abroad, may perhaps, in a measure, be traced to the coveted volume thus acquired; and in his Journal of 1805, when sailing in the Indian seas, he quotes King *Mehrage* of " Sindbad the Sailor " as a prototype of the *Maha Rajahs* of more modern times.

No sacrifice was too great for Leyden when demanded by the love of knowledge. He would have subjected himself at any period to the utmost privations to purchase such books as were not otherwise to be procured ; and sensitive as he was to ridicule, especially in youth, and unwilling to be seen by his companions riding on a donkey which his father had bought to carry him in severe weather to and from school, so soon as he found that a copy of " Calepini Dictionarium Octolingue" was to be included in the bargain, he at once dropped all objection, and thankfully accepted the obnoxious quadruped, prepared to surmount the *pons asinorum*, or any other kindred erection with which the learned have sought at once to illustrate and bridge over the rudiments of science.

It was in November, 1790, that Leyden left home to enter the Edinburgh University, escorted half-way by his father, but with no other companion during the remainder of his journey than his " obsequious " shadow.[1] His ultimate destination being the Church of Scotland, his college studies during the first term were exclusively devoted to Latin and Greek, but his appetite for knowledge being omnivorous, dur-

---

[1] " Once more, inconstant shadow ! by my side
I see thee stalk with vast gigantic stride;
Pause when I stop, and where I careless bend
My steps, obsequiously their course attend :
So faithless friends, that leave the wretch to mourn,
Still with the sunshine of his days return."
Scenes of Infancy, Part IV.

ing the succeeding years of his career there were few subjects taught in either of the Faculties which did not to some extent engage his attention. His talent for languages, and ardor in acquiring them, was only equaled by that of his friend and contemporary, Alexander Murray; and before his college course was ended, he had made himself master of German, French, Spanish, Italian, Icelandic, Hebrew, Arabic, and Persian. When some one objected to the miscellaneous nature of his studies, he said, " Dash it, man ! never mind ; if you have the scaffolding ready you can run up the masonry when you please."

It was during his university career that Leyden won the friendship of Francis Horner, Brougham, William Erskine,[1] Dr. Thomas Brown, and many other distinguished students of that day. By the recommendation of Professor Dalzel, he became in 1796 tutor to the sons of Mr. Campbell of Fairfield, in whose family, Sir Walter tells us, he was treated with that respect and kindness which every careful father will pay to him whose lessons he expects his children to receive with attention and advantage. Leyden's manners in society were not such as to produce at first a favorable impression ; but Scott, who knew him well, says that " the apparent harshness of his address covered a fund of real affection to his friends, and kindness to all with whom he mingled. To gratify the slightest wish of a friend he would engage at once in the most toilsome and difficult researches." Sir John Malcolm tells us his " temper was mild and generous, and he could bear with perfect good humor railing on his foibles."

In 1800 Leyden was ordained, and preached thereafter occasionally in the churches of Edinburgh and the neighborhood. His style of oratory was not pleasing, especially when he became excited, and what he himself called the " saw-tones " prevailed ; but it was impossible to listen to him without being convinced of his great learning, his knowledge of ethics, and sincere zeal for the interests of religion.

His acquaintance with Mr. Richard Heber, which began in

[1] A distinguished civil servant of the East India Company.

1799, soon ripened into friendship, and to it, among other great advantages, Leyden was indebted for his introduction to the best literary society, and above all, for his intimacy with Walter Scott, and through Scott, with George Ellis. He labored zealously in assisting Scott to procure materials for the " Minstrelsy," his earliest publication, in which Leyden was equally interested by friendship for the editor and patriotic zeal for the honor of the Scottish Border.[1]

Many of the friends of Leyden were anxious to see him settled in a ministerial charge ; and there is no doubt that ere long a suitable opening would have occurred; but though he still preferred the clerical profession to any other, he had no certain prospect of a living ; his expectations had been twice disappointed, and as he saw his contemporaries one after another either provided for in the Church, or successfully pursuing some other profession, he grew weary of the routine of private tuition, and impatient of the drudgery of literary employment. In these circumstances his thoughts turned to Africa and the patronage of the Sierra Leone Company. Alarmed for his safety in that dangerous climate, his friends bestirred themselves to find a more desirable opening, and by the influence of Mr. Dundas, then a member of the Board of Control, an appointment as assistant-surgeon was offered. His energy and success in at once qualifying himself for examination before the Medical Board at the India House is graphically set forth in the following letter to my father from the late James Wardrop, M. D., on hearing of Leyden's death : —

---

[1] The manners of Leyden, if not graceful, were certainly as easy as his heart was frank and free. Mr. Ellis thus announces Leyden's first appearance at his villa, near Windsor : " His whole air and countenance told us, 'I am come to be one of your friends,' and we immediately took him at his word." To Scott, just before sailing for India, Leyden writes : " Assure your excellent Charlotte, whom I shall ever recollect with affection and esteem, how much I regret that I did not see her before my departure, and say a thousand pretty things for which my mind is too much agitated. . . . . And now, my dear Scott, adieu. Think of me with indulgence, and be certain that wherever and in whatever situation John Leyden is, his heart is unchanged by place, his soul by time." The warmth and freedom of these utterances speak volumes for all parties.

" MY DEAR SIR, — When I heard of Dr. Leyden's death, and more particularly when I read the short but interesting account given of his life by General Malcolm, I could not help being strongly impressed that a detailed history of his life and writings would be most interesting. I thought also that no one could do this so well as Mr. Scott, not only from his unrivaled reputation as a poet and an author, but from personal knowledge and his intimacy with Leyden. You may think it odd that I should write to you on this subject ; but as you may have the means of suggesting and getting such a work executed, I have ventured to take this liberty. I must also tell you how it happens that I am particularly interested in such a work. Leyden was my private tutor for two years, and to him I am indebted for pointing out the advantages and the pleasures of knowledge. I had spent the usual time at the Grammar School, and attended one season at the University, and never learned a lesson but with the hope of escaping the *tawse.* After this, Leyden instructed me in Greek and Latin, and in place of *driving* it into my head with awe and severity, he excited a passion for study by *practically* showing its utility, and the reasonable sources of pleasure and satisfaction to be derived from it. His immense stock of knowledge, gleaned by labor and a most retentive memory, and communicated in a most simple and familiar manner, at once opened before me new prospects and new passions, which I have ever since been proud gratefully to thank him for. At the time I first knew Leyden (fifteen years ago) his manners were extremely rude and unpolished, and even after he had mixed in some polite society their natural coarseness was little softened, and finding it incurable he kept them in their original purity. The powers of his memory were never more usefully and strongly called forth than in the means which he pursued for getting out to India. He went there appointed to the medical department, for which he had qualified himself by a few *weeks'* study ! He had previously acquired some very superficial knowledge of anatomy and chemistry, more with a view of increasing his general knowledge than of applying them to the

practical parts of medicine ; and finding that a medical appointment was necessary for him to get out to India to prose-
cute his other pursuits, he undertook to qualify himself in a
few weeks to get the necessary diploma. In going through
this preparation he was not altogether fearless of success ;
and I remember well his calling on me that I might show him
some surgical instruments, and enable him to distinguish a
scalpel from a razor, and an amputating-knife from a carver.
After two, or at most three, weeks' preparation, he was bold
enough to appear as a candidate for a surgeon's diploma, and
his attempt was successful. The merits of his poetry are such,
and of his investigations, though not completed, on the Oriental or other languages, that along with the history of his
life, the whole would form a most valuable volume. I am, etc.,

JAMES WARDROP.

"LONDON, *June*, 1812."

The intercourse between my father and Dr. Leyden was intimate and constant from the day when they first became acquainted until Leyden left for India in 1803 ; but though frequent it was for the most part personal, and has left behind
but few epistolary traces. Leyden's earliest letter to my
father is dated in June, 1800, and marks the confidence with
which he was regarded by his proud-spirited and independent
friend : —

"DEAR SIR, — As I find that during my tour I shall have
occasion for more cash than I had supposed, I must request
you to accommodate me with £10, if you can conveniently, till
my return. I own your late conversation has induced me to
give you this mark of confidence — a mark which most persons
would rather dispense with, but which I would not grant to
any other person in Edinburgh on any account. As I shall
hardly have an opportunity of seeing you again, except *en passant*, being so very much engaged, I leave this card. Yours,
etc.,   J. LEYDEN."

The tour to which Leyden here alludes was in the Highlands and the islands of the Hebrides, in company with two

young German noblemen, whose incognito has been strictly preserved, as their names are nowhere mentioned. They had studied in Edinburgh during the preceding winter. From Oban, on the 14th August, he writes as follows : —

"OBAN, *August* 14, 1800.

" DEAR SIR, — You may perhaps suppose from my long silence that before this time I have been shipwrecked on some desert island, or that I have gone on a visit to the Celtic green isle of the Blest. I assure you, however, that no supposition can possibly be worse founded. I have this moment returned from visiting Mr. Macnicol of Lismore, after having been driven into that island by a dreadful storm which had very nearly made both me and my companions food for the fishes. I never recollect so complete a soaking, though I have often encountered perils by land and perils by water. There was no hope : I had begun to sing my death-song, and was roaring ' Lochaber no more,' to the utter confusion of my companions and the boatmen, who I believe thought they had got the devil in the boat with them, when we fortunately contrived to run upon the island of Lismore.

" I do not, however, intend to entertain you with an account of my own hairbreadth 'scapes when I have information of a different description to communicate.

" As we did not proceed by Glasgow, but by Stirling, my inquiries cannot possibly extend to that quarter concerning our literary antiquities. When I visited Inverary, though I had the Duke's permission to examine his old books, it was of no avail, for the books were shut up in a closet, and the steward, who was absent with the key, did not return till after my departure. I learned that very few fragments of the ancient library are extant in Inverary. Mr. Macnicol, however, has informed me that Carswell's treatise has been seen by himself and examined by the brotherhood of Gaelic scholars — Stewart of Luss, Smith of Campbelton, etc. It is not the Irish Liturgy, but a religious treatise in Gaelic, and not in very good Gaelic either, says Mr. Macnicol. The Propagation

Society intended once to have reprinted it from the Duke of Argyle's copy, but Mr. Macnicol thinks that they have now renounced that idea. It was printed at Edinburgh in 1567, as that gentleman showed me from a MS. note which he had taken down while it was in his custody. But what is of more importance to you —

"You have repeatedly expressed your desire of publishing something concerned with the Ossianic controversy. I have perused Mr. Macnicol's Remarks on Johnson's tour, and I sincerely believe that it would answer *your* purpose well to reprint it. Impressed with this idea, I have not only procured Mr. Macnicol's consent for you, if you think it will answer, but his promise to revise it, if it be undertaken. The local knowledge of Mr. Macnicol, who is himself descended from the Bards Macnicols of Glenorchy, who long preserved the Ossianic Poems in their country, is worth a great deal of argumentation, while his perfect knowledge of Gaelic, his literary friends in the Highlands, and the poems which he can repeat, which he has heard repeated, and which have passed through his hands in MS., render him by far the fittest antagonist to encounter Laing, of all the Highlanders, not excepting Campbell of Portree. If you choose to engage in the business you will find him by no means unreasonable in his demands, for the spirit of the Highlander is above that; besides, I have brought matters to such a length that you need only correspond with him yourself immediately on the receipt of this; and as you will not find him ready to quarrel about terms, you had better begin by sending him a copy of Laing's "Dissertation" for his use in the business, for which I engage to pay if nothing shall come of it. By this means you will anticipate Sir John Murray and the Antiquarian Society, who appear to me to be blundering in the dark. Sir John was anxious to meet Mr. Macnicol, but failed by accident; perhaps he may repeat the attempt, therefore no time is to be lost. I have likewise secured the coöperation of Mr. A. Macnab of Glenorchy, of the family of smiths who have resided on one little hill for four hundred years; and before my return, when I

shall willingly superintend the republication of Macnicol's
Remarks, I hope to establish such a chain of correspondence
in the Highlands as shall far exceed the efforts of both the
Antiquarian and Highland Societies. I am laboring at Gaelic
like a dragon. Write to me immediately to Inverness Post
Office, where I shall soon be, and lose no time to correspond
with Mr. Macnicol. Compliments to Mrs. Constable. I am,
etc., JOHN LEYDEN.

"*P. S.* — Mr. Macnicol comprehends very well the Irish
claims to Ossian, but has neither read Hill, in the 'Gaelic
Magazine,' Young in the 'Irish Transactions,' nor Campbell on
the 'Ecclesiastical and Literary History of Ireland.'"

To this tour we owe the beautiful ballad "The Mermaid of
Corrievrekin," included in the Border Minstrelsy, and it was
also in the course of it that Leyden came to know Dr. Beattie,[1] and was permitted to transcribe "Albania," a poem in
praise of Scotland, which, along with "Wilson's Clyde," was
published in 1802, under the title of "Scottish Descriptive
Poems."

About this time Leyden also edited for Mr. Constable "The
Complaynt of Scotland," a scarce and ancient political tract,
written in 1548, to which he prefixed a very able dissertation
on various points in Scottish history, and a glossary. In
1802 he edited for a time the "Scots Magazine," to which he
contributed both in poetry and in prose ; he was also occupied
on his celebrated poem, "Scenes of Infancy," which was published before leaving this country for India. It was on the
7th April, 1803, that Leyden sailed for Madras, which he
reached on the 19th of August. He thus graphically describes his landing : "We landed after passing through a
very rough and dangerous surf, being completely wetted by
the spray, and were received on the beach by a number of the
natives, who wanted to carry us from the boat on their naked,
greasy shoulders, shining with cocoa oil. I leapt on shore

---

[1] Author of *The Minstrel*, etc., etc.

with a loud huzza, tumbling half a dozen of them on the sand."

From " Puloo Penang, *alias* Prince of Wales' Island," he writes to my father on October 23d, 1805 : —

> " Prince of Wales' Island, *alias* Puloo Penang,
> " *October* 23, 1805.

" Dear Constable, — I would with great pleasure apologize for not answering sooner your very brief note accompanying a volume of the ' Edinburgh Review,' but really it is not a couple of months since I received it, and the last of these has been spent at sea between Travancore and Achin. I had almost forgot that it is very probable these names are not quite so familiar to you as York and Newcastle, or any other two places one might pitch on between Edinburgh and London, on the great high-road. Be it therefore known to you, that the one is the name of a kingdom on the Malabar coast, and the other of a sultanship on the western coast of Sumatra, the Sultan of which styles himself Lord of heaven and earth, and of the four-and-twenty umbrellas. ' But how came you to be so long in receiving my card and volume ? ' you will say. Why so ? — because I have been stationed in Mysore during the greater part of the time I have been in India, and during a considerable part of the time amid the jungles of Coimbatore and on the confines of the Wynaad, where neither mail-coach nor post-chaises ever come at all ; and during a considerable part of that time the communication between Mysore and Madras has been cut off by the Gentoo Polygars, and between Mysore and Malabar by the Nairs of the Wynaad, into whose hands I nearly fell about five months ago, when I descended into Malabar through the passes of Coory. Besides all these obstacles, you must take into consideration that ever since I left Madras, which was a few months after my arrival, it has seldom been an easy matter to tell where I should be in a few days, or even within a few hundred miles of it.

" You already perceive I have not imitated your laudable brevity in every kind of information. I hope therefore you will take the hint, and as you write a good bold hand, and as

I know there are few persons in the world more curious, and few persons more full of anecdote, be a little more communicative in your next epistle. I am not, any more than you, of a disposition to forget old friends, and to convince you of it, though I could tell you many adventures of the most marvelous description, nay, such as would make your very wig stand on end — for I presume you wear one before this time — you shall not hear a single circumstance that, with all your logic, you can contrive to call a *gun*, aye, or a *pistol*.[1]

"You say you will be glad to hear that I have found Madras according to my wish. Why then rejoice *therefor*, as ancient Pistol says. I assure you that I have found it exactly the field for me, where, if I stretch out my arms, I may grasp at anything no fear but I show you I have long hands. There is, to be sure, one terrible drawback with all this — the pestilent state of health I have enjoyed, or rather suffered under, ever since I came to the country. This, however, I think I may expect to triumph over, though it has even at this very time brought me from Mysore to Puloo Penang. In spite of all this I think I may venture safely to say that no person whatever has outstripped me in the acquisition of country languages, whether sick or well. I have nevertheless been given up by the physicians three or four times within these last eleven months, as any one might very well be, afflicted at once with the four most formidable diseases of India, *i. e.* liver, spleen, bloody flux, and fever of the jungles, which is reckoned much akin to the African yellow fever. Notwithstanding all that, I am the old man, a pretty tough chap, with a heart as sound as a roach, and moreover as merry

---

[1] We are reminded in reading this letter, and others written by Leyden while in the East, of the poet Campbell's remark to Scott, to whom Leyden had introduced him: "When Leyden comes back from India, what cannibals he will have eaten, and what tigers he will have torn to pieces!" Although associates, and at one time *quasi* friends, there must have been something antagonistic in these two men. They had quarreled; but when Scott repeated to Leyden the poem of *Hohenlinden*, he said, "Dash it, man! tell the fellow that I hate him, but, dash him! he has written the finest verses that have been published these fifty years." "I did mine errand," says Scott, "as faithfully as one of Homer's messengers, and had for answer, 'Tell Leyden that I detest him, but I know the value of his critical approbation.'"

as a grig, — 'so let the world go as it will, I'll be free and easy still.' I shall only add that my first medical appointment has been worth more than any possessed by three fourths of the medical men on the Madras establishment. I have been extremely successful in all my medical and surgical practice, so that at Madras my medical reputation is at least as high as my literary character. This I may say without vanity after some of the services I have been employed on. So you see I have fairly written myself out of my sheet, whereas you left 2½ sides blank in yours. You can therefore have no reasonable objection that I now subscribe myself yours sincerely,   JOHN LEYDEN.

"*P. S.*— Admiral Trowbridge is just arrived, and I have been giving him information of a Frenchman that had nearly taken me on my voyage, and a frigate is dispatching after him. Our vessel was a Malabar Grab manned with Mapillas and Muldivians — the rankest cowards in nature. We should certainly have been taken had the sea not run so high that they could not come aboard of us. For my own part, wearing a long red beard, a turban, and the other dress of a Mussulman, and speaking Arabic and Persic fluently, I had little to fear, and should probably not have been discovered. Admiral Trowbridge fell in with the *Marengo*, which Dan [*paper torn*] defeated formerly, as he came along with the fleet. He was terribly eager for action, and in order to blow her to the devil at once he opened all his ports, notwithstanding the immense surges of our Indian seas, and that a hard gale was blowing. At his first broadside he shipped such a sea at his lower ports on the opposite side, that he had nearly foundered ; two men were drowned in the orlop. The *Marengo* got off before he righted, and made her escape.

"Pray do not forget my good friend Mr. Willison, whom I often think of, nor yet Mrs. Constable. After a damnable march under a burning sun, I have often wished to have been able to eat a beefsteak with them as in the days of old. When we have finished the Mahrattas we expect to have a vigorous hit at Mauritius and Manila, so that we are all agog for prize-money.

"*PP. S.*— I have forgot two things which ought to have been mentioned : the first is, when you are disposed to re-member old friends, and my name comes athwart you, direct to the care of Messrs. Binnie and Dennison, Madras, who are my agents, and consequently always better apprised of my motions than others, else your letters may chance not to reach me in a couple of years, or perhaps never come within a thou-sand miles of me. I should be well pleased if you were to send me the 'Scots Magazine' from the time I was first con nected with it to the present, and continue ; I lost the copy in London of the first year ; also the 'Edinburgh Review,' for I have only odd numbers of it, and Murray's 'Bruce's Travels,' when published. Let this, however, be entirely at your own pleasure : I cannot transmit you the value till I have opened a communication with London direct, which cannot be till I revisit Madras, which may perhaps be some time, as after the Mysore survey is closed I am to be employed, I under-stand, as a Mahratta interpreter, as well as physician and sur-geon at one of the Mahratta residences or courts. So you see I cannot immediately answer that you will be paid for them ; therefore, do as you think fit ; if they come in my way I shall provide myself. Is 'Sir Tristrem' published ? I have not seen a Review better than a year and ten months old. The wars of Wynaad are nearly finished ; when I was there the Nairs could not venture to show themselves, though they sometimes kept up a rattling fire from the bushes. The re-bellion of the Nairs in Travancore has been quashed by the skill of Colonel Macaulay, the resident. The war in Ceylon goes badly on, from our own misconduct. We lately took Candy a second time, and were obliged to leave it from not having provided magazines. The wars with the Mahrattas are more glorious than advantageous : had the Marquis Wellesley remained half a year longer they would have been crushed to pieces : but M. Cornwallis is unfit for such active service, and besides, he is just dying of the dropsy in the chest. We are tigers among hares here. J. L."

The only later letter from Leyden that I have found among my father's papers is dated from Calcutta, January 10, 1810. As being his last, and in his lively if not humorous style, I give it here. Scott says Leyden had no "humor," and I think he is right : —

"CALCUTTA, January 10, 1810.

"DEAR CONSTABLE, — I have desired the accompanying parcel for Mr. Heber to be forwarded to No. 10 Ludgate Street, London, where I understand you are flourishing like a green bay tree. Go on and prosper, and, above all, do me the favor to let this parcel be delivered as soon as convenient. Pray, whether do you now intend to rival, the great Whittington, or the great Lackington, or are we to see the Life of Hannibal Constable, Knight, some of these days, to match the lives of Lackington and Phillips ? I now begin seriously to think you will inevitably have the start of me in the order of *knighthood*, for you are positively outdoing all your former outdoings. I have, however, some hopes to be sheriff of Calcutta before you can possibly contrive to be Lord Mayor of London.

"Now, *apropos* of the Lord Mayor of London, there has been a splendid translation of Confucius published here with the original Chinese text, under the patronage of Lord Minto, Governor-general, which, it is thought, will render it as easy to read Chinese as Latin. The translator, Mr. Marshman, intends sending home about 100 copies. He asked me the other day whom I could recommend as a bookseller, adding that the translation of the 'Ranayar' and Carey's 'Sanscrit Grammar' had lain like waste-paper at London. I told him, that as there was only one Bonaparte in the political world, so there was only one Hannibal Constable in the bookselling world, and that the best thing he could do would be to consign them entirely to your management. This he promised to do, and you will of course receive them soon from *Mr. Burls*, No. 56 Lothbury Street. Yours, etc.,

"J. LEYDEN."

Details of Leyden's career in India are to be found in the sketches of his life by Sir Walter Scott and Mr. Morton. His first employment, after his arrival, was in the General Hospital at Madras. In January, 1806, he was promoted to the office of surgeon and naturalist to the Commissioners appointed to survey the provinces in the Mysore recently conquered from Tippoo Sultaun. In 1807, in consequence of a memoir written by him in the Indo-Persian, Indo-Chinese, and Dekkani languages, he was elected to a Professorship of Hindustani, and made a member of the Asiatic Society. The Professorship was soon exchanged for the office of judge of the twenty-four Pargunnahs of Calcutta. Whatever that may be, the situation is an arduous one, uniting the functions of a soldier and a magistrate, and it is recorded that he discharged these with great credit to himself and benefit to the public. In January, 1809, when he had held this situation for two years, he was appointed a Commissioner of the Court of Requests in Calcutta, and towards the end of 1810 he was preferred by Lord Minto to the situation of Assay Master at the Mint, where he enjoyed a very considerable salary, and had easy duties to perform. "I have laid aside," he says in a letter to his father, "the scales of Justice for those of Mammon ; and instead of trying men and their causes, I have only to try the baser, but much less refractory, metals of gold and silver."

In March, 1811, Leyden's services were required in the expedition against Java. On August 4, the British troops landed at a village six miles east from Batavia, and three days afterwards entered that celebrated city. Amongst other objects there, calculated to excite and gratify his favorite passion, was a library, said to contain valuable Oriental manuscripts. Shutting himself up in this room without taking the precaution to have it aired, he was seized with shivering and sickness, and three days later, on the 28th of August, died of fever, in the thirty-sixth year of his age.

Mr. Erskine, in a letter to my father, writes as follows : —

"His dashing into matters that he had not fully studied exposed him to blunders, which numbers were eager to catch at,

5

and, in consequence to represent him as a pretender. But with all this, his real talents were so great, his industry so indefatigable, that he soon repaired and covered his mistakes by new accessions of knowledge. He was restless in suggesting topics of research, and in urging those best qualified to undertake them. He quite revived the Asiatic Society, which for some time before had slumbered, and infused new life into it by what he did himself, and still more by what he was the cause of others doing. There was no work of learning or utility projected in his time in which he did not take an active part."

Sir John Malcolm, in a speech delivered shortly afterwards, at a visitation of the College of Fort William, thus expressed his estimate of Leyden : " No man ever possessed a mind more entirely exempt from every sordid passion, more negligent of fortune and all its groveling pursuits — in a word, more entirely disinterested — or ever owned a spirit more firmly and nobly independent. I speak of these things with some knowledge, and wish to record a competent testimony to the fact, that within my experience, Dr. Leyden never in any instance solicited an object of personal interest, nor, as I believe, ever interrupted his higher pursuits to waste a moment's thought on these minor cares. Whatever trust or advancement may at some periods have improved his personal situation, have been without exception tendered, and in a manner thrust upon his acceptance, unsolicited, uncontemplated, and unexpected. To this exemption from cupidity was allied every genuine virtue worthy of those smiles of fortune which he disdained to court ; and amongst many estimable features of his character, an ardent love of justice and a vehement abhorrence of oppression were not less prominent than the other high qualities I have already described."

The monument erected on the green at Denholm, in memory of Leyden, bears the following inscription : —

William Godwin

(From Maclise Gallery.)

TO THE MEMORY OF
THE POET AND ORIENTAL SCHOLAR
WHOSE GENIUS LEARNING AND MANLY VIRTUES
WERE AN HONOR TO HIS COUNTRY AND SHED A LUSTRE
ON HIS NATIVE TEVIOTDALE
THIS MONUMENT WAS ERECTED BY PUBLIC SUBSCRIPTION
A D. 1861.

" Dear native valleys, may ye long retain
The chartered freedom of the mountain swain ;
Long 'mid your sounding glades in union sweet,
May rural innocence and beauty meet ;
And still be duly heard at twilight calm,
From every cot the peasant's chanted psalm ! "

SCENES OF INFANCY.

" His bright and brief career is o'er,
And mute his tuneful strains ;
Quenched is his lamp of varied lore
That loved the light of song to pour ;
A distant and a deadly shore
Has Leyden's cold remains."

SCOTT.

"Grata quies patriæ, sed et omnis terra sepulchrum."

WILLIAM GODWIN.

A valued friend of mine — himself Conservative in politics — once gave a curious and characteristic illustration of the conservatism of a distinguished Tory, by supposing, if it might be supposed without irreverence, that had the Almighty asked his concurrence in the creation of this world, he would probably have said, " No ; Chaos is an institution — it is respectable ; I would not disturb it." The subject of our present chapter would probably have been of another mind, and certainly would have counseled arrangements, moral and social, differing widely in many respects from those which have been ordained by Him who doeth all things well. A moralist William Godwin undoubtedly was, according to his own theory of morals ; but that theory involved the setting aside of many of the safeguards to society which have received an expressed heavenly sanction. The marriage ceremonial he considered an unnecessary service, only to be observed in deference to the unenlightened requirements of the age ; but I have been assured on undoubted authority that he spoke with "strong condemnation" of the association of his daughter with the poet Shelley, whose wife ended her days by her own act. Godwin's first wife, Mary Wollstonecraft,[1] brought an illegitimate daughter into his family when she married him in 1797. Yet was he strictly faithful to his engagements, social and domestic,[2] and lived in his own peculiar and limited sphere, both loving and beloved. Born in 1756, the son of a Nonconformist minister, Godwin prepared himself for the same calling at the Dissenting College of Hoxton, and officiated for five years near London, and at Stowmarket in Suffolk. In 1782, when he finally abandoned the clerical profession, he devoted himself to literature and the promotion of political reform. For his "Inquiry concerning Political Justice, and its Influences on General Virtue and Happiness," he received in 1793 the sum of £700 ; he acquired a further addition of fame, and probably of fortune, by the publication of "Caleb "Williams" and "St. Leon." Besides other works, he wrote two unsuccessful tragedies, and a Life of Chaucer ; but in 1809, the period when his correspondence with my father began, he had established himself as a bookseller and publisher in London, zealously aided by his second wife, and eventually by her son, Charles Clairmont, of whom some mention will be made hereafter. Godwin's first letter to my father is dated 12th July, 1809, and is as follows : —

---

[1] Author of the *Vindication of the Rights of Woman.*

[2] In the preface to *St. Leon*, Godwin writes: " Some readers of my graver productions will, perhaps, in perusing these little volumes, accuse me of inconsistency ; the affections and charities of private life being everywhere in this publication a topic of the warmest eulogium, while in the *Inquiry concerning Political Justice* they seemed to be treated with no great degree of indulgence and favor. In answer to this objection, all I think it necessary to say on the present occasion is, that for more than four years I have been anxious for opportunity and leisure to modify some of the earlier chapters of that work in conformity to the sentiments inculcated in this. Not that I see cause to make any change respecting the principle of justice, or anything else fundamental to the system there delivered ; but that I apprehend domestic and private affections inseparable from the nature of man, and from what may be styled the culture of the heart, and am fully persuaded that they are not incompatible (!) with a profound and active sense of justice in the mind of him that cherishes them."

"London, *July* 12, 1809.

"MY DEAR SIR, — You can scarcely imagine how much encouragement I felt in my arduous undertaking from the kind and friendly manner in which you expressed yourself on the subject. Indeed, I am sensible that in sober calculation it was too much for me to attempt, at my time of life, to become a tradesman. The habits of a literary man — and there never was a creature more purely and simply a literary man than myself — are the most adverse that can be conceived to those of mercantile life. Yet I have a good will, I have very powerful motives spurring me forward, and I am not wholly without understanding and observation of life. Perhaps I want nothing but such a man as you to take me by the hand and launch me on the ocean of commercial enterprise, to be able to enter the lists with the best of my competitors in such undertakings.

"I have just executed a plan which has been urged again and again by the different conductors of schools that frequent my counter. They say that a want universally felt by them is of a Dictionary which should be freed of pedantical, obsolete, and unusual words, and thus fitted to be used by them as a book of daily lessons. They complain that in all the Dictionaries now in use, the memories of the children are loaded with a useless number of words, not worth the being stored in the memory, and that of consequence scholars often leave them by the time they have acquired one half the alphabet. If this hint be of value, you will immediately perceive that as a commercial speculation it is of no ordinary value. A book wanted in all schools must sell a numerous impression ; and this one publication might (in the phraseology of Garroway's Coffee House) make a man of me forever.

"When I had made some progress in this undertaking, I was informed that Sir Richard Phillips had thought of the same thing two years ago. I printed a pretty large parcel of bills of my publications, in the list of which this stands foremost, of which ten thousand have gone to Ludgate Hill, under your kind encouragement, to be stitched into the 'Edinburgh Review;' and Sir Richard saw one of these bills in one of the London monthly publications. He accordingly told me, the day before yesterday, that he was surprised that I should have undertaken a thing which he had undertaken already, that his work had been two years in the press, and that he was printing 15,000 copies. He added that he could only be sorry for me, as it could not but happen that he should have possession of the market. For myself, I do not believe that his book has gone to the press at all; whether he will be stimulated to send it by my actual execution of the project I know not. I am however resolved, and am desirous of calling on every friend who is able to assist me in the plan, to make my utmost exertions to promulgate what I have done, and to get possession of the public, as in fact I have a right to do, before any competitor enter the field.

" I have now, sir, devoted myself for more than three years to this ungrateful and difficult undertaking of creating a little provision for my family by the publication and selling of books. I have written several myself expressly for the use of young persons ; I have procured others to be written by friends of no common abilities. I am placed in the most tantalizing situation, neither wholly successful nor wholly without hope of success. Nothing has happened to be decisive either way ; and I am most earnest to profit to the utmost of the advantages, such as they are, that I have already obtained. Every day that passes over my head, I flatter myself that I am less of a novice, and that my roots strike the deeper. Though not without my drawbacks, yet by the possession perhaps of some sort of ability, experience and sobriety, I must be better circumstanced than some others that engage in the same career ; so well that probably I should be the less in danger of disgracing the partiality and activity of any one who might think me worth his encouragement. . . . .

" I stand now as to my concerns in a critical kind of situation, and every step that I take at present is of great importance to my success. My manufactures are now somewhat various, but my means are very limited ; and if I cannot gain considerable encouragement to my productions, and strike a deep root, all my efforts, by the course of which I have consented to devote the latter part of a studious and sequestered life in some measure to considerations of profit and loss, will be fruitless. Thus circumstanced, the uncommon kindness with which you appeared to enter into my concerns seemed to me like the auspices of a brighter day. My own exertions have been, and certainly shall be, strenuous ; for I hold that to be the most contemptible of characters which, having chosen a purpose, does not make every honest sacrifice, and apply the whole of its ingenuity and force, to accomplish the thing chosen.

"I should certainly be glad to see my 'Essay on Sepulchres,' and still more any of my school-books, noticed in the 'Edinburgh Review,' provided the reviewer was of opinion that they merited to be mentioned for honor.

"Apologizing most sincerely for the nature and length of this epistle, I remain, my dear sir, your much obliged and most obedient servant, W. GODWIN."

To this, and to a subsequent communication now to be quoted, my father appears to have made no immediate reply ; but Godwin still persevered, and at a later period wrote a letter which had the effect of bringing about those closer relations to which we owe a correspondence that will not, I believe, be without some interest for the public : —

" 41 SKINNER STREET, *November* 23, 1809.

"MY DEAR SIR, — I am just returned from calling on Mr. Hunter at your shop in London. He said incidentally that you were, he believed, the greatest letter-writer in the world. This impressed me forcibly, and instantly inspired me with the resolution to try whether, by a line written at the instant, I could break the spell which has hitherto withheld you from answering mine of the 7th of July last. I can easily conceive how the thing has happened. My letter arrived when you were unfortunately ill, and incapable for a short time of attending to the calls either of business or friendship. By the time you got well, it was grown old, and went with many others ' to the tomb of all the Capulets.'

"I do not particularly recollect the contents of that letter, but I know that I opened my whole heart in it, as my heart then was, — for there was something in your manner when I saw you about three weeks before, more than in that of almost any man I ever saw, that tended to inspire communicativeness and unreserve. I own I was grieved when a short time after I found I had been declaiming in a pleasing scene, but where there was no echo.

"I have just forwarded to the proprietors of the 'Edinburgh Review' a 'Grammar' I have given to the public, written by one of my inward friends, Mr. William Hazlitt. He is a man of singular acuteness and sound understanding, and I think he has brought some new materials to elucidate a most ancient subject. I never saw the Parts of Speech so well defined (I could almost say at all defined) before. I need not say that it would be of the greatest advantage to me if the writers of the 'Edinburgh Review' felt disposed to speak of the book according to what I hold to be its merits.

"I have never fallen under the notice of those awful censors of literature, since the period in which they had vowed personal hostility to me and all my kindred. A few months ago I published a book, though small, not least in my affections, entitled an 'Essay on Sepulchres.' I have been persuaded to be vain of a book I wrote for the use of my juvenile establishment, called "Baldwin's Fables, Ancient and Modern," in two volumes, twelves. Would it be of any use to send those to the 'Review?' Lead me not into temptation, but deliver me from evil.[1] I am not disposed

' To kiss the ground before young Malcolm's feet,
And to be baited with the rabble's curse,'

but if your confederacy were inclined to notice me, and to

---

[1] Mr. Godwin and his theories had been (not too) severely handled in vol. i., iii., vi., and vii. of the *Edinburgh Review*.

notice me impartially, such an event would be welcome. Believe me, my dear sir, your obedient and faithful servant,

"W. GODWIN."

" LONDON, *September* 28, 1811.

" MY DEAR SIR, — I wrote to you twice, once a very long letter, shortly after I had the pleasure of seeing you in town, but received no answer. I had hoped, knowing your literary propensities, to have cultivated some friendly intercourse, and that the man who was in terms of intimate familiarity with Anna Seward and Walter Scott might have been inclined to amicable feelings towards William Godwin. I am even still willing to persuade myself that it is rather hurry of business that has driven from your recollection so casual a circumstance as our personal intercourse, than that you have deliberately reversed the partiality you had once the kindness to profess for me.

" My present letter is a letter of business, and therefore, I hope, will be honored with an immediate answer.

" The proposal to which it relates is one in which you can by one simple act be of eminent service to me, without, as I hope, the smallest disadvantage to yourself.

" Mrs. Godwin has a son, now in the seventeenth year of his age, whom I have educated thus far with a view that he might be a relief to us in the commercial enterprise in which we are engaged. I entered into the concern with habits of fifty years' standing of a totally different sort, and am very far from being a perfect man of business ; and Mrs. Godwin, who wastes her strength more than I do in the detail of the undertaking, finds her health sinking under the effort. Nothing can therefore be more consoling to us than to look forward to the relief I have mentioned, and the young man has every promise of answering our warmest expectations in this particular. But we are decisively of opinion that it will conduce greatly to our purpose, and to his benefit, that he should first see somewhat of the world before he fixes at home. Hitherto he has been with us as a boy ; but after an absence of a year or two he will no longer be upon an equivocal footing, but will return home to us a man. It is also from home that he will learn most perfectly the ideas and the habits of a man of business ; and these, I believe, will be more perfectly acquired, and in the best style, in your house, than in any other place to which he could be sent.

"I am persuaded, my dear sir, that if you felt inclined to coöperate with our views in this matter, you would find no reason to be dissatisfied with the young man. I kept him for five years at the Charter-house School, where he has made all due improvement. More lately I have placed him for some months under one of our first arithmeticians, to perfect himself in accounts and calculations ; and his arithmetical master says he would never desire to meet with an apter or more attentive pupil. Besides this, the young man is of an obliging and kind disposition ; and his natural and unassuming manners have long prepossessed every one in his favor who has had intercourse with him. I should hope, therefore, that his services, which he would be eager to render you to the utmost of his power, would be found an adequate compensation for your expense in subsisting him. It would, indeed, be a consideration of great anxiety to us, particularly at his critical time of life, that he should reside under the roof of his employers, which would of course afford us the best security against his being seduced into such habits as might be utterly subversive of our views and his future welfare in life.

"Thus, my dear sir, I have laid before you a case in which it is in your power to afford me the highest gratification, and confer on me the most essential service, who am, with real respect, your obliged and obedient servant,

"WILLIAM GODWIN."

To this letter my father sent the following reply : —

"EDINBURGH, 3d *October*, 1811.

"MY DEAR SIR, — I am happy in the opportunity which your letter of the 28th ult. affords me of renewing our correspondence. I was in a very poor state of health for several months after I had the pleasure of seeing you, and your letters, which I am quite ashamed at never having acknowledged, being received at a time when I was quite unable to attend to business of any kind, were somehow or other laid aside, and have remained so ever since ; but I beg of you to believe that I am still much disposed to forward the objects of them.

" I very much approve of your plans with regard to your young man. They are similar to those which I have just adopted with my own son, and I shall be very happy to lend you my aid in enabling you so far to follow them out, provided the terms which I shall now name should suit you. We have at present four young men as apprentices, from fifteen to eighteen years of age.

" I am willing to add your son to them, but unless it should suit you to fix him for four years, I really could not assure you that his residence here would be of much importance to him, as it is only by degrees that I could promise to introduce him into the most important parts of the business. Indeed, in justice to our other young men, who I am glad to say are all deserving, I could not (with every desire to meet your wishes) say I would take him for a shorter period.

" I myself pay 100 guineas a year to Mr. Cochrane of Fleet Street with my son (who is sixteen years of age), besides finding him in clothes and washing. If your young man is intrusted to my care, I shall consider it my duty to look after him as far as possible, but for a shorter period than four years I really do not think his coming to Edinburgh would be of much use. I have stated all these things entirely from a wish that you should have the best chance of obtaining your object. I remain, my dear sir, yours sincerely,

" ARCHD. CONSTABLE."

MR. GODWIN TO MR. CONSTABLE.

" LONDON, *October* 7, 1811

" MY DEAR SIR, — Mrs. Godwin and myself both feel extremely gratified by your very obliging letter, and the disposition you profess to assist us in an object which we regard as of the last importance.

"In one point, however, I hope you will allow me to expostulate with you, — the length of time which you propose for the young man's remaining at Edinburgh. My period of life, and Mrs. Godwin's weak state of health, render this a point of the greatest moment to us. We look forward with extreme eagerness for the relief we hope to derive from introducing this youth into our affairs ; and in that state of mind a vista of four years looks to us like an eternity.

"Allow me to state over again the object we have in view in sending him from home. First, and foremost perhaps, that having seen somewhat of the world, he may return to us with confidence and somewhat of the feelings of a man, having thus weaned himself from the character of a child, which it is difficult for parents to dismiss from their habits and thoughts, when it is most essential it should be dismissed. Secondly, that he may be formed to habits and hours and the activity of business first under an impartial and stranger authority. These are the principal points. I should further be glad that he got as much insight as he could into the general principles of business ; and I have a reliance in his capacity and observation, that he would learn these things much more quickly than the average of the four or six young men you happen to have with you would be likely to do. And, after all, I should feel no disappointment if he came away uninitiated into a few of the highest points of business which must belong to such a house as yours, and which after all perhaps might never apply to so comparatively petty a concern as mine. My favorite objects on the present occasion, as I have already stated, are, an interval of absence, and that he should acquire those habits of diligence, assiduity, and constant application to the details of business which must be in a certain degree new to a youth who has just left school, however well disposed.

"Though I was desirous of setting before you as favorable a picture as I could of the youth in question, yet I am not altogether sure that I have not failed in my point. His qualifications are certainly extraordinary. I have no doubt that if I thought proper to introduce him into a counting-house, I could procure him an immediate salary, with a promise to increase it at the end of the first year, without his becoming bound in any way with regard to time. But this, though it might be pleasant at first, would not answer my purpose of preparing him to be useful to me and independent for himself.

" I hope, my dear sir, that nothing I have here said will have a tendency to mar our negotiation. Nothing, in my opinion, can tend with so great certainty as an introduction into your house to secure the future respectability of the youth, and by consequence the comfort and tranquillity of the remainder of mine and his mother's life. There is no obligation, therefore, that can be laid on myself and Mrs. Godwin that would be so sure to be remembered by us with complacency and delight so long as we continued to exist. Believe me, my dear sir, your obliged and faithful servant, WILLIAM GODWIN."

On receiving my father's consent to the desired limitation, Mr. Godwin expressed his gratitude as follows : —

" LONDON, *October* 16, 1811.

" I know not how adequately to express my sense of your kindness in thus liberally subscribing to all the conditions, which to Mrs. Godwin and myself, under our peculiar circumstances, appear to be of so great importance. I hope you will find the qualities of the young man such as to make it pleasant to yourself and the various persons concerned in your house to encourage him and bring him forward, and to leave a pleasing and approving recollection of what you have done for him behind, when this temporary connection shall no longer subsist. I intrust him implicitly to your management, and have no doubt that the employments you shall find for him, and the situation you shall provide, will be such as to meet my perfect approbation. WILLIAM GODWIN."

Charles Clairmont gave perfect satisfaction. In February of the following year he was authorized to offer the coöperation of Constable and Company in the circulation of the works for Juvenile readers, and the Educational books published by Mr. Godwin under the pseudonym of Edward Baldwin, and the following extract (October 30, 1812), refers to Mr. Godwin's expectations of advantage from that arrangement : —

" MY DEAR SIR, — After all the interest you have professed to take in my concerns, and all the kindness you have shown to my son-in-law, I cannot help having a warm expectation of benefit to arise from this opening connection. You seemed to think that my school-books might have less chance in Scotland than the children's books. But then, in opposition to that, you will have the kindness to recollect that my school-books, many of them (those under the name of Baldwin), are written by myself, and the others formed under my eye. It was in reality an anticipation that I could write something better than the school-books in ordinary use that first reconciled me to the plan in which I am embarked. In Scotland there is a party friendly to my name, and entertaining a partiality for what comes from my pen ; and throughout the country there is a spirit of good sense, and a serious attention to the lessons in-stilled into young persons, that have always given me an im-pression that my writings of that sort, if I were fortunate enough to have an agent in Scotland to do them justice, would stand a better chance for vogue and popularity there than per-haps in any other part of the king's dominions.

" I am afraid of mentioning anything more respecting my little concerns, in which, however, the existence and future prosperity of my family are involved. Is it not probable that the booksellers of Edinburgh itself would take some ? You are a mighty body in the Scottish sphere, round which these little planets move, and from which they receive their light. Could Clairmont himself wait on them, and make the proposi-tion ? If this suggestion is inadmissible, excuse my ignorance, who am anything but a tradesman, for making it.

" I have just received a most extraordinary account of a triple alliance of the houses of Longman and Cadell with Sir

Richard Phillips, for promoting the vent of the books formerly the property and publications of the latter. This is the most mighty step towards a monopoly I ever heard of. Oh that reviewers, instead of strewing the couches of innocent, and often meritorious authors with thorns, could expose and put down such grievances as these ! Very truly yours,

" W. GODWIN."

So satisfactory had Charles Clairmont proved, that when the period of his engagement approached, a proposal was made that he should remain in Scotland in connection with Constable and Company. The terms of the proposition are not within my reach, but that they had not been such as to induce Mr. and Mrs. Godwin to forego the comfort and advantage expected from his assistance in the conduct of their business is manifest from the following letter : —

"LONDON, *September* 8, 1813.

" MY DEAR SIR, — It is now more than a fortnight since I received a letter from Charles, respecting a very kind and liberal proposal you have made to him for the purpose of detaining him at Edinburgh. I determined that I would not immediately take any step upon this. His letter was filled with the particulars of what you said, and scarcely contained anything by way of expressing his sentiments on the subject. I wrote to him by return of post, desiring that he would express to me fully and freely his feelings on the question, without giving any opinion of my own. Whatever I thought of the matter, I was most anxious not to take any step on such an occasion without being fully assured of his concurrence. Being now satisfied on that point, it is necessary that I should write to you explicitly on the subject.

" It is now six or seven years since the concern in Skinner Street has been in existence. During the whole of this time it has been an up-hill undertaking, and has not yet ever reached the state in which I have wished to see it. You, my dear sir, can understand better than almost any one, the reason of this. I have spent the best of my days in the unprofitable trade of an author, and am incurably disqualified for a man of business. I have made many arduous struggles against this defect, but with no adequate success. Mrs. Godwin, pitying the efforts I made, and whose plan the concern originally was, has devoted herself beyond the strength of her constitution to give it all the success which the most industrious exertions on her part could put into it. But such a husband and such a wife do not make one man of business. I early became impressed with this conviction, and more than two years ago we agreed to fix our hopes upon Charles as the only means by which our concern could ever be rendered sufficiently stable, and adequate to all our wants. I frankly laid the true state of the case before you, and requested your concurrence. As the best scheme I could devise for giving effect to our hopes, I ingenuously told you that we could on no account wait more than two years for the proof of our experiment, and you kindly consented that that point should stand as I and his mother pleased. The two years for which we parted with him expire in the first week of November.

" All our efforts, my dear sir, have for some time been directed to that point. I am in the fifty-eighth year of my age. With great exertions and anxiety I have contrived the means of keeping up the business to the present moment. I have now an advantageous opportunity afforded me of raising a loan that shall place the concern so that the efforts of our young man may be attended with every possible favorable circumstance, and this loan now is on the point of being concluded. Mrs. Godwin, whose health and strength were arrived at the last ebb by her incessant exertions, has been for some weeks at a watering place recruiting, and preparing herself to meet her son with fresh spirits at the commencement of the winter, to transfer the detail of the business to him, to introduce him to our set of customers, to explain everything that requires explanation, and to consult with him respecting that more productive footing upon which I have no doubt his ability, his experience, his industry, and his zeal will place the whole concern.

"This, my dear sir, is the final effort we shall be able to make. It is by looking forward to November, 1813, that our courage to struggle with commercial complexities has been kept alive. To us it is a question of life and death. I am sure Mrs. Godwin's constitution would not enable her to sustain another year of such efforts as the last. I am truly sorry if the loss of Charles just at this time should be productive of inconvenience to you; but you will do me the justice to admit that I specifically stated the limitation from the first. The loss, too, will after all be productive of inconvenience to you; and his coming here I regard as the preservation of the lives of myself and his mother. She could not, I am sure, survive the delay of another year; and the concern, in fact, has long required that infusion of vigor which only a young and properly trained conductor can give it. The whole would be lost, and I should be thrown a naked adventurer upon the world to seek my fortune, if we could admit of any delay in this point.

"You will perceive, my dear sir, from the whole tenor of this letter, that the question is by no means of a sort to admit of discussion or uncertainty, I thought, however, it was justly due to you that I should fully explain the whole affair, and show you that it is with regret, and from absolute necessity only, that we set ourselves in any respect in opposition to your wishes. Very truly yours,   W. GODWIN."

Several letters succeeded the above in the same strain of troubled anxiety for Charles's arrival, and fear lest he should be even one day later than the 3d January, 1814, in setting out for London. From the following letter it appears that he travelled by sea, and must have been nearly three weeks on the passage between Leith and London! —

"LONDON, *March* 12, 1814.

"MY DEAR SIR, — We have been in daily expectation of seeing you in London; but I am just informed that your journey is put off, and that probably you will not be with us before the beginning of April.

"The favor you conferred on me in November last was of

6

the most essential service. I then informed you that I was negotiating a loan upon landed security, which a friend had generously accommodated me with, for the purpose of increasing my capital, and giving the diligence of my son-in-law, when he arrived, every possible advantage for producing the benefits we looked for from it. The negotiation has taken up a much longer time than I contemplated. I regard it now, however, as fixed in every essential particular, but the money will not probably be forthcoming for some weeks to come.

"It was certainly, my dear sir, an act of pure generosity in you, — the fruit of the esteem and good-will you had the kindness to bear me, — that led you to comply with my request in November in the very liberal way in which you granted it. The bill I sent to Edinburgh falls due on the 18th instant, at a moment when it will be extremely inconvenient to me to take it up. Shall I therefore be intruding too far on your good-nature if I ask you whether by means of the inclosed you could not, without occasioning yourself any material injury, enable me to put off the payment a short time longer?

"Charles Clairmont reached us, after a very tedious passage, on the 22d of January. His mother and I have found him a very diligent and active tradesman, and we can neither of us ever forget to whom we are indebted for all the advantages we are confident we shall reap from his exertions. He is not yet a master tradesman, looking with a comprehensive eye into everything, and forwarding everything from his own energies ; that, it would be unreasonable to expect at his years ; it will infallibly come, and in the meantime he executes with edifying zeal and exemplary perseverance whatever plans we concert between us.

"Have the goodness to answer by return of post. I am, dear sir, very sincerely yours,   WILLIAM GODWIN."

Mr. Godwin's letters from this date till December, 1815, are full of apologies for inability to repay money which appears to have been advanced to him. On the 13th of that month he writes : "Why do you not smile upon me in my literary character? We might then change places; you might then be my defendant instead of my plaintiff, my debtor instead of my creditor. The thought of this unfortunate remnant of obligation has hung on my thoughts and made me afraid to see you." Five days later he proposes to write a novel.

"December 18, 1815.

"MY DEAR SIR, — Several of my literary friends, and persons of eminence, among whom I may mention Madame de Staël, Lord Byron, and Mr. Curran, have importuned me to write another novel. I have generally answered that I was afraid I could not do better than I had done in "Caleb Williams' and 'St. Leon,' and that therefore I had no motive of fame to undertake it. Sir James Mackintosh in particular replied to this argument, that if by such a work I did not add to my fame I might at least add to its vigor and freshness. I am the least in the world of an obstinate man in refusing to do that which my conscience does not forbid me to do, and I must own that the multiplied remonstrances I have received have somewhat moved me.

"In 'Caleb Williams' and 'St. Leon' I was excited to write by a strong idea occurring to my mind, which I conceived, if worked up into a story, with the vein of thinking most congenial to my habits, was capable of a powerful effect. It is, perhaps, but a few times in any man's life that such an idea offers itself to his mind. Seven years ago, in the wantonness of literary reverie, a fresh idea of this sort presented itself to my thoughts, which I immediately conceived would furnish an excellent foundation for a superstructure of fiction. I allowed myself a week to make notes upon this thought, and sketch it out in all its ramifications. Three or four years ago I set myself down to the regular composition of this work, and wrote about the quantity of four sheets; but after a pretty obstinate experiment I found that my various commercial avocations, and still more the embarrassment of seeking for means to support an establishment not sufficiently freed from the want of extraneous aids, rendered it impossible for me to proceed. A work of fiction, especially when it consists in the capacious unfolding of a single idea, requires (speaking from my own experience) continuous application, and that a continuous number of hours, the flower of every day, should be uninterruptedly devoted to its prosecution.

" I am now willing to enter upon this undertaking with the whole bent of my mind. But to induce me to do this I must have some encouragement. I never did sit down to write a work of any magnitude upon speculation merely, and probably I never shall. It was my fortune early in life to meet with spirited and warm-hearted booksellers, disposed to give me the encouragement I wanted. 'Political Justice,' 'Caleb Williams,' and 'St. Leon' were all written as the result of a previous engagement formed with my bookseller before a line of the works was produced. I know from experience that this is the only way in which I can write with satisfaction and spirit. If while I am writing I say to myself, The book on which I am employed may be worth something or nothing : when it is finished I must go into the market, as if I were going to Smithfield, and see what any hard-hearted tradesman will beat down the price of my work to, when I have spent upon it infinite thought and anxiety, — this deadens all my exertions. I feel in such a case like a slave, or as if I were cultivating a field, and my landlord were to come at harvest-time and decide for himself what portion he would carry away of my crop. But when I have a contract beforehand I am like a farmer on a lease, — I know what I am working for, and am not at the mercy of any man's bad passions, or superior skill in driving a bargain.

" There is a still further reason, however, why this question of a pre-contract is of the utmost importance to me. When writing all the works above spoken of, I lived upon the produce of them at the very time I was writing, and if I had not met with a spirited bookseller who enabled me to do so, most probably no one of them would ever have been written. At present my situation is considerably similar. I have got rid indeed of the embarrassments of my business for the most part; but unless I can obtain the present use of £500 on account of this novel, I cannot promise myself that uninterrupted application which is necessary to carry it into effect. With that aid I shall certainly be able so to devote the flower of every day to the work, as to finish it with the effort of the best powers of my mind.

"For what remains of the question, my own idea was of a specific bargain for a given sum of money. In the case of Madame D'Arblay, Miss Edgeworth, and even Miss Owenson, £1500, £2000, and £3000 were prices asked, and in most instances given. And however modest it may become me to be in the courts of literature, when the question is of price in the courts of Paternoster Row, I dare not dissent from the opinion of my judicious friends, — that my talent for novel-writing is not inferior to that of any known author now living. I own I should be best pleased with a specific price. But in this point I do not refuse to yield to your opinion, and to be put upon a footing with the author of 'Waverley' and 'Guy Mannering.'

"It remains to speak of time, and this I am enabled to do with some confidence from experience of the past. 'Caleb Williams' and 'St. Leon' took exactly four months to a volume. The present work I propose should consist of three volumes, and will therefore occupy twelve months. It has been my habit, however, to write with so much deliberation and thought that I have never hesitated to send my work to the press by the time the half of it was completed, and as it drew to its conclusion, the printer and the author generally finished within three days of each other.

"Thus, my dear sir, I have laid before you the naked feelings of my heart. The present booksellers of London are statues merely, incapable of one thought but of gain ; as far as they are concerned, the author of 'Caleb Williams' may cease to be an author as soon as he pleases ; and if he had been born thirty years later, and had depended on their patronage, he would never have been an author at all. But such men outwit themselves, and by too keen an attention to what they call the main chance, in many instances miss the main chance itself. You are the only person in whom I recognize the image of that genial climate which first warmed me into production, that sort of bookseller who, while he was willing to found his fortune upon the labors of authors, felt some sympathy and loving-kindness to the artists with whom his fortune and his habits connected him.

I am, my dear sir, with much regard, and a lively feeling of past favors, yours,   " WILLIAM GODWIN."

Though my father received this proposition with favor, he expressed a desire to see a portion of the manuscript before entering on a definite agreement. Godwin appears to have been possessed with morbid apprehension at the bare idea of letting the precious pages out of his sight. How this was settled I know not, but a question of incognito, which, from the following passage, had evidently been mooted, eventually received a negative solution : [1] —

" January 30, 1816.

" I have amused my imagination a thousand times since last we parted with the masquerade you devised for me. The world is so fond of wonder. An old favorite is always received with ˙coldness, merely because his claims are of old standing, have often been urged, and almost as often received. Pooh ! they say, Godwin has worn his pen to the stump ; he is nothing like what he was in the heyday of his novelty ; what he gives us now is merely dregs, *crambe decies repetita.* But let me once be equipped with a significant mask and an unknown character from your masquerade-shop, and admitted to figure in with the ' Last Minstrel,' the ' Lady of the Lake,' and ' Guy Mannering,' in the Scottish Carnival — gods, how

---

[1] Mr. Godwin, before this time, had traded for some years in Skinner Street, and written and published books for children, and educational works, under the pseudonym of Edward Baldwin. These are said to have been insidious productions, intended to inculcate his own peculiar opinions, and, *e. g.*, in the Dictionary alluded to, we are told in a state paper quoted by Mr. Denis Florence MacCarthy, that the only meaning given to the word " revolution," is " things returning to their just state !"

the boys and girls will admire me ! 'Here is a new wonder,' they will say. 'Ah, this is something like ! Here is Godwin beaten on his own ground. Our true-born Caledonians will put the fusty English to shame in everything. Who shall say that genius and the art of writing are on the decline ? Here starts a novice-candidate that in a moment outstrips the gray-beards. Here is for once a Scottish writer that they cannot say has anything of the Scotchman about him.' "

The pecuniary necessities of Mr. Godwin seem to have interfered sadly with his literary power, and some slight delay in giving effect to that part of the contract which involved the immediate advance of £500, altogether discomposed him. The following quaint remonstrance is amusing : " Allow me to mention that a reasonable dispatch is of considerable moment in the question. The sooner I sit down seriously to the work, the sooner will the harvest grow up, and the sooner shall we reap the fruits of it. You were very kind and punctual in contriving that I should receive your letter on the 10th of February, the very day I mentioned ; but to speak frankly, my occasion on that day was a pecuniary occasion, and your letter, though extremely satisfactory, had no direct tendency to pay any one demand on me."

He was enabled ere long to satisfy all such for a time, and a month later, in acceptance of an invitation from my father, Godwin visited Scotland, and from the following letter would seem to have been much gratified by a tour which had introduced him to many eminent literary persons, among others to the author of " Waverley " and " Dugald Stewart " : —

" May 21st, 1816.

" MY DEAR SIR, — You have two qualities which will be of service to me, in pleading my excuse for not having written to you sooner on my return to London : first, I may venture to affirm that you are not the complete model of a punctilious and immaculate correspondent in your own person ; and secondly, you know what it is to return home after an absence of some weeks, and find a thousand things that have stood still

in the meantime for want of your counsel and superintendence.

"It was on Friday the 26th of April that I lost your agreeable company, and watched you and Mr. Ballantyne across
the ford of the Tweed at Abbotsford. Notwithstanding the
heavy loss, however, with which the day commenced, I am
bound to confess that I never spent a more agreeable nine
hours than this said 26th of April. In thirty minutes after
your departure Mr. Scott and I set out for Melrose ; and, the
poet excusing himself on account of his lameness from as-
cending the broken stairs, I had, in addition to my other
pleasures, the gratification of looking down on the poet of
Melrose, seated, with a book in his hand, on a stone in the
centre of the ruins. When we returned to our chaise at Mr.
Charles Erskine's in the town of Melrose, we found Lord
Buchan's chariot standing next to it. His lordship was somewhere wandering about ; but he knew that we were there, and
so our names crossed each other, which is the newest and
most approved way of paying a mutual visit. In the evening
Mr. Scott sent me on in his carriage to Selkirk, where, without a minute's delay, I got into the coach for the south.

"On Saturday and Sunday I dined with Mr. Wordsworth,
and on Tuesday with Mr. Walker of Manchester. My visit
to Mr. Thomas Moore at Ashbourn was a miss, as little Anac-
reon had set off for London the very day I left Edinburgh,
and though he has called on me I have not seen him since.
I therefore slept on Thursday at Leicester, and on Friday arrived in Skinner Street, exactly one week from our parting at
Abbotsford.

"One of the first things I did after my arrival was to read
'Guy Mannering,' which I regard as, on the whole, inferior to
'Waverley ; ' but I have since read the 'Antiquary,' which I
judge to be superior to both. It is full of character, humor,
observation, and learning, and fixes the attention of the reader,
and inspires him with delight, from one end to the other.
The author has disdained to call in even the aid of a story to
keep up the enchantment. In this respect the 'Antiquary'

has a striking resemblance to my old friend ' Humphry Clinker.' In his other novels the author is perpetually laboring after a tale, and we feel that he does not always reach the thing he strives to attain. There is, indeed, scarcely a novel in the world where we do not occasionally find the author missing his mark, and falling short in act of the thing he meditated to reach. He stands below his subject. But in the ' Antiquary' the writer shows himself confident and at his ease ; and the very circumstance of daring, and successfully daring, to write a novel without a story, deeply impresses us with the notion of the wonderful mastery in the man that has done it.

" Remember me most kindly to all friends at Edinburgh. If I were to attempt an enumeration, I should be sure to be guilty of injustice — they were so many, and the attentions of all so gratifying. I feel myself, however, particularly indebted to Mr. Constable and Mr. Cadell, since they were not contented to feed me with pudding and praise, and to exhilarate my spirit with the juice of the grape and the wine of homage ; besides this, they satisfied the imaginations of my heart, filled my portfolio with good things, and dismissed me from their metropolis contented with my fortune.

" Mrs. Godwin begs me to add that she hopes you will not think her insensible of your kindness, and requests to be allowed to join me in the acknowledgment of it. Very faithfully yours, W. GODWIN."

The following letter of September 12, 1816, has reference to an offer, apparently made by my father, through Mr. Godwin, to Mrs. Inchbald, well known as a novelist, a dramatist, and an actress. The negotiation had no practical result, beyond introducing my father to a remarkable woman, whose life had been full of romantic incidents from the time when, at the age of sixteen, she ran away from home, and made her *début* at a theatre in a country town. Finding her position not altogether pleasant, she applied to Mr. Inchbald, a brother actor, for advice. On his counseling matrimony, she objected

— " But who would marry me ? "   " *I* would, if you will have me ! " he replied.   " That I will," rejoined she, "and be forever grateful to you." [1]   The marriage is said to have been a very happy one, but Mr. Inchbald did not live many years, and after acting with much distinction in Edinburgh, London, and Dublin, his widow finally retired from the stage in 1789.

In her tastes and habits Mrs. Inchbald was simple almost to parsimony, while splendidly liberal to others, — cleaning her own apartment, and allowing an invalid sister £100 a year. There seem to have been various competitions during her life for the honor of publishing her memoirs, yet they never appeared, and by her express direction the manuscript was burned after her death. The two volumes edited by Mr. Boaden were compiled from her autograph journal, and are by no means a satisfactory performance. Mr. Godwin's letter is as follows : —

" LONDON, *September* 12, 1816.

" MY DEAR SIR, — I have seen Mrs. Inchbald. She tells me (which is curious enough), that her memoirs have twice been sold, and that for the same sum — one thousand pounds ; first, to George Robinson, immediately before his death, when his successors, alarmed at so great an undertaking, wished to be off, to which she readily consented ; secondly, to Sir Richard Phillips, immediately before his bankruptcy ; but the bargain being a verbal one merely, she locked up her memoirs in her drawer, and said no more about it.

" To my overture on your part she said that she was never so rich in her life as now ; two poor sisters, whom she supported, having lately died, and therefore she had no occasion to sell her manuscript ; but she confessed that a thousand pounds tempted her. She could not, however, reconcile herself to the sending it to Edinburgh ; a thousand accidents might happen ' by flood and field ; ' could you not examine it when in London, or had you no literary friend in this metropolis whose judgment you could trust ?

[1] See Chambers's *Cyclopædia of English Literature*, vol. ii. p. 128

" I confess I was a little surprised that you were not contented with mine. But I ought to be glad ; such judgment is
always a sort of responsibility. I ought to add, from my recollection, that the merit of the work does not consist in its
treating of great people, and dealing in scandal, but simply in
that fascinating naïvete of manner which charmed the whole
world in ' The Simple Story,' and which is still more enchant-
ing when not employed in a fictitious story, but in relating the
history of the life of such a woman.

" This is a letter of business merely. I had a morning visit
from Mr. Skirving,[1] who was to leave London in a day or two
after. He sat, I believe, an hour, and I was a good deal entertained with him; he offered to lay me twenty bets upon passages in the poets, and other things, in which his memory, I
dare say, was better than mine.

" Remember me very kindly to Mr. Cadell, and any one else
to whom your doing so will be acceptable.

" Very faithfully yours, W. GODWIN."

My father had several interviews with Mrs. Inchbald on the
subject of her memoirs, and we may conclude from the following extract of a letter, written under apprehension for his
health, that he had at least made a favorable impression. This
letter is addressed to Mr. Godwin, and is dated February 7,
1818 : —

" I have neither heard from nor seen Mr. Constable since
20th January. I have his address, but as I cannot think of
troubling him with a letter while I dread he may be suffering under some severe sickness or other calamity, I apply
to you, who introduced him to me, for an explanation. The
business part of the question is a *subordinate* matter ; for I
am concerned for his welfare, and I never take up any newspaper without great agitation, for fear I should read of his
death. Yet he was quite recovered when he last called, and
looked remarkably well. Pray answer this note immediately."
Mrs. Inchbald died in 1821.

[1] An eccentric but very clever artist.

The title proposed by Mr. Godwin for his novel was "Mandeville, a Tale of the Seventeenth Century in England." To a proposal by my father that the last two words should be omitted, the author thus replied : —

"October 7, 1816.

" MY DEAR SIR, — I most willingly subscribe to your alteration in the title of my novel, to be made in your announcing it in the ' Review.'

" My object in adding the two words you object to (in England), was to give a more clear idea of the plan of the work. My second book of this sort was entitled ' St. Leon, a Tale of the Sixteenth Century.' The subject of the book was the ideas entertained by the alchemists, and the scene was variously in different parts of the Continent. The scene of my present novel is at home, and the subject relates to the manners of the English nation in the seventeenth century. So much intelligence I intended to convey by the title I sent you ; but I am aware that sense must sometimes be sacrificed to graceful phraseology.

" I am deep in the fury of composition.

" Ever faithfully yours, W. GODWIN."

On the 29th December, Mr. Godwin wrote again as follows : —

"December 29, 1816.

" MY DEAR SIR, — I have recently experienced so much kindness from you, as ought to operate doubly as a motive why I should not trespass on your good-will. I cannot, however, refrain from once more putting seriously to you the consideration of where the novel of ' Mandeville ' shall be printed.

" In finally looking over the manuscript for the press, I have been struck with the complexity of my insertions and reinsertions in the few places where I found it most difficult to please myself in writing. They are all sufficiently marked, so that the editor of the book, as a posthumous work, would be able exactly to ascertain the place of every line, and a printer who would be as careful as such an editor would of course be equally successful. But I never met with a printer who was not sure to make some blunders in such matters ; and then what a piece of work we should have, if eight or ten pages were occasionally misplaced backward and forward, so as to require revises and re-revises four hundred miles each time, and the author not sure at last that his intentions had been executed !

" This is a new consideration that has occurred to me ; but you must give me leave once more to urge to you that which I have repeatedly pressed on your attention. Few authors who have much regard to their own reputation have the courage to send any part of a work to the press before the whole is finished ; and most authors with whom I have conversed have been astonished at my boldness in venturing on such a process. Yet I have done so in former instances, and have not seen reason to repent. But then, as I told you, my printer was in London ; the manuscript was at the distance of three streets ; and upon any unforeseen emergency I could immediately have recourse to and consult it. In stories, at least such as I write, there are so many subtle links and conjunctions of incidents that lie remote from each other, that it seems as if such a privilege could not be dispensed with.

" If you give up this point, I will to-morrow deliver the entire manuscript of the first volume to any printer you shall name, and enter into any engagement you please, not to withdraw any part of it. You shall order him to proceed with whatever rapidity you shall think proper ; and I will not attempt to countermand your orders, but will reënforce them to the utmost of my abilities.

" If you think this request of mine utterly without foundation in reason, I desire no more than that you will set it aside without ceremony. But in reality it rests on the most cogent arguments — and the merit and success of the work may materially depend upon your agreeing with me on this point, you surely then will not think proper to refuse me. I wish only that the reason of the case should prevail, and have not the smallest desire that you should concede an inch in the matter from any inclination to oblige or to gratify me.

" Very sincerely yours,   WILLIAM GODWIN."

My father having appeared willing to concede the point thus urged, but without an actual pledge, Godwin addressed the following remonstrance to him on the 5th of January, 1817 : —

" An author, I should say, judging from my own experience, is a sensitive animal, a very barometer ; and to be kept to work, should be kept in tone. Do not allow me to harbor the slightest suspicion that what was settled last Monday can be unsettled again."

The question as to the place of printing having been decided in favor of Edinburgh, and the early sheets of the work having been transmitted to London for revision, Mr. Godwin wrote as follows : —

" January 20, 1817.

" MY DEAR SIR, — I thank you for the quickness with which you have forwarded to me the inclosed sheets, though I am much grieved, and ever shall be, that you have removed the manuscript four hundred miles from my occasional inspection. In a week or ten days I shall greatly want to refresh my memory as to what I have said of certain persons living on the verge of Beaulieu Forest, but God knows when it will be in my power to do so.

" The correctness of these sheets certainly far exceeds anything I could have expected — except in one point, the punctuation. If the printer would have had the goodness to adhere to the manuscript in this matter, he would have saved me and himself infinite trouble. You cannot suppose that I have lived to sixty years of age without having formed a set of obstinate notions in this particular. But the printer has introduced a Scotch system of punctuation into my sheets, which is by no means agreeable to my taste, and which, to my eye, greatly disfigures my periods. He should have kept this air of his for a greener author. Very sincerely yours,

" WILLIAM GODWIN."

The sad history of Percy Bysshe Shelley, that erratic and erring son of genius, has been so often told, that it is happily unnecessary to enter on it here, excepting in so far as it involved the family of Mary Wollstonecraft Godwin, for whom he had deserted his wife, poor Harriet Westbrook, whose sad life closed on the 18th November, 1816.[1] On the 3d of February, 1817, Mrs. Godwin wrote as follows to my father : —

" MY DEAR SIR, — I have had the pleasure of seeing your late communications with Mr. Godwin. But what will you think of me as a wife, or as an inhabitant of this London, in an age so advanced in the fashion of reading, when I tell you I have not yet perused a syllable of ' Mandeville ' ?

" My time and my thoughts have been employed to even a painful degree upon the question, so interesting to the comfort and the peace of this family, which I took the liberty to mention in confidence to you in our last interview. I have now the pleasure to announce that Mr. Godwin's daughter, Mary, has entered the marriage state with Mr. Percy Bysshe Shelley, eldest son of Sir Timothy Shelley, Baronet, of Field Place, Horsham, Sussex. We are now endeavoring to forget preceding sorrows, and to enjoy the flattering prospects which seem to present themselves. The young couple have been in town several weeks, principally under our roof, and my poor nerves begin to cry quarter from the bustle and feasting occasioned by the event. They have taken a house in Berkshire

---

[1] We seek anxiously for palliating circumstances in considering this dark tragedy, and such circumstances I have been assured did exist. The poet's daughter-in-law, in her *Memorials*, quotes the following words of Mary Wollstonecraft Shelley, his second wife : " This is not the time to relate the truth ; and I should reject any coloring of the truth. No account of these events has ever been given at all approaching reality in their details, either as regards himself or others ; nor shall I further allude to them than to remark that the errors of action committed by a man as noble and generous as Shelley, may, as far as he only is concerned, be fearlessly avowed by those who loved him, in the firm conviction that, were they judged impartially, his character would stand in fairer and brighter light than that of any contemporary." For the sake of his contemporaries we may hope this is untrue. Theorists of Godwin's school would tear the existing picture from the framework of society, and paint their own ideal on its canvas. Their ideal, in the present instance, did not preclude adultery, suicide, or injustice, and in a late publication on the early days of Shelley we are told that " poor Fanny Imlay or Godwin (the daughter of Mary Wollstonecraft and Gilbert Imlay), like Harriet Shelley, committed suicide by drowning.'

for the spring months, and will probably pass the summer in
Italy. Mrs. Shelley's health appears very delicate, and I
hope will be quite set right by the efficacy of so fine a climate.

"Mr. D. Constable has done us the favor of an evening call
more than once, and is so obliging as to convey this scrap of
agreeable intelligence to your hands. You will not be surprised if I add that Mr. Godwin will retain a very pleasing
recollection of this circumstance, as this less ceremonious
kind of intercourse afforded the opportunity for ascertaining,
what he before supposed, that your son is a young man of considerable and valuable acquirements and tastes. We both
hope that on all occasions of making visits to London he will
allow us to improve the acquaintance.

"I doubt if Mr. G. will be able to spare a moment for sending you a line by the favor of this conveyance. You will, however, my dear sir, be pleased to hear of his good health of
body and the unceasing perseverance of his *spiritual* activity.

"I had a word or two of a little matter of business to address to you, but with your leave I shall propose it to Mr.
Shaw in preference, being unwilling to mix the *holy* with the
profane in this friendly communication.

"We had a letter from Miss Curran (oh, 'profane' topic !) a
few days ago. I am sorry to say she speaks of continued ill-
health, which compels her to delay the accomplishment of her
father's wish for her return to the Priory till the fine season is
advanced.

"Believe me, my dear sir, your much obliged,

"M. J. GODWIN.

"LONDON, *February* 3, 1817."

The events alluded to in Mrs. Godwin's letter must have
been still more exciting for her husband than for herself, and
were doubtless among the "vexatious circumstances" to
which he refers in the following communication : —

"*February* 28, 1817.

"MY DEAR SIR, — 'Mandeville' goes on, in my opinion, well.
I have, for a considerable time, been employed upon him

every day, with scarcely a single intermission. You recollect, no doubt, that I was upon the whole well satisfied with my first volume. I am much better satisfied with the second, as far as it is advanced. I find the work growing in interest under my hands. I find the opportunities increase for the exercise of my peculiar powers, if I have any that are peculiar ; and I am daily more convinced that the Godwin of sixty years of age is not less of a man than the Godwin of five-and-thirty was formerly. I am resolved, as I find inscribed among my late memoranda, to ' consider this as my last work, — like Virgil's bees to leave my life and soul where I strike, and — to change the figure — that I will view myself in it as engaged in planting the foremost banner over my tomb.'

" Thus, my dear sir, I frankly tell you the state of my feelings. How far they will coincide with yours I know not. You perhaps had rather have a work that should be speedily at its close than such a work as I contemplated. If so I am sorry to say that I cannot accommodate you. I *must* write slow ; I must work up to the standard in my own mind, or I cannot write at all.

" It unfortunately happened that I could not altogether dismiss the first volume till far onward in December. This was very different from my calculations. Many vexatious circumstances happened to retard my progress. I was not for a considerable time thoroughly in my subject. I wrote several passages four or five times over before I could satisfy myself. The case is now widely different. I am now devoured with my subject. Mandeville and his associates are to me now the only realities of life ; and the people I am obliged to talk with every day mere creatures of the imagination. I therefore go on regularly and sure, but what the author of " Waverley," and men of his kidney, would call damnably slow. I calculated upon recent experience that the second volume will be finished in the three months, and the third in three months more, — in other words, the second in March, and the third in June. I shall be sorry if this materially thwarts you ; but the Muse that inspires me is an object of more perfect adoration to me,

7

and requires to be more implicitly obeyed, than any bookseller, nay, than any friend on earth.

"Believe me, my dear sir, very sincerely yours,

"WILLIAM GODWIN."

"*March* 18, 1817.

"When you last received at my hands the duplicate of the inclosed, you predicted that at the period of its expiration I should want its renewal. This I stoutly denied. The period is come round ; and, as all human intellects are estimated by the event, it turns out that you are a wise man and I am a fool. I had, I thought, very good reason to believe that the affair to which this bill belongs would have been liquidated by this time ; but for the present I am disappointed. Is it that you are so much better acquainted with my affairs than I am myself, that you turn out in this instance to be right, and I to be wrong ?

"I should not however have the confidence to address you at the present moment, but for the extraordinary circumstances in which I am placed. I have looked back at the little record of my daily industry, and I find, to my surprise, that I have scarcely been interrupted for two days together since I began my second volume. The beginning of the year 1817, to which I looked forward with some alarm, has proceeded with particular smoothness. It needs, however, a nice management, and the good offices of all my well-wishers, to keep me quiet. Among these on the present occasion I venture to number you ; and in that confidence alone have taken the liberty to forward the inclosed. Forgive, and assist me, I entreat you ! "

"*April* 16, 1817.

"I have two remarks to make upon your advertisement of 'Mandeville.' First, my title was 'A Tale of the Seventeenth Century in England.' In civility to your objection I made a verbal alteration in this phrase ; but I am grown less modest and pliant now, as my book proceeds towards its termination, and I request that the first and more significant title may be restored. Secondly, it is a dignity I have always retained in my titles, to stand 'William Godwin' merely, and not as the author of one or more particular works. If you are very tenacious, you may do as you please about the *advertisements;* but I think it but just that I should be the sole emperor of the *title-page*, as of every other part of my book.

"Believe me, my dear sir, very sincerely yours,

"WILLIAM GODWIN."

MR. CONSTABLE TO MR. GODWIN.

"EDINBURGH, 16*th May*, 1817.

"MY DEAR SIR, — I have the pleasure of sending you clean copy, as the printers would say, of the second portion of the second volume of 'Mandeville;' you have also a proof of the title-page, altered, I hope, to your wish.

"I anxiously wait the arrival of the MS. of the third volume, the season for publication being rapidly going past; and to say the truth, in these times both the active and intellectual worlds require something new to cheer and instruct them; your work, my dear sir, is well calculated to produce both effects.

"'Mandeville' will have many attractions and claims to popularity; there is an additional attraction, however, that has struck me in ruminating on the subject, which may probably never have occurred to yourself, and which I now beg to suggest. Would an engraving, from the admirable picture of the author by Mr. Opie, not be reckoned a very suitable embellishment? What I mean, however, would not be a finished engraving of the whole, but rather a head in the style of Dr. Adam Smith, prefixed to Mr. Stewart's 'Biographical Memoirs,' of which I now inclose an impression. Much however, as I should like this myself, I would not propose delaying the publication on account of it, but I presume there would be time sufficient for having the engraving made while the third volume is at press. If this be your opinion, I would request you to employ an artist without delay; but it must be done in a manner to give us at least three thousand good impressions.

"My faith and my spirit you will say keep pace when I tell you that three thousand copies is the first edition of 'Mandeville.'

"I am, with much respect and regard, my dear sir, yours most sincerely,   ARCHIBALD CONSTABLE.

"WILLIAM GODWIN, Esq."

MR. GODWIN TO MR. CONSTABLE.

"LONDON, *June* 12, 1817.

"MY DEAR SIR,— I shall give you some pain, in which I most truly sympathize, when I tell you that the third volume of 'Mandeville' is not in as much forwardness as by this time I expected it would be. I have found one difference in my present work from any other of similar extent in which I have ever before engaged. In those it uniformly happened to me, at some time or other in their progress, that my mind shrunk from them with fatigue, the bow refused to be forever bent, the spirits seemed used up by being continually turned to one subject, and I was compelled to give myself a month or two of holiday. That has never been the case in the present instance. I have not once felt sated or wearied ; nor have I for one day refrained from working upon my book, unless unavoidably prevented by indisposition, avocation, or those accursed embarrassments and entanglements of circumstance, which too often reduce me from a man of genius (as by courtesy I am called) to a hunter of beggarly expedients. I have always preferred the story on which I am engaged to any other amusement that could be offered me.

"In the first three months of the present year I was singularly fortunate ; nothing occurred to impede my progress, or disturb the smoothness and tranquillity of my mind. I therefore finished a volume in three months, which I had always been accustomed to consider as the work of four. But since the last day of March my prosperity has by no means been so uniform. I have more than once been suspended for days together on the caprice of a discounter, or on the hoped-for success of a negotiation, in which my son-in-law is a party, that it is to put an end to these discounts altogether. In fine, the volume, I foresee, will not be completed till the end of July or the beginning of August.

" To turn from this distressing theme, allow me to say one word on the subject mentioned in your last, of a portrait. I beg leave earnestly to deprecate this proposal, and I trust you will think no more of it. Mrs. Godwin contemplates it with horror. My own sensation immediately was, if the proposal had been to prefix a portrait to a new edition of a work which had already been attended with a certain degree of success — 'Political Justice,' or 'Caleb Williams,' — I should have submitted ; but in a new work, where my ambition is to sustain the reputation which the public has in former instances kindly awarded me, I come forward with unfeigned diffidence, and I hope no one will wish me to use the forms of arrogance, and prefix an *ecce homo* from which my soul so unequivocally revolts. I am always, however, distrustful of my own judgment, and have therefore mentioned the question to one or two friends, who all decidedly agree with me. Mr. Hazlitt said at once, ' Such an impertinence suits wonderfully well with Lady Morgan, and is indeed a copy of the lady's mind, but it would completely let you [W. G.] down from the rank to which you justly have a claim. It would be downright quackery.'

" I have already mentioned that the negotiations that are to extinguish forever these vexatious discounts are not yet brought to perfection. I trust, therefore, you will not think me unreasonable in requesting you once more to entertain the inclosed in continuation, for the purpose of replacing its predecessor by the same parents, which expires on the 20th instant.

" I suppose you have seen by these impertinent newspapers — that will not let any one stir from their fireside in quiet — that Mrs. Godwin is in France. I expect her home the first week in July. I am, my dear sir, with much regard, yours,

" WILLIAM GODWIN.

" Davison complained to me the other day of your breach of the expectation you had given him of printing ' Mandeville.' "

MR. CONSTABLE TO MR. GODWIN.

" EDINBURGH, *17th June*, 1817

"MY DEAR SIR, — I inclose your draft on Brooks and Dixon at 65 days, p. £99 1*s*. 5*d*., as the value of annexed state of Joseph Hume's acceptance, 3 m d., per £100.

"I am greatly disappointed at the prospect of ' Mandeville ' not being out till the end of July or beginning of August; and must also acknowledge my regret at the remarks contained in your letter of the 12th on the subject of my proposal of attaching a portrait to ' Mandeville '; in my view of the matter such a thing would neither have been considered as an impertinence nor looked upon by the public as quackery; this is my decided opinion, and I may, I hope, add without offense, would have been useful to the undertaking; the idea was not new, but I regret having troubled you with it.

"I suppose you by this time have heard of a new work announced by the Author of ' Waverley ' — ' Rob Roy '; it will consist of three volumes, and from the progress already made in the printing, I expect it will be out in little more than two months, certainly in the course of September. I am naturally anxious that ' Mandeville ' should precede ' Rob Roy,' as it would not be useful to either should two works of similar importance come out in the same day, or even month, particularly from the same publisher. I think it right to mention this to you candidly, but while I do so, believe me, my dear sir, I hope it will not offend.

"I am surprised that Davison should express himself as you mention respecting the printing of ' Mandeville.' I believe I said to you, and perhaps to Mr. Davison himself, that if the work were printed in London he should have it; but surely when I found it more convenient to have the work done here, neither Mr. Davison nor any one else is entitled to say anything of breach of expectation. I have forwarded the copy of vols. I. and II. of ' Mandeville ' by mail to-day as you requested.   I am, etc.,   A. C."

Before the 9th of August incipient asperities appear to have been nipped in the bud, and the author continues from time to time to report progress : —

"August 9, 1817.

"I duly received your letter of the 2d instant, and for a few days delayed returning an answer, as I intended that that answer should be accompanied with the manuscript of the first half of the third volume. But I have altered my mind : I cannot part with my sheets without one more revisal, and that revisal would probably occupy me for a couple of days. I am at this moment in excellent tone ; I am unintermittedly engaged in the grand development of my story ; and I am convinced that it would be to the last degree impolitic to draw off my attention at the present crisis. I also judge, from my experience of your activity, that the sending half the volume just now is by no means necessary for the purpose of ultimately forwarding the publication."

"August 23.

"Though I wrote to you this day fortnight, yet I think I know you well enough to know that you will be glad to hear from me again. I have written the 97th page of my third volume, and 120 I consider as my regular stint. My mind at this moment revolts from every other subject. I write cautiously ; but I write every day. All depends on the conclusion being wrought up in a full and faultless manner.

"I have not a moment's leisure to call myself off from meditating what is to come, for the purpose of revising what is already done."

"September 6, 1817.

"Since I wrote to you last, I ran my head against a post, and got all wrong. You cannot conceive what a piece of work I was making of it! But that is over now ; and I am proceeding as if upon velvet."

"October 16, 1817.

"You have seen, of course, that Mr. Curran is dead. It is grievous that this should have happened at all. It is grievous that it should have happened at this time. I am sure you have warmth of heart enough to feel the interruption that this event must necessarily have given to my literary occupations. I still hope that I shall send off the last leaf of ' Mandeville ' on Saturday."

"October 22, 1817.

" Forgive me ! I believe every letter I write you ought to begin with that word. Certain proofs of ' Mandeville ' arrived here yesterday ; and if I had been at home should have been returned to-day. But after the application I have exerted, — though the world, I daresay, will judge that I might have written it in my sleep, — I ventured to take two days' relaxation at my son-in-law's in Buckinghamshire. Therefore I cannot send the proofs till to-morrow."

"December 16, 1817.

" MY DEAR SIR, — A fortnight ago I took the liberty of suggesting to you the question of certain urgent necessities in which I stood of pecuniary aid, and mentioned to you one or two projects by means of which I hoped to obtain your friendly interference in that object. You answered me at that time with a degree of quickness that was somewhat distressing to me ; but our conversation ended with your desire that the question might be put off to the present time. I have hardly the courage to meet you again however on the subject, and therefore prefer writing.

" And now, my dear sir, I throw myself entirely on your liberality and your mercy. The success of my poor novel has far exceeded any expectation that you had formed from it ; and perhaps you will hardly think the moment of that success a fit time in which for the author to be consigned to insurmountable difficulties and sufferings. You generously aided me in this way when I was in Edinburgh in April, 1816, and that aid enabled me to sit down to my work. In the close of 1816 I frankly owned to you that without some further assistance I should be wholly unable to persist, and that difficulty was also overcome. Twelve months have elapsed since the latest of these periods. Those twelve months, I assure you, have not passed without embarrassment and perturbation ; but I devoured my own sorrows. I felt that I ought to finish my work in silence. And then I relied, when my work was actually performed, and especially if, when published, it appeared to be received with encouragement, that I should not be likely to make an application to you of this sort in vain.

" I ought to have written this letter yesterday, but I was not well enough. Besides, as you are to take a friendly slice of mutton with us to-day, I thought it ungracious to interpose a discussion on this subject between. As it is, have the goodness to put this letter in your drawer, and we will, with your permission, enter into the necessary explanations sometime to-morrow. I am, my dear sir, very faithfully yours,

" WILLIAM GODWIN."

In a letter of condolence on the death of Mrs. Robert Cadell, dated August 3, 1818, I find the following : —

" I have just read the new volumes of the ' Tales of My Landlord.' My opinion is of little consequence, as the public seems to be quite crazy for the novels of this author. I will however just mention, that I think the new tale superior to ' Rob Roy,' but inferior to four novels of the writer that went before. I suppose we may now, without fear of contradiction, affirm them to be the productions of Walter Scott ; and assuredly nothing can be more astonishing and admirable than the facility and felicity of his pen in this species of composition.

" What a ridiculous fellow is our friend Jeffrey ! Is it not so ? I think he and I can hardly meet again. I suppose a new number of the ' Edinburgh Review ' is by this time out in Scotland. I have not seen it. I am told I am not in it. ' Præfulgebant Cassius atque Brutus, eo ipso, quod effigies eorum non visebantur.' "

In default of access to the books of A. Constable and Co., I am unable, on this occasion as on others, to be as particular as I could wish in details of commercial success, but I have evidence that a profit of upwards of £1100 was divided as the result of the first edition of " Mandeville." The last letter in my possession from Mr. Godwin to my father is dated February 18, 1819, and has reference to the settlement of that account : —

"SKINNER STREET, *February* 18, 1819.

" MY DEAR SIR, — On the other side you have my letter of business, which I thought might as well not be mixed with my feelings towards my friend and the hospitable host of Craigleith.

" You stole a march upon us all in the sudden way in which you left town in December last. I was grieved to find, on looking back, that I had not seen you for more than a fortnight previous to departure. I hope and trust the illness of your young folks, which I believe was the cause that shortened your stay, has left no permanent effects behind.

" Remember me, I pray, with kindness to all my friends, Mr. David, Mr. Cadell, etc., etc., etc. If you see Fairley, have the goodness to tell him that I got his letter of the 3d instant, in which he announces that I shall hear from him again in a day or two with some important documents for my answer to Malthus, but that these documents have not reached me to the present hour. Believe me, very faithfully yours,

"WILLIAM GODWIN."

No subsequent correspondence of Mr. Godwin has come into my hands. He survived my father nearly nine years, and died in his eighty-first year, on the 7th April, 1836.

LORD JEFFREY.

The relations between Mr. Jeffrey and my father, as editor and publisher of the " Edinburgh Review," were so close, and their intercourse so uninterrupted, that I had expected to find many valuable records in their correspondence ; all more important matters, however, appear to have been settled by personal communication, and there is little interest in the private letters in my possession. Before sailing for America, on 29th August, 1813, on his matrimonial expedition, Mr. Jeffrey writes as follows with reference to the conducting of the " Review," — a matter of the deepest interest to both : —

" I have had many anxious thoughts about the ' Review' since the possibility of this measure occurred to me, and I have neglected nothing that I could think of to put it on as safe and prosperous a footing as possible during my absence. Sir James Mackintosh, with whom I have corresponded largely on the subject, is inclined, I think, to be very zealous ; and if it were not for certain jealousies, and the risk of imprudence in other quarters, I should leave it without apprehension in his hands. As it is, I shall do what I can, though something must be trusted to the prudence of those who remain at the helm. . . . . You will consult chiefly with Mr. Thomson in any emergency that may occur. I have the most perfect confidence both in his judgment and in his friendship for me, and I believe you are sufficiently acquainted with the liberality of his character to make this reference more agreeable to you than any other I could have suggested. . . . . I hope to find you less hurried and anxious and fat, and still more rich and famous on my return. If I have good luck I shall be back early in December."

Mr. and Mrs. Jeffrey did not reach England till the 10th February in the following year, and their arrival was announced as follows by Mr. Morehead : " This moment a letter from Mr. Jeffrey from *Liverpool*, and suppose we shall see him in a few days. You should go to church to-morrow to return thanks." Whether this injunction was obeyed I know not, but of my father's gratitude I have no doubt.

In the following month of August an arrangement was concluded by which Mr. Jeffrey became my father's successor in the charming residence of Craigcrook, whose beauty and attractions were thenceforth every year increased by the exquisite taste and ever-mellowing character of its inmates. I quote the following extract from a letter to my father, 25th August, 1814, to show the unfailing consideration and the liberal kindness that were Mr. Jeffrey's eminent characteristics : " I could have no use for the place before next Whitsunday, except perhaps to begin the repairs, and I suppose I could pay the money at that time; but if the accommodation of my name would be of any use to you for as much more, I should not hesitate to grant it. Indeed, that or any moderate accommodation in money I shall be very ready to grant for old acquaintance' sake, whether we make a bargain at present or not — I mean when it is at all in my power, and there is any exigency in your affairs that requires it. I only say this that you may not have any difficulty in applying to me."

A few other instances of Mr. Jeffrey's liberality I cannot refrain from adding. The payment for an article in the " Review " had been through negligence delayed : " Here, by God's grace, is Mr. L.'s honorarium. Pray let it be sent off instantly to him at Longman's and Co., and desire them to pay him or offer him ten guineas for the delay and disappointment. I *mulct* myself in this fine, and you have nothing to do with it but to enter it to my debit in your account. I deserve this for my negligence, and besides it is right that the ' Review ' and its management should not be liable to the imputation of shabbiness, even from the shabby."

My father had been anxious to secure, and succeeded in securing, funds for completing the education of the son and only surviving child of Dr. Alexander Murray. To an appeal for help, he received from Mr. Jeffrey the following reply : " I shall willingly join in any good work with such coadjutors as you and Sir Walter. I have more of those things, however, upon my hands than you are probably aware of, and in general I do not like to engage for *future* gratuities. However, I will give £6 for the time you mention, and more if you think it necessary. Certainly the son of a man like Murray should not be left without a liberal education."

As a model in style and spirit for editors at the present day, I cannot resist quoting here two letters from Mr. Jeffrey to Mr. Hazlitt, the first chiefly in answer to a request for advice, and the other with reference to an action at law which Mr.

Hazlitt proposed to raise against the proprietor of "Black-wood's Magazine." They are eminently descriptive of the generous yet wise and honest nature of the writer.[1]

MR. JEFFREY TO MR. HAZLITT.

"EDINBURGH, 3d *May*, 1818.

"MY DEAR SIR, — I am sorry you ascribe so much importance to the omission of your little paper on Dr. Reid's book. I did certainly intend to have inserted it, but the monstrous length of some other articles, and your unavoidable absence from home when the No. was finally filled up, prevented me. I think I shall give it a place in the next, though there is not much interest in the subject.

"I feel that I am extremely to blame for not answering a former letter of yours on a subject more personal to yourself, and assuredly I do not feel it the less for your delicacy in saying nothing about it in your last; but I can safely say that it was not owing to indifference or unwillingness to give you all the information I had, but to a feeling of great uncertainty as to the justness of any information I had, and the hazard of great error in any advice I might found on it. This made me hesitate, and resolve to reflect and inquire before I made any answer, and then came in the usual vice of procrastination and the usual excuse of other more urgent avocations, till at last it was half forgotten, and half driven willingly from my conscience when it recurred.

"Perhaps you care nothing about the subject any longer, or have received information to decide you from quarters of higher authority, but I still think myself bound to answer your questions as they were put, and therefore I say that in general I think Edinburgh the very worst place in the world for such

[1] William Hazlitt and Leigh Hunt, for whom, in 1818, Constable and Company published *The Round Table*, a Collection of Essays on Literature, Men and Manners, were occasional writers in the *Edinburgh Review*, and contributors to other periodical publications of the house. They were men of great talent and of strong political sentiments, which they were not careful to conceal, — Mr. Hunt, indeed, as he expresses it in a letter to my father, having suffered imprisonment "for not thinking the Prince Regent slender and laudable," and they were both persons whom certain writers in *Blackwood's Magazine* specially delighted to dishonor.

experiments as you seemed to meditate, both from the extreme dissipation of the fashionable part of its population, and from a sort of conceit and fastidiousness in all the middling classes, which, originating at least as much in a coldness of nature as in any extraordinary degree of intelligence, makes them very ready to find fault and decry.

" Most lectures have accordingly failed entirely in this place, and the only exhibitions of the sort which have taken have been such as pretended to reveal some wonderful secret, like Feinagle, or to give a great deal of information in a short and popular way, like some teachers of Astronomy and Chemistry, though their success has been always very moderate.

" Estimating the merit of your lectures as highly as I am sincerely inclined to do, I could by no means insure you against a total failure ; but I think it much more likely that you might find about forty or fifty auditors — not of the first rank or condition — and be abused as a Jacobin and a raving block-head by a great many more, if you seemed in any danger of — [*MS. torn here*]. We are quite provincial enough for that, I assure you, notwithstanding the allowance of liberality and sense that is to be found among us. If this prospect tempts you, pray come. I shall willingly do all I can for you, but I fear it will not be very much.

" In the meantime I am concerned to find your health is not so good as it should be, and that you could take more care of it if your finances were in better order. We cannot let a man of genius suffer in this way, and I hope you are in no serious danger. I take the liberty of inclosing £100, a great part of which I shall owe you in a few weeks, and the rest you shall pay me back in reviews whenever you can do so without putting yourself to any uneasiness. If you really want another £100 tell me so plainly, and it shall be heartily at your service. Believe me always, with the greatest regard, your obliged and faithful servant, F. JEFFREY."

The legal action referred to is the subject of the letter which follows ; but it was abandoned, the offense having been made the subject of a compromise.

"Edinburgh, *20th September*, 1818.

"Dear Sir, — I have just received your letter, and shall willingly hold myself retained as your counsel. It is quite impossible, however, that I should either employ or recommend a solicitor for you. It is against all professional etiquette, and would besides imply a responsibility and a personal concern in the suit, which it would be absurd for me to assume. I know you to be a man of genius, and I have no reason to doubt that you are a man of integrity and honor, and most certainly my good opinion of you is in no degree affected by the scurrilities of Mr. Blackwood's publication, but you are aware that I have no personal acquaintance with you, and that beyond what I have now stated, I have no power to testify to your character.

"I have scarcely read the libel to which you allude. From what you say I can scarcely doubt that it is actionable, and by our law the truth of the imputations would not absolutely justify their publication. At the same time, the question of truth or falsehood will be allowed to be gone into, as affecting the amount of damage, and the jury may give one farthing.

"It is proper that you should be aware that by bringing such an action you put your character in issue — at least as to all the matters alluded to in the libel, and therefore it will be of the utmost consequence to prove the statements to be false. Unquestionably it is *quite false* that you have been expelled from the E. R., though, as it is against our principle to proclaim or acknowledge any name among our contributors, I cannot give you a formal warrant for saying so.

"If I can find room for Reid I shall insert him, and if you have anything brilliant or striking to say on any other subject, I shall be very thankful for it. I am told you are profound on the Fine Arts ; if you could get up a dashing article on that topic I should be glad of it.

"I shall always be glad to hear from you, and to do you any service in my power. Ever very truly yours,

"F. Jeffrey."

In the correspondence of my father's firm many important letters from Mr. Jeffrey would probably be found ; but I have given in these few pages all in my possession that I think would interest my readers.

The following sketch by my brother David was written a few days after Lord Jeffrey's death, and had been called forth by the inadequacy of a notice in one of our local journals : —

" This notice strikes me as scarcely equal to the occasion. It might easily have been more encomiastic and not a whit the less truthful as a picture or sketch of the individual. With what a different tact, and with how much more of heart-kindliness and delicacy of touch would the subject of it have put on record the leading characteristics of the man, had he been called to discharge the same duty to some departed contemporary of kindred ability and undoubted worth !

" Lord Jeffrey was no ordinary personage. His standing was high both as a public man and in the qualities which grace the more private intercourse of social life. There seemed to be a measure of his own sprightly and vivacious temperament communicated to those highly polished and intellectual re-unions where he delighted to relax himself sometimes, as well as among the fashionable and the gay. Wonderful was the ease with which he could mix business and pleasure. Without neglecting the serious realities of life and diligent attention to professional duty in the Parliament House during a long summer's day, he could find time in the afternoon to attend consultations and receive consulting clients, write law-pleadings, dine out, attend his evening parties, flutter with the lively and the gay, pay homage to beauty, till the night was far spent, and then return home to write an article for the ' Review,' until the morning light found him still awake and working in his study.

" Together with undoubted professional eminence as a lawyer and pleader at the bar, he held a first rank in the literature of a period which was peculiarly fertile in men of genius and high talent. His intellectual features were of a pleasing kind — like the playful smile unmixed with bitterness which was the ordinary expression of his countenance — and animated that conversation which was the element in which he evidently delighted. But he was endowed with powers of a far higher order ; his sound and discriminating judgment made him a lover of good men wherever he found them — whatever was generous and disinterested he could duly appreciate. He was a sincere hater of whatsoever was base, time-serving, or ignoble, but while he possessed powers of withering and contemptuous reprobation and reproof where it was due, these powers were always tempered by an amiable humanity, and he could make full allowance for the ignorance and frailty and corruption of poor human nature. Though his love for his fellowmen sprang less, perhaps, from a divine principle than from the ideal or notional and airy region of the τὸ καλὸν, which seems to have been the floating isle, the Hesperian groundwork and criterion that regulated much of his philosophical as well as critical opinion, he may be commended as a man in whom the elements were so kindly blended and commingled, that take him for all in all, we shall find few survivors to equal, and still fewer to surpass him.

"As a lawyer — highly accomplished, though others were more profound — he well knew gracefully and judiciously how to wield an argument, and to make the best of it for the interest of his client. As a judge, his decision in the case of the poor barber's apprentice at Dundee — were there none other to appeal to — proves that he knew how to apply a great principle *in radicibus*, we might almost say *in apicibus juris*, for the public good and for the protection of the humblest subject in the realm. His well-regulated but earnest zeal in the cause of constitutional liberty led him rather to favor the just claims of lawful authority, while he was nevertheless wisely jealous of the encroachments of power. When the occasion demanded, he was ever firm and resolute in defense of all lawful privilege, civil or religious, and ever ready to vindicate public or private rights on behalf of his fellow-subjects, when they appeared to

8

be violated or tampered with by the political tools or underlings of a party in the state."

DUKE OF ROXBURGHE.

It appears to have been the chief distinction of John, third Duke of Roxburghe, that he was an indefatigable and judicious collector of rare books, a bibliomaniac who had method in his madness, as was undeniably evinced at the sale of his wonderful library. The account given by Dr. Dibdin in his "Decameron" of that exciting forty-two days' auction, in spite of its abounding and mysterious coxcombry, is interesting even to the uninitiated ; while to those who have taken part in similar contests, or who penetrate the *alias* of *Glaucus, Atticus,* and other modern Romans, the magnificent rivalry on the occasion, especially between Earl Spencer and the Duke of Devonshire, must have an added charm. "Caxton's Mirrour of the World," which cost the Duke of Roxburghe £9 9s., was knocked down for £351 15s., apparently to Mr. Nornaville, a Bond Street bookseller, to whom other rare volumes fell at equally extravagant prices, including " Caxton's Recuyell of the Historyes of Troy " for £1060 10s., which the Duke bought in Edinburgh in 1792 for £50 ; but the crowning marvel was when the Marquis of Blandford, in competition with Lord Spencer, acquired for £2260 the Valdarfer Boccaccio, which had been bought in 1740 for one hundred guineas. The total sum realized was £23,397 10s., 6d.

The Duke of Roxburghe's correspondence with my father, from 1798 to 1803, though frequent, is for the most part too technical to be interesting to the general reader. The following letter has reference to Mr. George Paton, a humble but assiduous brother collector, and I quote it chiefly because it gives me an opportunity in the appended note of showing the high estimate entertained of his worth, and the anxiety my father at all times manifested to be useful to his friends : —

DUKE OF ROXBURGHE TO MR. CONSTABLE.

"LONDON, *April* 26, 1800.

"SIR, — I have received your letter of the 20th, and am obliged to you for the offer which you make to me of the books mentioned in the list, which came inclosed. It is still more ancient poetry that I wish to collect, and what would give the books mentioned great merit with some people — namely, the music — has none with me. If I meet with any person wishing to have the books, I will inform you of it.

"I received your letter containing a list of the 'Black Acts,' which I have not had leisure to compare with my copies. In answer to what you write respecting Mr. George Paton,[1] I be-

---

[1] "Mr. Paton was born in 1721. His father was a respectable bookseller in this city, and his mother a granddaughter of George Mosman, a celebrated printer to Her Majesty Queen Anne. In the early part of his life he assisted his father in his commercial concerns, but about the year 1760, being deeply engaged in a cautionary obligation, which they were obliged to fulfill, both were under the necessity of retiring from business, so entirely ruined as to disable them ever after from resuming their former pursuits. In the meantime Mr. Paton, through the interest of his father's friends, obtained the place of clerk to the Customs, with a salary of £30 per annum on which, by means of the most rigid frugality, he contrived to support himself and his two aged parents. The salary was afterwards raised to £70 per annum, at which it remained for several years, and then, owing to some new regulations, was reduced to £55, which has long been the full amount of Mr. Paton's annual income ; nevertheless he, with incredible care and economy, saved £200, which being deposited in the Bank of Bertram, Gardner, and Co., went with the general wreck of their affairs ; thus he saw himself, after the age of seventy, deprived of what he had thought would enable him to spend his advanced years in comfort, when he should be unable to discharge the active duties of his office ; and, in a manner beginning the world anew, he bore this heavy misfortune with resignation, and was never heard to complain. Notwithstanding all this, with the greatest industry he has collected a library, relative to British Antiquities, more particularly those of Scotland, greater, perhaps, than any individual in the same circumstances has ever made. With the merit and utility of this collection I am convinced your Grace is acquainted, from the assistance it has afforded to the researches of Mr. Pennant, Mr. Gough, Bishop Percy, and many other antiquaries whose names are well known to your Grace. In this laudable pursuit Mr. Paton has employed most of his leisure time. His whole income, as I have said, is only £55, the rent of his house, city taxes, and insurance £20, and his servant's wages, three guineas (your Grace will excuse me for entering on such *minutiæ*) ; so that he has little more than £30 to supply the necessaries of life in this time of scarcity. He still pays the most unwearied and assiduous attention to his office. The goodness of his character is acknowledged by all, and the reason that he has been in the same situation for near forty years is because in those offices

lieve him to be a very worthy man, but from certain circumstances regarding myself, which it is not necessary to mention, I really cannot be of the use to him which you wish me to be.

"I am, sir, your most obedient humble servant,

"ROXBURGHE."

It is mentioned in my father's "Autobiographic Fragment" that the Duke of Roxburghe's favorite volume was his copy of "The Complaynt of Scotland." In 1800, this volume wanted several leaves, which his Grace was very anxious should be supplied, and he frequently alluded to the subject in his letters. On one of his flying visits to Edinburgh he writes as follows : "The Duke of Roxburghe wishes much to see the copy of 'The Complaynt of Scotland,' in which there is a leaf supposed not to be in other copies, and as it will take some time to compare it with his own copy, he would be glad to see the copy alluded to this evening if possible." [1] Again : "In looking at some books in my library yesterday, I was surprised to find a *perfect* copy of the 'Satyre of the Thrie Estates,' the same edition as that which I lately got from you. If you have a chapman for the copy which I got from you, you shall have

there is no room for preferment. I trust your Grace will forgive me for presuming to solicit your interest in his behalf. His great age (seventy-nine years) renders it probable that the burden will not long continue ; his extreme delicacy prevents him from importuning any one with his case, and this application is entirely unknown to him. He has survived all his friends, and I am sure there is no one besides myself who is intimately acquainted with the confined state of his circumstances ; but if it should please your Grace to procure him any pecuniary addition, however small, I may venture to affirm you will find it has been bestowed on a worthy object."

[1] After examination he writes: "The only MS. leaves in the Duke of Roxburghe's copy of the *Complaynt of Scotland* are fols. 84 and 85.

"Fol. 84, recto — Empriour Henry brotht ane grit armye to seige the toune, etc.

"Fol. 85, recto —. . . . rous of tribulation allou quhou is justice.

"I am afraid therefore that fol. 85, in this imperfect copy, will be the only leaf of use. But as some leaves are misplaced, fol. 84 may perhaps be discovered, though it has escaped my search." The copy of this treasure was at length made perfect, but the fact seems to have been unknown to Mr. George Nicol, for in the Sale Catalogue of the Duke's library, it is stated as wanting five pages in the middle, which may account for its having been bought for my father by Mr. David Laing for £31 10s. As a perfect copy excepting the title-page, which could not be supplied, it was supposed to be unique. It afterwards came into the possession of Mr. Heber, and is now, with the Grenville collection, in the British Museum.

the refusal of it, and the wanting leaf shall be supplied in MS. from my copy."

In the year 1801 my father had acquired the Gordonstoun library by purchase for a very small sum, and he sold it shortly after for a not much higher price to Mr. John Clerk, afterwards Lord Eldin, who, finding the accommodation in his library insufficient, had placed the new acquisition in an upper room, and had the intention of weeding his collection before its final arrangement. Among the books laid out for dismissal was

"The Historie of Ariodanto and Jeneura, daughter to the King of Scottes, in English verse by Peter Beuerley. Imprinted at London by Thomas East for Fraunces Coldocke." *n. d.*

Only two copies of it are known. One sold at the Gordonstoun sale in 1816, for £31 10s., and the second occurred at Sotheby's in 1856, fetching £30. Mr. Phelps was the purchaser in 1816.

The Duke of Roxburghe was most anxious to possess this volume, and my father sent it to his Grace, informing him, at the same time, that Mr. Clerk had not yet determined which of the Gordonstoun books he would dispose of. To this communication the duke sent the following reply : —

"LEVEN GROVE, *December* 30, 1801.

"SIR, — In answer to your letter of the 7th inst., Mr. Clerk certainly must take his own time to determine on what books he means to throw out of his collection. But in the meantime I wish you would send me a list of the plays in his collection, whether he means to cast them or not. You will be so good at the same time to mention the dates. I wish also to know which of Shakespeare's plays he has in the collection, and I desire that you will be very particular in giving me the full title of that play which you mention as being bound up with it. Mr. Clerk shall have a copy of the reprinted ' Acts ' if he wants it. Please direct your letter to London.

"I am, sir, your obedient humble servant, ROXBURGHE."

Mr. Clerk of course accepted the copy of the reprinted leaves of the " Acts ; " and with reference, doubtless, to some

forgetfulness on the part of my father, the Duke of Roxburghe
wrote as follows : —

"FLEURS, *November* 6, 1802.

"SIR, — As *I* always keep a promise, I have ordered two
copies of the reprinted 'Black Acts' to be sent to you on
Monday by the Kelso fly. One copy is for Mr. Clerk, the
other for yourself. If you have occasion to write to me, direct
for me in London, as I leave Fleurs this day.

"I am, sir, your obedient humble servant,   ROXBURGHE."

Mr. Clerk having at length decided to retain the entire Gordonstoun Collection, my father was reluctantly compelled to
require the restoration of the prized volume. The duke replied : —

"LONDON, *December* 2, 1803.

"SIR, — . . . . I am not only vexed but much surprised at
the latter part of your letter respecting the little volume of
poetry, which is a translation from 'Ariosto.' Upon the good
faith of the book being mine, I had it bound and my coat-of-
arms put on it. I now should be sorry to part with it, and I
should hope that Mr. Clerk would yield it to me. I am very
willing to pay the fair price that you will put on it, or give him
any book of equal value in lieu of it. Possibly I may have
some duplicates of some books in my library that may be
equally agreeable to him. I know that I have some duplicates
of 'Hearne,' also duplicates of old Plays, and perhaps some
of old Poetry, but of this I cannot be certain, from memory.
Any modern book I can easily procure. But it is unnecessary
to say anything farther on the subject until you have conversed
with Mr. Clerk, which I desire you will take an early opportunity to do. I am, sir, your obedient humble servant,

"ROXBURGHE."

The above is the last communication from his Grace which
I find among my father's papers. The Duke died in 1804,
and was succeeded by William, seventh Lord Bellenden, who
was also called away from his temporal honors only one year

later, when the Dukedom became an object of competition between Major-general Walter Ker, heir-male of the first Earl,
the Right Hon. W. Drummond, heir-male of the second Earl,
and Sir James Innes Norcliffe, Baronet, in whose favor the
House of Lords decided in 1812. From him, the fifth Duke
of Roxburghe and father of the present Duke, my father in
1817 received a letter which contains interesting reminiscences
of troublous times in which his infancy and early life were
passed.

George Chalmers.

If it be true that George Chalmers was, what in a letter now
before me he claims to be — "the best antiquary and not the
worst historian that Scotland has produced " — he deserves
ample notice in a work like the present, professedly illustrative of the authors and literature of his country ; though it
was manifestly unnecessary that he should be included in such
petitions as that offered up by the pastor of a congregation
who were oppressed with disquieting humility, that they might
be "blessed with a better conceit of themselves." It is doubtful whether he would have stood first in a competitive archæological examination at the present day, or have been admitted
to the front rank among our historians ; but it is certain that
in either department he deserves to be honorably mentioned.

Mr. Chalmers has another claim to tender and respectful
treatment at my hand, as having been among the earliest, most
active, and most constant of my father's patrons, always ready
not only to show kindness to himself, but for his sake to be-
friend those whom my father's helpful disposition led him to
recommend for notice. He has been accused, and not without
reason, of discourtesy and unwarranted contempt in his treatment of those who opposed his theories and presumed to con-
trovert his views ; but there was little upon either side of the
charity that "endureth all things," and although he may not
always have endeavored to fulfill the Divine injunction by over-
coming evil with good, he was sweet as summer to his friends,
and in his thirty years' uninterrupted intercourse with my

father, I find no action nor expression save of perfect kindness.

Mr. Chalmers was born at Fochabers in 1742, and was educated partly at King's College, Aberdeen, and partly in Edinburgh, where he studied law. Twelve years of his early manhood — from 1763 to 1775 — had been passed in America, where he practiced in Baltimore as a lawyer, and he was only driven back to this country by the strength of his royalist tendencies, which rendered him obnoxious to those among whom his transatlantic lot was cast, and led him to sacrifice professional prospects for the attainment of a more congenial atmosphere. He had been more than ten years at home when, in 1786, he was appointed to the office of Chief Clerk to the Committee of Privy Council for trade and foreign plantations, the duties of which he continued to discharge until his death in 1825. Although sixty-two of the eighty-three years of his life were thus passed out of his native land, Mr. Chalmers's love for Scotland was unimpaired, if indeed, absence did not make the heart grow fonder ; and his principal literary undertakings were all in illustration of the history, literature, and topography of his country.

Mr. Chalmers's acquaintance with my father began in 1795, and in his earliest written communication to the young bookseller he orders *thirty-three* articles from his first printed Catalogue, and in conclusion, wishing him success, and commending himself to Mr. George Paton, who, I believe, had the credit of making them acquainted, he adds, "Say nothing about my writing to you ; 'the still sow eats up the draff.' " From each successive Catalogue some rare volumes are commissioned ; my father is more and more warmly thanked for literary intelligence imparted ; the formal " Sir " passes through " Good Sir," into " Dear Sir," and ere long the correspondence concludes in accordance with its uniform tenor, as from an " affectionate friend." It contains much that would be interesting to lovers of bibliography, but it is far too voluminous to admit of anything beyond a selection of passages which may be presumed to have a more general interest. This, therefore, I shall now proceed to make.

Mr. Chalmers was a great admirer of Allan Ramsay, and his zeal appears to have extended beyond the poet's reputation, to the success and respectability of his commercial position and relations. With reference to his " Life of Ramsay," published in 1800, and for which my father zealously assisted in collecting materials, he says, 4th October, 1799: " The authority for Ramsay's bankruptcy is very bad. Lord Gardenston, and his crony Callander, were both unprincipled men, without regard to truth or propriety. I conceive it impossible that Ramsay could have had any hand in the Critical Club lucubrations in 1738. He had left off writing some years before, as you may remark in his letter to Smibert, and was only busy with his shop. I think Ramsay's relatives are right in denying that the poet ever was a *barber ;* it is demonstrable that he never was ; he was only a wig-maker ; and the two trades were not in that age coincident."

In a letter of a later date Mr. Chalmers writes : " After washing my hands of ' Lyndsay,' I shall employ a week or ten days in giving a lift to my ' History of the Poetry of Scotland.' I have made a great progress, and some curious discoveries. I agree in opinion with you, that we have of late too much neglected our old poets, and paid too great attention to the moderns. I am sorry to see a sort of sacrifice of Ramsay at the shrine of Burns. The ' Gentle Shepherd ' has never been equaled, and some of Ramsay's songs are unrivaled." The past was usually superior to the present in the estimation of our antiquary, and in this instance posterity has not indorsed his decision.

In 1800, Mr. Chalmers also published his conviction that Hugh Boyd was the writer of the " Letters of Junius " — a theory never very widely entertained, and long ago abandoned. In this matter also my father appears to have taken some trouble ; for in a letter of May 23, 1800, I find Mr. Chalmers writing thus : —

" I am particularly obliged to you for your information about Mr. J. P. Wood's knowledge of the handwriting of Junius. If you be sufficiently acquainted with him, I wish you would borrow Dr. Stenhouse's copy of my ' Appendix,' which contains the fac-simile of Boyd's hand, which I am assured is very like — as indeed it must, having been taken from a real letter of Boyd's — and show it to Mr. Wood, in order to hear what he says. I cannot be persuaded that the copy of ' Junius' sent to Woodfall was in the real handwriting of the author. I shall be glad to hear what Mr. Wood thinks upon the point." In a letter of January 20, 1801, he adds on the same subject : " Mr. Wood may be assured that I would make no bad use of what he may say from his recollection, as the controversy is decided in favor of M'Aulay Boyd." ! !

On February 8, 1803, my father writes from Edinburgh : —

" DEAR SIR, — A particular friend and customer of mine has a copy of the first edition of Shakespeare in folio, *London,* 1623 ; it is in fine condition, but unfortunately wants some leaves. I need not inform you of the value of this book, if perfect. I have been told that some London bookseller has an incomplete copy, which he has cut up, and sells by the leaf. If this is really a fact, I have no doubt you must know who the person is, and if it should happen that he has the leaves mentioned in the inclosed paper, my friend would not grudge sixpence or even a shilling (!) a leaf to have his book completed. Could you manage this for me ? I am sensible that by proposing such trouble to you, I am using great liberty, but your attention to me on former occasions induces me to hope that you will forgive it."

To this Mr. Chalmers wrote in reply : —

" I lost no time in executing your commission. There certainly were, as I have heard, some booksellers who retailed the pages of Shakespeare at a pretty high price ; but, though I put your commission into the hands of Egerton, whose coadjutor Harris knows more of Shakespeare than anybody, we cannot learn that there is any bookseller who retails the pages of the first edition. What you want for a customer, therefore, can only be obtained by some lucky hit."

October 27, 1803. — "The friends of Ossian are infatuated. The last publication of the Highland Society promises something by way of the result of their inquiries very soon. Mr. (Henry) Mackenzie has a large collection of mine upon this subject. John Mackenzie, who had a thousand pounds to print the Gaelic Ossian, is dead, without saying a word about either the publication or the money. His son, who acts as his executor, is now called on by George Nichol the bookseller to pay for the paper which was bespoken for the work.

"Both old John and this boy have been so infatuated by their avarice that they could not be persuaded that they may do their duty to the public and serve themselves by leaving the matter to the bookseller.

"I shall keep an eye on poor Ritson's Remains ; and if I can retrieve what I fear is gone you shall know. I would give more for the MS. than any bookseller, because I would make it a groundwork.

"I was surprised to learn from you that I should have been considered by anybody at Edinburgh to be the author of the 'Vindication of the Celts,' which is so unlike anything that I ever wrote. If I had written on that subject, I would have beaten Pinkerton's brains out in one half the space. Pinkerton's 'Goths' is a tissue of interpolation and falsehood, fiction and impertinence ; but I have never published anything upon the matter. The 'Vindication' is the hasty production of a man who writes many books. I have heard the reviewer laughed at for the logic in his conclusion that because Pinkerton has been convicted of falsehood and interpolation, honest men should be suspected, and not Pinkerton disbelieved, even when he does write truth, according to the common maxim about liars. But there seems to be a Pinkerton mania in Scotland. I am glad that I had influence enough with Dr. Jamieson to get him to collate Barbour with the MS. in the Advocates' Library, when he found what I told him was true, namely, that there is some falsehood in every line. The same is true of every other book of Pinkerton's, though I think his History is his best book. I should thank you, if you would say to everybody that I have nothing to do with the ' Vindication of the Celts.' "

In the following letter of the 27th December Mr. Chalmers again alludes to Ritson's 'Bibliographia Scotica,' and mentions his intention to edit the works of Sir David Lyndsay, and to write a Life of the author : —

" You have heard of the fate of Ritson's ' Bibliographia Scotica,' which was said to have been burnt, but appeared in his Catalogue. I wished for it, that I might have completed it, and given it to you, as Ritson intended. I offered upwards of forty guineas for it ; and Longman and Rees bought it dearly, either for you or Mr. Walter Scott. If they find it a dear bargain they have themselves to blame by not acting in concert for the good of the whole. Longman and Rees must at last come to me for help.

" But of this enough ! I write you now about a new and complete edition of the works of Sir David Lyndsay of the Mount. I obey the call of your Edinburgh Reviews. I am so powerful when I set to work that I have already almost completed my task.

" It will make three small crown 8vos, I think. The first will be Prolegomena, with the Life, criticisms on his works, etc. The second will contain his Poetry, comprehending his Drama, whereof I have a fine copy. The third volume will be a copious Glossary, with a Concordance of the old English poets. Such is my plan. Would you like to be the proprietor of such a work ? Every curious library must have it.

" In the meantime I want some help. Leyden, in his ' Complaynt of Scotland,' often quotes an addition of Lyndsay by Henry Charteris, 1592. I would give the world for a sight of this edition, for the purpose of collation. Try to buy it for me, or try to borrow it for me. Surely if my design be avowed, nobody at Edinburgh would refuse to lend it to me. If you can get it in either way, pray send it to me by the mail-coach. I have a great many editions of Lyndsay of the very oldest. But this edition of 1592 I specially want. Let me beg your activity in procuring me this, either for love or money."

On September 2, 1805, Mr. Chalmers writes to Mr. Hunter : —

" I envy you the discovery you lately made in Mr. Maule's library. This ' History of Alexander the Great ' is unique. I never saw or heard of this book before. We know when Alexander Arbuthnot lived ; but we did not know before that he had printed such a book. I thank you for the specimens of it.

" You talked of a new edition of Mr. D. Herd's Songs, to be edited by Mr. W. Scott. Is this almost ready for the public ? I hope Mr. Scott will not *touch the text*. I am sorry that I have nothing which could be of any use to you. My collections are all of a different kind. I see you are to have a superb selection of Jacobite Songs. I shall be glad to see them. The Jacobite songsters sung the best. George II. did not pay for song, nor, indeed, for anything else."

The following letter from my father, relating to Sir Ralph Sadler's Papers and other matters, may be read with interest : —

" EDINBURGH, *4th June*, 1806.

" I do not know if Mr. Hunter ever mentioned to you that we some time ago had the inspection of a most valuable and various collection of original papers in the reign of Queen Elizabeth, preserved since the time of Sir Ralph Sadler, chiefly addressed to himself, or connected with public or official matters in which he was concerned. They begin just at the period where the printed volume of Sir Ralph's letters ends. They are the property of Mr. Clifford of Tixall, in Staffordshire, — one of the Chudleigh Cliffords, and whose younger brother has them at present in Edinburgh. They descended to this family through the Lords Aston of Forfar, one of whom married Sir Ralph's granddaughter. We have got leave to publish either the whole or part, and for that purpose they are now in the hands of Mr. Walter Scott, from whom we expect a valuable selection, to make (perhaps) two respectable quarto volumes, to be printed by Ballantyne, embellished with portraits, autographs, etc. There are among the papers a good many particulars about Queen Mary when in confinement (I think) in Tutbury Castle, some extracts from which Mr. Clifford informs me will be found in a recent 'History of Forfarshire,' by a Mr. Shaw. This book you no doubt have already in your library, or can easily command. What think you of this for a speculation ? Mr. Clifford has projected a work to be executed by himself, which I feel an equal anxiety should be brought forward. This work would make a quarto volume, and would be embellished with portraits, views, ancient funereal monuments, etc. Are you acquainted with Mr. Todd, the editor of Milton ? I am told he has a volume of MS. unpublished poetry of my namesake Constable, whose history I am disposed to believe would fall to be illustrated in this work, as I hope to find him a noble author of Scotland, the first 'Viscount of Dunbar,' a great friend and favorite of King James, of whom Ritson has published some scanty particulars. Would Mr. Todd be tempted to part with this volume ? I should not grudge the value of a good many tomes in the acquisition of it ; but how that can be brought about is a difficult matter. Can you assist me ? "

MR. CHALMERS TO MR. CONSTABLE.

"*9th June,* 1806.

"DEAR SIR, — I have had the pleasure of receiving your obliging letter of the 4th inst. I was, I will avow, grumbling in my gizzard, that neither you nor our friend Hunter would write me a word about 'Lyndsay,' though I had written to him of its speedy publication. But from you I learn that Longman and Co. have informed you that he is now published.[1]

" I presume Dr. Jamieson will wish that the 'Glossary' had never been conceived in the brain of your humble servant, for it leaves not an inch of ground to support his two quartos of 'Glossography.' But he has been cutting the ground from under my 'Caledonia,' so the hardest head might fend off ! But, according to your rule, of bulk, his two quartos will beat

[1] *Poetical Works of Sir David Lyndsay of the Mount, Lyon King at Arms under James V., with Prefatory Dissertations, and a Glossary.* 3 vols. crown 8vo. 1806.

out the brains of my 'Lyndsay,' three crown 8vos, at only 32*s.*
My whole 'Life of Lyndsay,' 'Dissertations,' and 'Glossary'
are such slaps in the face to the scholars and critics of Scotland, that I am already like the fly on the wheel, crying out,
'What a dust we make!' One of the greatest lawyers and
orators (Sir W. G.) has written me on the occasion, 'that I
have made a very valuable present to the scholars and antiquaries of our country.' This is exactly as the said scholars
and antiquaries may take it. If they take it by the right
handle, my 'Lyndsay' will certainly give an entirely new turn
to the modes of thinking in Scotland about the vernacular
language there.

"You have quite dazzled my eyes with the splendor of the
quartos — of 'Shrewsbury Papers' — of 'Sir Ralph Sadler's'
— of 'Cliffords' and 'Constables.' Happy, if they were all
out, that I might enjoy the voluptuous feast! How can I
help you out with them?

"Yes, you say: the Rev. H. Todd, the editor of Milton
and Spenser, for the last of which he was so scolded by the
Edinburgh Reviewer, has a MS. of Henry Constable's poetry.
If he has, I think it likely, I presume to believe, that you will
get this MS. I will go to him to-morrow upon this business.
I know him well to be not only one of the most ingenious but
most worthy of men; and I am sure he will not hesitate a
moment to gratify me, if he have no special purpose to answer.

"I think you may venture to give it as a piece of literary
news in your next Magazine: The Rev. Mr. H. Todd, the
editor of Milton and Spenser, has it in contemplation to favor
the public with an octavo volume on the 'Life and Writings of
Chaucer.'"

MR. CHALMERS TO MR. CONSTABLE.

"*12th June,* 1806.

"MY DEAR SIR, — I have already written you a few posts
ago, that I would speak to the Rev. Mr. Todd about Henry
Constable's MS. poetry.

"I met him in great tribulation, for there had been the night before a fire next door to him, which had put his all in jeopardy. He told me he had such a MS. collection of poetry ; that he had refused pretty large offers for it ; that I was very welcome to the use of it ; but that this rare MS. was finally destined for the Marquess of Stafford's library, to whom he owed so much. Such, then, seems to be the decision of Mr. Todd with regard to the MS. of Henry Constable. It is for you to consider how I can serve you in the business, knowing your own project, and seeing what is disclosed by my communication with Mr. Todd. You perceive that I may have the use of the MS., and of course may take notes from it for your use in any work you may have in contemplation. I can only add, that it will give me great pleasure to be of any use to you.

"I ought to have thanked you for the 'Journal of Ballendyne.'[1] I was amused with an observation of the learned editor : that the criminations and inquiries of two hundred years had not proved Mary Stuart guilty of the murder of her husband ; yet he wished she were proved innocent. I have been applying this to Lord Melville. No crime is proved against him, yet some folks think him guilty.

"Before this comes to hand, you will have heard and seen that he was yesterday found *not guilty* of all the charges and matters of the impeachment. I never saw so much joy expressed by all ranks as I witnessed yesterday on Lord Melville's acquittal. It seemed to be the avowal of the public sentiment on the discharge from persecution of a man who has served his country.

"Health and success attend you! Such are the wishes of your friend and servant, GEO. CHALMERS."

TO MR. CONSTABLE.

"*22d January*, 1808.

"Beloe and Todd dined with me yesterday. Beloe, who is publishing more 'Anecdotes of Literature,' constantly kept crying out 'Oh what a rare book !' But Todd knows books bet-

---

[1] Richard Ballatyne, Knox's secretary — published by Sir John G. Dalyell in his *Illustrations.*

ter. *Apropos* of these two knowing men, I said a friend of mine had some thoughts of reprinting the ' Palace of Pleasures,' would it do ? Beloe said Yes ; Todd said No. I concurred with Todd, as republications seldom take. Scarcity is valuable, but plenty is cheap."

It had long been believed that Mr. James Chalmers, who had been for many years devoted to his uncle, would be his heir, but on the death of the old gentleman no will was found, and strong suspicions were entertained that the document, which was known to have been executed, had been maliciously destroyed by a dependent of Mr. Chalmers, who was ill-disposed towards the intended beneficiary. The library, which was curious and extensive, would probably have been purchased by the Edinburgh Faculty of Advocates, had Mr. James Chalmers had power to dispose of it. As it was, it remained under his care until he died, when it was sold by public auction. It is thought that it had at one time been the intention of Mr. Chalmers to bequeath his books to the Faculty of Advocates, but that he was so much dissatisfied by the election of the late Dr. Irving as librarian, instead of one or other of two of the candidates he thought much better qualified for the office, that the learned body forfeited his good-will. His library was sold in London in the year 1841.

DR. DUNCAN FORBES.

This Reverend Doctor died a bachelor nearly half a century ago, and I am not aware that there is any one now living whose feelings would be wounded were I to use the extremest freedom of speech with regard to him. I doubt if any man ever existed who was more determined to win the favor of fortune than Dr. Forbes, but though her faithful follower throughout life, she does not seem ever to have granted one of the smiles he sedulously courted. He had studied at the University of St. Andrews, and had been licensed as a preacher in connection with the Church of Scotland ; but in distrust of a judicious exercise of patronage, and thinking it well that his bow should

9

have a second string, he attended medical classes in Edinburgh, and obtained the degree of Doctor of Medicine there. In mind and manners he was an unhappy compound of Dominie Sampson and the Rev. Duncan M'Dow, without the loveable qualities of the one, or the self-serviceable qualifications of the other. Like the Dominie, he had depths of unavailing scholarship, and he was as awkward and ungainly as insignificant proportions would permit; he credited himself — I believe in all sincerity — with more than Mr. Sampson's devotion to my father, and conceived himself of important use in advancing his professional interests. Like his prototype in "Destiny" — though he could scarcely be said to be "an easy, good-humored, sensible, moderate man, who troubled nobody," as Miss Ferrier represents Mr. M'Dow, — he certainly excelled in "minding his own affairs;" and had the untiring effort been crowned with equal success, he would assuredly have followed Mr. M'Dow's example in making instant demands for augmentation of stipend, enlargement of glebe, and additions to the manse. He was not, however, like Mr. M'Dow, "possessed of that sort of callous good-nature which rendered him invulnerable to all rebuffs," for he was delicately, though not sweetly, sensitive on personal matters, and ready at all times to render railing for railing.

At what period my father became acquainted with him I do not know, but the earliest letter in my possession is dated in 1797, while he was pursuing his medical studies at Edinburgh University, and he seems subsequently to have contributed occasionally to the "Scots Magazine," and other periodicals with which my father had concern. In 1802, the Doctor requested him to bring under the notice of Mr. Longman a work whose name I do not find recorded, and which, though at first favorably considered, finally failed of acceptance — to the annoyance and indignation of its author.

In 1804 my father had introduced him to the acquaintance of Lord Buchan, who, believing himself entitled to make appointments to Chairs in the projected University of Wilna, presented Dr. Forbes to that of Logic, but, as it proved, without effectual result. Disappointment encountered the poor man at every turn of Fortune's wheel, and his social experiences were not brighter or more encouraging than those professional. His temper was hot, and he was very sensitive to ridicule, an infliction to which his eccentricities offered strong inducement.

He made strenuous efforts to obtain an appointment in the Institution founded in Calcutta by the Marquis of Wellesley, for the instruction of the junior servants of the East India Company, and when he failed in that, he vainly besought the directors to send him to India in any situation whatever. He endeavored afterwards, with no better success, to find an opening as a physician in some county town in England. In 1806, however, his hopes were kindled and raised very high by the accession to power of the Liberal party, of which he deemed himself a deserving member, and he wrote to an influential friend a letter which begins thus : " Jam nascitur ordo novus rerum," and concludes as follows, " I commit my future destiny, as far as the affairs of this world are concerned, into the hands of your political friends. This surrender I make with some confidence ; and if it shall please them to place me in a situation where any little ability I may possess shall have scope, brand me as one of the unworthy if I act not true to my principles, and be always found ready to evince my gratitude. Let me yet again assure you that my predilection for the Church has not been effaced, or indeed weakened, by frequent disappointments, and that a situation in it would be congenial to the best dispositions of my heart. My attention and my hopes were early directed to the functions of a clergyman, and first impressions are with difficulty obliterated."

How frequently, previous to 1806, he may have presented himself as a candidate for vacant benefices, I do not know ; but he had certainly applied for Moulin, Dunkeld, and Little Dunkeld, and loudly blamed the Duke of Athole and others for their blindness in passing him by.

It were too tedious to give a detailed account of the energetic measures taken by him during the last twenty years of

his life to obtain what he was wont to term "a resting-place
for the soles of his feet;" but in his letters now before me I
have a record of the following unsuccessful applications, in
which he had claimed my father's help, viz., for the parishes
of Cathcart, Creich, Kilconquhar, Tealing, Inchture, Flisk,
Glencairn, Abbotsrule, and Kells! Besides these, there was
one in Angus, and another in the gift of Lord Lauderdale,
which he made vigorous efforts to secure; and in the year
1815 he was a candidate for the Chair of Moral Philosophy at
St. Andrews, vacant by the death of Mr. Cook. How many
other posts he coveted I know not; but so fully was he aware
of the trouble he caused, that he used to say that were he to
try for Ultima Thule, he should be sure of earnest support,
and on one occasion he promised to " burn the bond " should
his application prove successful.

In all his difficulties and trials, and on his own showing they
were great and frequent, he seems to have come with confidence to my father as to an earthly Providence, and his per-
sistent solicitation must at least have been tolerated if not
encouraged, for until the close of life he never allowed many
months to pass without assailing him, either for the books
which he pedantically calls his *intellectual desiderata*, or to use
his influence in securing a parochial charge or professorial
chair.

With my mother Dr. Forbes was the reverse of a favorite,
though very anxious to cultivate her favor, and he was impru-
dently fond of obtruding medical advice, which her low opinion of his skill did not lead her to encourage. One scarcely
ever failing mode of pleasing parents he liberally practiced, —
by praising her children on all occasions in her hearing, as
"the sweetest little cherubs in town or country;" while to
my father he expatiated on the charms of his mother, to whom
her son was devotedly attached. When this old lady was
eighty years of age he writes as follows: "I never saw your
mother looking better; the roses are in full bloom on her
cheeks, notwithstanding this fading season of the year, and
the very advanced period of her life." Let us hope these
raptures were sincere.

Dr. Forbes frequently reproached my father for his coldness towards him, dwelling by way of contrast on the warmth of his own attachment — an attachment which he conceived entitled him to expect that his friend and patron's time and money and influence, and — above all — his books, should be entirely at his service. Acting upon this impression, he had been in the habit of visiting the establishment at the Cross whenever he stood in need of any article its stores could supply, and was so much startled on one occasion, in 1811, when he was not permitted to carry off the paper he had chosen without leaving an equivalent in money, that he wrote an indignant remonstrance to my father on the subject. He says : " Is it really so ? is my credit now so very low with you ? have you actually directed one of your menials — a base-born fellow — educated in a charity work-house, and whose sole importance is derived from his standing behind your counter, openly to insult me, whom you have known these twenty years ? " Not long after, he was both startled and *alarmed* when an account of nearly £20 was handed to him for books and stationery which he had carried off from time to time. I do not think he himself regarded such appropriations as theft, but they were certainly unwarrantable, and my father's affairs having about this time come under more vigilant superintendence, the worthy Doctor had become an object of careful attention whenever he came within the premises.

I remember to have been told by Mr. Charles Kirkpatrick Sharpe of another frequent visitor of the establishment at the Cross, a noted bibliomaniac, and a man of good position in society, whose conscience, like that of Bryce Snailsfoot,[1] was a timorous creature, apt to retire at sight of an *editio princeps,* insomuch that whenever he appeared my father received this warning, " The gentleman with the brown great-coat is in the gallery ! "

---

[1] " My conscience," he said, " is as tender as any man's in my degree, but she is something of a timorous nature, cannot abide angry folk, and can never speak above her breath when there is aught of a fray going forward. Indeed, she hath *at all times* a small and low voice." — *The Pirate.*

Our Doctor had so long regarded it as a prescriptive right to call for any work of which he conceived himself to stand in need, that I find him writing to my father in the following terms of indignation on meeting a refusal : —

"On calling at 10 Princes Street on the 26th ult., to inquire after the recently published number of the 'Medical Journal,' I was not only refused that 'Journal,' but rudely and insolently treated before a number of people and all your shopmen by that popinjay and pert pragmatical coxcomb who stands behind your counter, who asked me in a very uncivil and impertinent tone, 'If I were a *subscriber* to that work ?' — a very gratuitous question surely, as he well knew that I was not a subscriber to it. He said, moreover, that he would not give me the 'Journal' without Mr. Cadell's orders or permission, and desired me to apply to Mr. C. on Monday. You may suppose I feel no disposition to make such an application, and that I choose rather to forego the use of the 'Journal.' Here the matter stands awaiting your decision, and let me earnestly entreat you to give effect to your liberality in as far as you intend to supply the *desiderata* mentioned in my last, before I start on my autumnal pilgrimage."

Finding that he was no longer to be allowed to help himself at will, Dr. Forbes betook himself to almost peremptory supplication of the principal, and did not hesitate to demand copies of the most expensive works when fancy prompted, or he believed that he had need of them. Pride of a certain kind he had in abundance, but to obtain a book he coveted he would threaten, wheedle, beg, borrow, or appropriate. The plea of poverty was his favorite argument, but one way or other he had collected a very considerable library, and I remember hearing my father say to him one day, when he complained of wholesale plunder that had been committed in it during his absence in the country, " Ah, Doctor ! I suspect if we all had our own, your library would be still smaller." [1]

I know not to what extent my father's influence was used in

---

[1] I have been told that on the sale of this collection there were found an unusual number of odd volumes !

promoting the professional views of Dr. Forbes, but I am sure he cannot have done much with a clear conscience, for I find him on one occasion saying of an unreasonable author that "he ought to be put to death without benefit of clergy, — even Dr. Duntikin." Our Doctor was certainly a man rather of ready acceptance than of acceptability, and although his attainments were considerable, — he indeed stood so high in the estimation of some of his clerical brethren that he was strongly recommended for preferment by such eminent persons as Principal Baird and the Professor of Logic and Rhetoric in Edinburgh University, — their united testimony in his favor proved unsuccessful. In the Rev. Mr. Wightman of Kirkmahoe, in Dumfriesshire, he also had a faithful and most hospitable friend, in whose house he was accustomed for many years to spend the autumn months.

Wherein our Doctor's power of fascination lay I have failed to discover, but with my father and Mr. Wightman it certainly was strong, — for the long-suffering hospitality of the one was never-failing, and to the other he applied with the confidence of affiliation in every difficulty until the close of life. The occupation by which he earned what he was wont to call his *pittance* was "grinding" youths while preparing to take a degree in Law, Medicine, or Theology, and I am inclined to believe that his labors yielded him a very sufficient livelihood; but in applying to my father for his half-yearly dividend he usually represented his finances as reduced to half a crown, and in his annual pilgrimage to Kirkmahoe he avoided what he termed the expense of "wheels and hoofs,' and trudged over hill and dale along "Cheapside·" with knapsack on his back. It was his wont on such occasions to favor my father with a narrative of his adventures by the way, although he generally expressed a doubt whether his friend would read the letter. These communications were always characteristic, and sometimes amusing.

Each year, before leaving Edinburgh for his autumn holiday, he enumerates, and almost demands, a list of books required, as he says, for an "intellectual viaticum," and bitterly complains when any of the number are denied him. Those were not the days of cheap books, and he was never restrained by the value, but only by the weight and bulk of the publications. The "Encyclopædia" and "Supplement" he reserved for winter demand ; these also he succeeded in obtaining.

In the autumn of 1825, destined to be his last, we find him again at Kirkmahoe with his long-suffering friend, his hopes of preferment not yet extinguished, and manifested in urgent appeals to my father to exert himself to secure a presentation, either to Abbotshall, Glencairn, or Kells, all of which had become vacant. He expresses high approval of my father's project of the "Miscellany," and mentions the subjects he desires to undertake in connection with it !

I hope I have not presented too cruel a view of my subject. He was kind to an aged sister in Dunkeld, and his last letter to my father shows warm interest in a young relative whose career he entreats him to promote.

Early in March, 1826, my father hearing that Dr. Forbes was seriously ill, requested the excellent Dr. Abercrombie to give him a report upon his case. The following note, dated March 7th, was the result : —

"DEAR SIR, — I have seen Dr. Forbes several times, and you may depend upon me paying him every attention in my power. He is affected with great depression and a degree of fever, bad sleep and impaired appetite, and his strength is considerably reduced. I have sent him some wine, but have found difficulty in ascertaining the state of his pecuniary resources. I have reason, however, to fear that they are very deficient. I shall mention to him your kind inquiries after him. Sincerely yours, JOHN ABERCROMBIE."

On the 11th April Duncan Forbes breathed his last, and two days later my father addressed the following letter to the gentleman who had undertaken to arrange the funeral : —

" *Confidential.*

"3 PARK PLACE, 13*th April*, 1826.

" SIR, — The interest which I understand you took in the late Dr. Forbes, of whose death I heard yesterday with much real regret, must be my apology for the freedom I use in addressing these few lines to you.

" I have not heard who takes charge of the funeral, but under the presumption that you are to be kind enough to undertake that duty, I request leave to say that I shall consider myself as answerable, at a future day (not very distant, I hope), for the amount of the expenses which may be necessarily incurred on that occasion.[1] I have the honor to be, sir, your obedient servant, ARCH. CONSTABLE.

" R. W. NIVEN, Esq., Writer to the Signet."

On the next day my father received from Mr. Thomas Thomson, who had also been a patron of this eccentric man, a note which contained the following announcement, for which my father was altogether unprepared : —

" Poor Dr. D. F. ! I daresay the charitable world are charitable enough to think that he has died of hunger. It may be so ; but our queer friend will cut up for nearly £1500, of which £1000 is on heritable security ! On the Sunday before he died he dictated a Will which he did not live to execute, containing minute directions for the disposal of his body, in lead, timber, earth, stone, and iron ! ! and directing myself and two other executors to establish a Bursary at St. Andrews, to be in all time coming called Dr. Forbes's Bursary ! "

JOSEPH RITSON.

Some years ago a friend of mine, when visiting at Fulham Palace, enjoyed the honor, not often vouchsafed to Scottish laymen, of passing a night under the same roof with five prelates of the Church of England, and witnessed the departure next morning of two of the right reverend gentlemen, in the brougham of their host, who quaintly expressed a doubt whether one horse would be able to draw so great a load of dignity. My friend remarked that he believed horse-power alone could draw together two prelates so diametrically opposed in politics, both lay and clerical.

[1] The crisis in my father's affairs had occurred two months earlier.

A faculty exists, however, of wielding and welding, for a time and end, the powers of very various minds ; and by no one has this faculty been manifested in more eminent degree than by Sir Walter Scott. Mr. Lockhart tells us that in the preparation of the " Minstrelsy of the Scottish Border," he enlisted the united services of Richard Heber and the Ettrick Shepherd, George Ellis and William Laidlaw, John Leyden, Robert Jamieson, and Joseph Ritson, individuals whom perhaps no other man could have associated in a common cause. Even among the "happy families" that earn a living for themselves and their conductors by a public exhibition of mutual forbearance — if we may not say agreement, — there is frequently a perverse monkey in disgrace for abstracting feathers from the peacock's tail, and apt to bring the exemplary community into disorder by his malicious freaks. Such an one — but for Scott's controlling, sweetening influence — Mr. Lockhart would have us believe that Ritson might have been. He tells us that " this narrow-minded, sour, and dogmatical little word-catcher had hated the very name of a Scotsman, and was utterly incapable of sympathizing with any of the higher views of his new correspondent. Yet the bland courtesy of Scott disarmed even this half-crazy pedant ; and he communicated the stores of his really valuable learning in a manner that seems to have greatly surprised all who had hitherto held any intercourse with him on antiquarian topics." The biographer elsewhere dwells with evident complacency on the eccentricities of the " half-mad pedant," as he calls him, and details an invasion of them by John Leyden, in devouring, merely for the horror of the rigid vegetarian, a raw beef-steak. On the authority of Mr. Robert Pearse Gillies, whom he designates as "a gentleman of the Scotch bar, well known, among other things, for some excellent translations from the German," Mr. Lockhart also tells us that on another occasion, Ritson had " expressed himself in such outrageous terms " to Mrs. Scott, in consequence of that lady having offered him a slice of cold beef, that Leyden threatened to "*thraw his neck,*" and thus "frightened him away." I confess my utter disbelief of the whole story, the more so as Mr. Lockhart describes the " Recollections of Sir Walter Scott," wherein it is related, as " a set of papers in which many inaccurate statements occur."

My father's correspondence with Mr. Ritson was uninterruptedly friendly, and his " Life and Letters," published by Pickering in 1833, ought to have restrained Mr. Lockhart from presenting him as an object of ridicule and dislike. He was a man of warm heart and honorable principles, and if he unhappily neither made the most of this world nor hoped for one to come, if his temper was irritable and his faith was weak, while yet he exerted himself strenuously in what he believed to be the cause of truth, and was kind and considerate to his friends and his dependents, he surely rather deserves compassion than reprobation at the hands of Christian men. If we are to credit the narrative of Mr. R. P. Gillies, his temper must have been far from unforgiving, for in letters written to Mr. Scott after the events therein detailed, Ritson mentions Leyden as their " inestimable friend," declares " there are no men in the world I am so desirous to see as your friend Leyden and yourself," and says, " Though I can hardly flatter myself with another pleasant and interesting visit to Lasswade Cottage, the stay [in London] of our amiable and accomplished friend Dr. Leyden is some atonement."

As a critic Ritson was certainly severe, and often repented of his severity, but he was always desirous to be just, and never hesitated to make the *amende* where he felt it was required of him. In his earliest letter to my father (1801), already printed in 1833, there occurs a characteristic passage, which I shall here transcribe : —

" I am sorry to say that I have looked over (for it is impossible that any one should read) your publication of ' Scottish Poems of the Sixteenth Century,' [1] with astonishment and disgust. To rake up the false, scandalous, and despicable libels against the most beautiful, amiable, and accomplished princess that ever existed, whose injurious treatment, misfortunes, per-

---

[1] Edited by John Graham Dalyell, advocate.

secution, imprisonment, and barbarous murder will be a lasting
blot on the national character to the end of time, and which
were, as they deserved, apparently devoted to everlasting
oblivion and contempt, — to stuff almost an entire volume with
the uninteresting lives of such scoundrels as Regent Murray
and the laird of Grange, — to publish, in short, such vile,
stupid, and infamous stuff, which few can read, and none can
approve, is a lamentable proof of a total want of taste or judgment, a disgrace to Scottish literature, degrades the reputation
of the editor, and discredits your own. I must be free to tell
you that I will not suffer such an infamous and detestable heap
of trash to pollute and infect my shelves ; it is therefore under
sentence of immediate transportation. I confess, at the same
time, that the libel against the Tulchan Bishop, though excessively scurrilous, has much merit, and would have been admis-
sible in any collection of a different description."

In the following extracts of letters from Mr. Ritson, I shall
preserve the peculiar orthography. The correspondence
mainly refers to a publication of "Select Scotish Poems,"
which he had intrusted to my father's care, of which, at the
time of the author's death, only two sheets had been printed,
and which, I believe, was never completed. The correspondence is unimportant, unless in so far as it tends to redeem the
character of Ritson from the imputation of acrimony, so liberally attributed to it by Mr. Lockhart and others, and to show
that Leyden's offense, if ever offered, had been soon forgotten.
In the earliest, dated December 19, 1801, after a kindly message to that *bête noire*, he offers my father the publication of
another work : —

" My annals of the Picts, Scots, Strath-Clyde Britons, Cum-
brians, Galwegians, and men of Murray, in Latin and Eng-
lissh, with which i have takein great pains, and which is certainly a very curious book for that sort of learning, is now
ready for the press.[1] If you think it would answer for your
shop, it is at your service ; but i do not wish you to venture

---

[1] It was eventually published by his nephew, in 1828 ; two vols. crown 8vo.

upon it, if you are not perfectly satisfy'd, though we should likewise have the name of a good bookseler in London. Think on this and tel me your mind."

In a letter of March 1, 1802, Mr. Ritson writes of " our amiable and excellent friend, Mr. Leyden," and expresses a desire for a copy of Pinkerton's — which he elsewhere calls " the *Goth-pik's* " — " History of Scotland."

On September 25, 1802, he writes as follows : —

" In consequence of two serious paralytick shocks, my physician has recommended me to go to Bath for a month, which is all the time i have to spare. If I hapen'd to make use of any improper expressions in my last letter, i sincerely beg your pardon, as i have and shal ever retain for you the utmost regard and esteem ; but unhapyly my mind is liable to be irritateëd by trifling circumstances.

" Dear Sir, earnestly and sincerely, your ever faithful friend, and obedient humble servant, J. RITSON."

Ritson's horror of animal food, and the diminutive *egotism* of his peculiar orthography, were eccentricities that could give no offense to others, while his many fine qualities of head and heart attracted the regard and admiration of such men as George Chalmers, Mr. Surtees of Mainsforth, and Walter Scott. The latter wrote of him after his death : [1] —

" I loved poor Ritson, with all his singularities ; he was always kind and indulgent to me. He had an honesty of principle, which, if it went to ridiculous extremities, was still respectable, from the soundness of the foundation. I don't believe the world could have made Ritson say the thing he did not think. I wish we had his like at present. . . . . I always received from him the readiest, kindest, and most liberal assistance in the objects of our joint pursuits."

In allusion to Mr. Ritson's dislike of animal food arising from a principle of humanity, Mr. Surtees says : [2] " I could

[1] See *Memoir of Joseph Ritson,* by Sir Harris Nicolas. London, 1833.
[2] *Ibid.* p. lxix.

mention a hundred instances of Ritson's unaffected feeling for the sufferings of the brute creation — their groans entered his soul. It is easy to ridicule such feelings, but I own I had rather possess them than laugh at them." And again, " In whatever singular habits or speculative opinions he might indulge, his deep and serious feelings were neither morose nor unsocial ; his attachments were steady and disinterested ; the associates of his youth were the friends of his age, and he lost the regard of no honest man whose good opinion he had once acquired. He neglected no natural tie of blood or connection, and to an only nephew his attention was parental. In society with those in whose characters he had confidence, Ritson was a lively, cheerful companion, frank and unreserved ; and, if tenacious of his own peculiar opinions, he was at least most tolerant of those of others, and would permit every one to . . . . jingle his bells to his own time."

Like Charles Lamb and Sydney Smith, and other Englishmen who have disparaged Scotsmen and their country, Ritson counted many of my countrymen as his most valued friends, and to one of these, Mr. William Laing, evidently in *badinage*, he thus expresses himself in a letter dated January 25, 1793 : —

" Shoals of Scotchmen are arriving here every day ; the difficulty, I should imagine, would be to find one going back. Edinburgh, at the same time, is so very small a place, that you may be easily acquainted with the motions of every individual from your shop door. Formerly, I have been told, when a Scotchman intended a journey to the South, he used to ring the cryer's bell for a quarter of a year beforehand, in order to indemnify himself against the enormous expenses of the Newcastle wagon, by the packets and parcels he got the charge of from his neighbors ; but at present, I suppose, the neighbors go too — not in the Newcastle wagon, but the mailcoach ! — *Tempora mutantur.*"

Mr. Ritson's ailments had been more serious and deeply seated than any one except himself supposed ; a crisis came, and on the 4th of October, 1803, George Chalmers wrote as follows to my father : —

" I know not if you have heard of the sad fate of poor Ritson. He was sent from Gray's Inn to Hoxton, sadly deranged, a fortnight ago, and from Hoxton has been sent to that bourn whence none return. He died last Saturday. Before he was sent from the Inn he was seen burning his papers a whole night. I hear nothing is left, except his copy of ' Shakespeare,' which he had been long preparing for the press. This leads me to ask if you ever got from him the biographical work on the historians and poets of Scotland, which he put into my hands, and intended for you. I intended to have corrected it for him and for you. But before I could do much he sent for it, in order to show it to Mr. Scott, when he was up here lately. Happy if he sent it to you by Mr. Scott ; if he did not, it is gone — forever. If you should happily have got it, I am still more ready, now that Ritson is gone, to do what I can to make the book as perfect as possible. The subject, and charity, demand this of me, amidst my many labors."

On the 27th of the same month Mr. Chalmers writes : " I shall keep an eye on poor Ritson's Remains ; and if I can retrieve what I fear is gone, you shall know; I would give more for the MS. than any bookseller, because I would make it a groundwork ; " and again, on the 27th December in that year : " You have heard of the fate of Ritson's ' Bibliographia Scotica,' which was said to have been burnt, but appeared in his Catalogue. I wished for it, that I might have completed it, and given it to *you*, as Ritson intended. I offered upwards of forty guineas for it ; and Longman and Rees bought it dearly either for you or Mr. Walter Scott. If they find it a dear bargain, they have themselves to blame by not acting in concert for the good of the whole. Longman and Rees must, at last, come to me for help."

The coveted MS. was, I understand, eventually presented by Messrs. Longman and Co. to Mr. Chalmers, in acknowledgment of some literary service rendered by that gentleman.

In the third number of the " Edinburgh Review " Mr. Ritson's foolish crotchet on " Abstinence from Animal Food " is very severely dealt with by Lord Brougham, and the author held up to contempt on account of it, and even to execration for a graver fault; but in the fourteenth number of the same journal the genial reviewer of his "Metrical Romances" takes a more lenient view, and sums up his notice in the following words: "Upon the whole, it occurs to us, from a careful perusal of his Essay, that Mr. Ritson's talents were better adapted to research than to deduction, to attack than to defense, to criticism than to composition; and that he has left us a monument of profound industry and extensive study, undirected by any attempt at system, and tarnished by the splenetic peculiarities of an irritable temperament. Still, let it be remembered to his honor, that without the encouragement of private patronage, or of public applause, without hopes of gain, and under the certainty of severe critical censure, he has brought forward such a work on National Antiquities, as in other countries has been thought worthy of the labor of Universities and the countenance of princes."

JOHN PINKERTON.

The true Ishmael among archæologists of that day was John Pinkerton, who seldom praises others, and of whom no one seems to have a good word to say. Neither shall I enter on his defense. My father's literary connection with him, in so far as I am aware, was limited to the "Iconographia Scotica, or Portraits of Illustrious Persons in Scotland, with Biographical Notes." Mr. Pinkerton was notorious as well for suppression as misquotation of authorities, for *suppressio veri* and *suggestio falsi*. In his collection of "Scotish Ballads," 1783, he inserted as ancient a Second Part of "Hardyknute," etc., which were proved to be modern; yet, in the Preface to his "Dissertation on the Scythians or Goths," he says: "In Germany or Scandinavia, if an author were to quote falsely, he would go near to incur the character of a scoundrel and a liar." He must have presumed too confidently on the greater lenity of his countrymen in estimating his own productions. Sir Walter Scott says of him that "he understood in an extensive sense Horace's maxim, *quidlibet audendi.*" In his " Recollections of Paris " in 1802 to 1805 we have abundant evidence of the low level of his moral standard. He died there in 1825.

ROBERT JAMIESON.

A very different and far higher man was Robert Jamieson. Of genial heart and honorable mind, he thought of himself not more highly than he ought to think, and was liberal in his esteem and consideration for others. Materials are slender for biographic illustration of Mr. Jamieson ; he was a native, I believe, of Elgin, and must have received a classical education, for in 1800, the time at which his correspondence with my father began, he was usher in the school at Macclesfield in Cheshire, conducted by the Rev. Dr. Davies. His earlier communications have reference to the " Popular Ballads," [1] published at Edinburgh in 1806, — a work which, according to Sir Walter Scott, "was not greeted by the public with the attention it deserved." Sir Walter describes Mr. Jamieson as " a gentleman of literary and poetical accomplishments," and was afterwards instrumental, by means of an arrangement with Mr. Thomas Thomson, Deputy Clerk Register, in bringing him back to this country, from Riga, where for some years he acted as tutor in the family of a merchant. Scott's kindly feeling for Jamieson was warmly returned, and it is pleasing to observe the interest that each felt in the literary work and reputation of the other. Jamieson writes to my father on 6th June, 1801 : —

" Send me ' Scotland's Complaint,' and the other Collection, if there are many things in it which have not been edited before. Mr. Scott tells me he is hard at work scouring the rusty panoply of ' Sir Tristrem.' Pray let me have him as soon as he has got his new *claiths* on. Will you have the goodness in the meantime to present my kindest and most grateful re-

---

[1] *Popular Ballads and Songs, from Traditions, Manuscripts, and Scarce Editions, with Translations of Similar Pieces from the Ancient Danish Language, and a few Originals by the Editor.* 2 vols. 8vo.

spects to Mr. Leyden, who, Mr. Scott tells me, has had the
politeness to undertake to transcribe some things for me in
the Advocates' Library ; tell him how sensible I am of the
kindness he does me, but that I am ashamed to think he
should have such drudgery on my account. It would be particularly agreeable to me if Mr. Leyden would have the goodness to point out any lyrical pieces yet unedited in the Ban-
natyne MS., or elsewhere, worth preserving, to commit them
to some careful transcriber, and glance over the copy, allowing
for the writing out whatever he may think reasonable, and an
amanuensis may agree to do it for. I will immediately, and
with much thankfulness, transmit the money to London, to be
paid as you shall direct ; and may I hope that you will do me
the favor to be my banker in Edinburgh ! As I am a poor
school-fag, he may perhaps be disposed to labor for me out of
charity. But I am not so very poor ; my income this half-
year being fifty and a half guineas, with board, lodging, coals,
candle, attendance, etc. This, though not opulence, is comfortable for a poor minstrel, and I mention it to take off the
delicacy and reserve which an apprehension of my incapacity
to pay might occasion on the part of my good friends in your
quarter, in letting the copies be taken for me at my own expense. I do nothing in the ballad way at present, nor have
had leisure to do this half-year ; but in ten days our six
weeks' summer vacation commences, and I must 'fecht like a
Turk and work like a man' to bring up my lee-way. I only
wait for a few things from Scotland to set to. I begin every
day to feel more and more reluctance to publishing my subscription, but have not yet finally determined. My paper has
been bought some time — wove, cream-colored, etc. I believe
I shall give few prints, if any ; — I must have so much music.
Tell Mr. Scott I 'll write to him forthwith. I have not yet got
the complete copy of the ' Baron of Brakely ' from Scotland.
The third stanza of his fragment of it made the tears start
into my eyes."

On the 29th of the same month Jamieson writes as follows
to Scott himself ; —

"Sorry I am, my dear friend, that you should have had such reasons for your long silence. Under such circumstances I know how irksome a task writing at all must be, and I value as I ought your kindness in making such sacrifices on my account. All the things you have had the goodness to send me are to my purpose. The third stanza of the 'Baron of Brakely' brought the tears to my eyes. I have got a complete copy of it, but much inferior in its dress to yours, which I would give a great deal to have complete and genuine. Pray, is the music of it come-atable? If I remember aright (for I have not heard it since I was a boy) the music of 'Lord Roslin's Daughter' is very decent. Could you procure it? I am much pleased with that piece, of which I remembered the greater part. Some of the readings, as I learnt it when a boy, are preferable, I think, to Herd's MS., *e. g.* —

> "'Whan the cherry is in the *flirrey*,
>   I wat it has nae stane,
> Whan the chicken is in the *egg*,
>   I wat it has nae bane;
> *And sin' the flood o' Noah*
>   *The dow she had nae ga*:
> Sae we'll baith lye in ae bed,
>   And ye'se lye neist the wa'.'

"You know the tradition in Scotland, that the dove which Noah sent out of the ark in search of land, flew till she broke her gall before she returned, and that that bird has never had a gall since?

"I am exceedingly obliged to you and Mr. Leyden for all your kind endeavors in my behalf; and am only sorry that my situation should not only oblige me to be troublesome to my friends, but preclude my making them any suitable return. On this head I lately gave a commission to Mr. Constable, which I presume he has delivered. By the bye, I have lost all hope about the books which I ordered of him. Why does he not write me, either to say that I shall or shall not have them? Will you have the goodness to ask him when you see him? You'll please tell Mr. Laing when you see him, that I have not yet received the 'Euripides,' which has been at the binder in London these four months ; but I shall transmit the money to Cuthil in eight or ten days.

"Did you ever hear ' Gregor's Ghost ? ' I have heard it, but I remember nothing of it. I should like much to have it as a companion to ' Fair Annie of Lochryan,' if it has any reference to that story, which I do not remember. Did Dr. Anderson receive a hasty scrawl from me, accompanying ' Lady Jane ' and ' The Gude Wallace ? ' What says he of them ? What have you made of ' Jellon Graeme ? ' You have two copies, concluding differently. Could you take the other, and leave Mrs. Brown's for me ? This is a very bold request ; but if the other is good also, both might be preserved, and I am very fond of it. Do you take ' The Wells of Slains ? ' There is a fine old ditty which I wish much to procure — do you know it ? The story is nearly the same with that of Glasgerion in ' Percy.' It begins in some such way as this : —

> "' Glenkendie was ance the best harper
> That ever harp'd on a string ;
> He 'd harpit fish out o' saut water,
> Or water out o' a stane ;
> Or milk out o' a maiden's breast,
> That bairn had never nane,' etc.

"In Ritson's ' Robin Hood, Notes and Illustrations,' p. lxxv., he mentions ' an old book in black letter in the Advocates' Library, sent to the Faculty by a gentleman from Ayrshire in 1788,' in which ' are fourteen leaves of *fits*, etc., of Robyn Hood.' Ritson could not get at the book. Pray is it still in the Library ? and what does it contain ? What are these *fits ?* Are they fragments of ' A Lytell Geste of Robyn Hode, in 8 fittes,' reprinted by Ritson ? You 'll much oblige me by inquiring.

"As it is at present vacation-time with us, I am quite at leisure, and wish to get my materials together as soon as possible, in order that I may work upon them before the labor of next session begins. Are there any interesting variations from the printed editions in your copy of ' May Colvin ' and ' False Sir John ? '

"How does 'Sir Tristem' come on? Is the good old knight's panoply genuine antique, or has some of the true mold of the rust been brushed off in passing through different hands? I long uncommonly to see him. When may we hope for the publication?

"How does Dr. Anderson come on with 'Drummond?' And Dr. Jamieson with his lexicographic work? Please remember me kindly to them.

"With best wishes for all health and happiness to you and Mrs. Scott and family, I am, my dear friend, your most obliged friend and servant, R. JAMIESON."

In illustration of the considerateness of Mr. Jamieson, I shall quote the following passage from a letter to my father, in which he seems to have good reason to accuse his correspondent of neglecting his commissions : "Pray let me hear from you *immediately*. I hope you have no sufficient excuse for your neglect. If it has been owing to ill-health, or any other disagreeable circumstance, I have only to beg pardon and be sorry for my impatience, and to assure you that I am sincerely yours."

In August, 1803, I find Jamieson writing as follows from Epsom : "Your last I received here, where I shall remain for some time with my friend Mr. Boucher,[1] assisting him with his 'Archæological Dictionary.'" Was this work ever completed? In 1805, on the 10th August, Jamieson writes from London : —

"I have sent my 'Ballads,' but in a miserably ragged state, to Mr. Scott. If you think that, even as they are, they may sell, I will, at the end of two years, indemnify you to the amount of £30, but no more, if you should publish a handsome edition of them, and be out of pocket by it. Let them not be printed at all, if it will be too great a risk to publish such an edition as that of the 'Border Minstrelsy.' Cadell and Davies lately made me an offer, through the medium of

---

[1] The Rev. Jonathan Boucher was a learned clergyman and philologist, born in Cumberland in 1738, and died in 1804.

Bulmer the printer, of publishing at their own risk, and sharing profits, if any.

"I have hardly time to tell you how sensible I am of the handsome manner in which you have behaved towards me on various occasions, since I had the pleasure of seeing you at Edinburgh."

Not long after this I apprehend that Mr. Jamieson must have gone abroad, for in 1806 we find Walter Scott already negotiating for his return, though it will be seen from the following correspondence that in June, 1808, he was still at Riga : —

MR. WALTER SCOTT TO MR. JAMIESON.

"EDINBURGH, *16th December*, 1806.

"ROBERT JAMIESON, ESQ., *Riga :* —

"*My dear Sir,* — I was yesterday surprised to find by a letter of yours, dated on the 15th November, that you have not got two of mine, written since the publication of your book. In the last I mentioned what I now have the pleasure to repeat, that the 'Ballads' have been very well received by the public, and Constable is pleased with the sale. Since that time there has been a pretty rough attack from the 'Critical Review,' arising, I suppose, from the connection which Mr. Pinkerton has with that Journal. He is returned from Paris, and probably was not particularly gratified with the notice taken of him in your Preface. This, however, is but a conjecture of mine. Constable long ago shipped for you the books you wanted, from Leith. The vessel was driven back, and the books relanded and shipped in another vessel. There were also several sets, four or five I think he says, of your own work, and I am truly surprised and sorry to find that the package has not reached you. I cannot but hope you have ere now received one at least of my letters. I wish with all my heart you were safe in Scotland. Mr. Thomson, who has been lately named deputy of the Lord Register, has great occasion for assistance from some person as well acquainted as you are with old hands and Scottish antiquities. He is a noble-minded fellow, and would strain a point to make your situation comfortable, if you would think of assisting him in his department, which is the Ancient Records and Diplomata of Scotland. I suppose that as this sort of labor is very well paid, you might be sure of from £150 to £200 a year to begin with, and every effort would be made to place you on a more permanent footing. When I say £150 or £200, I mean that as this is a kind of piecework, Mr. Thomson would put it in your power to execute work to that amount. You could easily combine this labor with that of teaching a scholar or two, if you were so disposed. We would, of course, keep the Library in our eye, as it must open one day. In short, you would be on the spot; and although my friends are not at present in power — so that, like Noodle in 'Tom Thumb,' I am on the side of the malcontents, — yet things may turn round again, when I will have some chance of being listened to. I am sensible this is a very small thing, but it gives you a footing in your native country, and connects you with a most excellent man, whom I am sure you would have every reason to be pleased with.

" I must not omit to mention that your Norse translations came safe, and are printed in your collection. The principal blunder in the work was the mutilating the Battle of Belrinnes, which has not been discovered by the Critical critic. As I am very uncertain as to this letter's fate, I will rather repeat what I have said in another than prolong it at present. All your friends are well, and the country is *one and all*. Believe me, yours most truly,   WALTER SCOTT."

MR. JAMIESON TO MR. CONSTABLE.

"RIGA, *June 7th*, O. S., 1808.

" MY DEAR SIR, — Having never heard a word about my collection of 'Ballads' since about a month after they were published, I am totally in the dark as to their fate, and the reception they have met with. Willing, however, to do justice to you, to such as may have purchased the work, and to myself,

as soon as I knew that it was to be published I resumed my
labors with the utmost zeal and industry. I have now by me,
fairly transcribed for the press, nearly thirty romantic ballads,
etc., translated from the Icelandic, Danish, Swedish, and German, all of them curious, and all of them, so far as I know, perfectly new, in any form or language whatsoever, to my countrymen. These, with the notes, etc. (which I hope will do me some
credit as they have cost me much pains), and glossary, will make
a third volume, larger than those already published. As sixteen of the ballads from the Danish are now in Mr. Scott's
hands, he will be able to give you some idea of what may be
expected from the volume. I have given him leave to let them
all be inserted in the ‘Scots Magazine,’ with my signature. If
the unfortunate volumes already published have been sold, the
third volume will, I hope, redeem my character for accuracy and
industry, and make my peace with the purchasers ; if they have
not sold, the third volume will make them sell ; and I have it
now in my power to prepare the work for a second edition, in
such a manner as will make it a necessary appendage, and less
unworthy companion, to the ‘ Border Minstrelsy.’ In the meantime, my dear sir, if it has sold, and if you owe me so much
money, you will oblige me very much by writing to Mr. Isaac
Forsyth, bookseller in Elgin, and authorizing him to pay my
poor old mother in Westfield, for me, the sum of £10 sterling.
He can give the money to Mr. Buchan, the Episcopal clergyman in Elgin, who will give it to the good old woman ; and
let him tell her that I got it for *old ballads*, which she often
thought it very silly in me to be so fond of. I can at present
devise no other possible means of conveying money to her ;
and there was so much blundering and so many delays before
she got the last, that I am very anxious that she should receive this, which, in these trying times, I fear she wants. This
is the fourth attempt I have made within these six months
to transmit it, and all have failed. On this account, my dear
sir, whether you owe me so much money or not, if you think
me deserving of so much credit, I hope you will trust me so
far. If I live, you will certainly be paid, and if I die, at all

events, thank God, my gear, though little, will be aboon my
debts — I shall leave you ten pounds' worth of books and
ballads, and my blessing. I shall be with you as soon as I
can possibly get away from this wretched place, but I despair
of that being sooner than next summer, by which time Buona-
parte will probably drive us out *vi et armis.* Have the goodness to tell Mr. Scott whether you have done me this favor,
as he may find means of having a letter conveyed to me, *via*
London, according to the instructions I have given him.

" It does me good to hear that Mr. Scott continues to grow
up and flourish like a green bay tree, and that the poet gets
rich and the bookseller gets fat upon it — lang be 't sae ! Be
sure to scold him well when you see him for his unmerciful
neglect in not writing me a single line these eighteen months,
while I have written volumes to him. But perhaps that is the
reason why he has not written to me, for fear of increasing the
evil and provoking me to further trespasses upon his leisure
and his patience ; and certainly his time has been much more
profitably employed. I 've sent him two more very curious
ballads, which you will see or hear of. I have in meditation
to translate for you a very entertaining and interesting work in
four duodecimo volumes, of travels among the Calmucks ; and
as the author is a clergyman in Livonia, I shall procure such
notes, drawings, etc., as will make the translation more valuable than the original, and will secure the property of it to the
bookseller as certainly as if it were an original work. I 'll
bring it with me, and we must get rich and fat upon it. If we
do, I shall go to Sweden with £600 in my pocket (if I can
raise so much), stay at Lund, Upsala, Stockholm, etc., ten or
twelve months, and return with a cart-load of books, MS., antiquities, observations, translations, etc., etc. ; then visit Ork-
ney, Shetland, the Hebrides, write a book as big as Johnson's
folio Dictionary, and astonish the world with the *greatness* of
my works. Adieu ; God bless you !   R. JAMIESON."

The exact time of Mr. Jamieson's return to this country I
do not know ; but in 1811 and 1814, I find him on such cordial

terms with our family, that he was a frequent and welcome
visitor at Craigcrook, and invites himself to dine at my grandfather's house on New Year's Day. In 1820, on the occasion
of his candidature for the office of Librarian to the Faculty of
Advocates, he refers to Walter Scott, Thomas Thomson, and
my father, as the best judges of his fitness for the post. He
was unsuccessful, the appointment having been conferred on
the late Dr. David Irving. It may be mentioned here, to Mr.
Jamieson's honor, as well as that of Dr. Benecke, Professor
and Librarian in the University of Göttingen, who was proposed by Sir William Hamilton to succeed Mr. Manners on
this occasion, but who declined to be nominated, that Mr.
Jamieson stated, in his letter of application, that he could not
offer himself as a *rival* of Dr. Benecke, though he would
gladly accept a smaller salary as his *colleagne.*

In his latter years Mr. Jamieson appears to have been unfortunate. His position in the General Register House became uncomfortable, and was at length relinquished. Mr.
Inness, in his " Memoir of Mr. Thomas Thomson," indicates
a belief that Jamieson was one of the *genus irritabile ;* " that
it was not in his nature to be content ; that he fretted extremely at the moderate pay and subordinate station." The
notice I have here been enabled to give of him is contradictory
of such a view. He died in London about the end of 1844.

THE EARL OF BUCHAN.

David Stewart Erskine, Earl of Buchan, along with much
that was conceited and absurd, had qualities of sterling excellence, both mental and moral. In friendship he was active and
sincere ; he appeared indeed *possessed* by a spirit of friendli-
ness, or perhaps I may call it friendly patronage, as it was
more frequently manifested towards individuals than to society
or the world at large. He had great confidence in the virtue
and influence of his own opinion when expressed in favor of
an individual or object, even where no reasons were adduced ;
he frequently gave recommendations like the following : —
" Lord Buchan begs leave to recommend Mr. Henning to the

attention of his friends," — and has been known to congratulate a youthful artist, after one or two turns in Princes Street, with assurances of success, that had no firmer foundation than the fact that he had been seen in public with the modern Mecænas leaning on his arm.

Lord Buchan's intercourse with my father seems to have begun in 1799, and continued without interruption till 1827. His Lordship was no great collector of books, but had much general interest in literary matters ; he contributed occasional papers of varying excellence, or rather worth, to the periodicals of the latter end of the last and the early part of the present century ; but though acute enough to discern good from bad in the writings of other men, the faculty of discriminating nonsense from sense appeared to desert him when the former flowed from his own pen. As an evidence of this, read the following lines by his Lordship, entitled " The Earl of Buchan Arriving in Scotland, to the Duchess of Gordon," printed in the " Scots Magazine " for 1802,[1] with an introduction by Leyden, the irony of which was recognized by all except the noble author : —

> " Thou beauteous star whose silvery light
> Enchanting came upon my youthful sight!
> Ah ! what a blaze has hid thy virgin rays,
> Whilst I, in woods retired, have past my days!
> Now, silvered o'er by time's eventful hand,
> I greet the evening beam on Scotia's strand.
> Clara ! this image is to picture thee !
> I saw thee rising from the Atlantic sea,
> Thy tresses dropping the cerulean wave,
> From whence thou didst the water lave ;
> The Graces and the loving Boy were there,
> And whilst they braided thy ambrosian hair
> I saw thee blushing, shrinking from my view,
> And thy quick footsteps brushing o'er the dew.
> Old Kaimes, like Vulcan, first proclaimed thy charms,
> And blest Alexis took thee to his arms,
> Clara ! thy charms surpass the Paphian Queen,

[1] Fearing probably to offend his Lordship by declining his production, and yet jealous for their editorial reputation, the editors placed it alone amid the prose, stating that from respect for Lord Buchan they had "assigned it a conspicuous place in their *Miscellany*, distinct from the mass of vulgar poetry."

Now Pallas' casque upon thy head is seen!
'T is not our hearts suffice to grace thy car,
The Muses come at last to close the war.
'T is fixt; behold the wreath thou well hast won,
I bear it smiling with my setting sun!
I ask no praise, no sympathetic tear,
Heaven is my home, I am a stranger here." [1]

The Earl of Buchan was manifestly not a poet, but he seems to have possessed the gift of calling forth kindred verse from others. The following *Impromptu* was composed by a Baronet of multitudinous sense and occasional nonsense, and sent to my father a day after Lord Buchan had been seen in his company on the race-ground at Musselburgh: —

"To make up the rout
Lord Buchan 'came out'
To see the Musselburgh Races;
But to keep 'himself in,'
And secure from all sin,
A 'Constable' watched all his paces.

[1] The following *Irregular Ode to the Duchess of Gordon by the Earl of Buchan* (Second Edition), is also, I believe, from Leyden's pen, but has never before been printed: —

1.

"Thou beauteous star,
Seen from afar,
Than Phœbe's silvery beam more bright, —
As yet a boy,
And somewhat coy,
I first beheld thy dazzling light.

2.

"Ah! what a blaze,
In thy young days,
Thy matchless beauty first revealed!
Hid that full blaze,
Thy virgin rays,
In deepest darkness lay concealed.
Whilst I in woods,
Midst streams and floods,
Have lived retired since days of yore.
I mind myself,
I count my pelf,
And now my head is silvered o'er.

" Oh why, my good Peer,
Should thus you appear,
With a male companion to chat,
When a sprightly young belle
Would suit you as well,
And would to your taste be more pat ? "

J. S.

As a proof that in 1816 his Lordship's admiration for his own productions had not diminished, the following, dated March 7th in that year, may here be quoted : —

" Lord Buchan returns Mr. Constable his hearty thanks for

3.

" As insect tribes, so bright and gay
Around the taper's quivering ray,
Are often burned or singed ;
So fluttering foplings, bards, and men
Of science, to your noble den
Allured, are quite unhinged.

4.

" Clara ! this image is to picture thee,
Like Venus rising from the sea.
I saw thee bathing in the briny wave,
I saw thy hands the water lave ;
Then Grace, thy maid,
Thy hair did braid,
Which her fingers most nimbly had weaved ;
When quick o'er the dew,
You blushed as you flew,
But my optics perhaps were deceived.

5.

" For, wherefore, and why,
Should we blush and look shy,
Because truth quite naked is seen ?
To be honest and civil,
And shame the old devil,
Not a rag should e'er cover her skin.

6.

" The village blacksmith first thy charms inspired,
When his strong frame at once was fired,
Not much unlike the red-hot iron he hammered,
While out 'midst sighs, some broken words he stammered.
So, to old Vulcan, Venus did her charms forego,
Jove's trusty blacksmith, many a year ago.

his obliging attention in sending him a copy of Anderson's 'Literary Miscellany,' for the purpose of marking his anonymous and other tracts, which having done, he returns the volumes, which may some years hence attract regard in Mr. Constable's son's library, when a great mass of modern poetry and rascally politics shall have gone to their own place. At any rate, together with the copy of his learned and worthy ancestor Sir Thomas Brown of Norwich's 'Posthumous Tracts,' which with an extemporaneous effusion in the front of the book, written by Lord B., was presented to Mr. Constable many years ago, they will serve to mark the regard of the donor.

"Dr. Robert Anderson of Windmill Street, a native of Lord Buchan's mother's native district in the west of Scotland, is possessed of a large mass of his correspondence, from whence perhaps hereafter it may be thought not uninteresting to the literary world to make a selection for publication, especially if it should be interspersed with Biographical Notes."

7.

"Clara! the Paphian Queen thy charms may dread.
Who, Madam, made the wig upon your head?
With noble ease and elegance it sits,
My taste in wigs — most critical, it hits.

8.

"La! what a wagon-load of hearts!
Six oxen, fed on turnips, stout and strong,
With force united, straining every nerve,
So huge a load could scarcely move along.

9.

"But now the Muses and the men of rhymes,
With modern song and tales of other times,
And odes, and elegies, and epigrams appear;
Loud squeaking voices pierce the ear;
While each in turn the verse recites,
The glowing verse the Muse indites,
I last, not least, shall close the war,
And celebrate thy glorious car.
I ask no praise, but let me have a dinner;
Far, far from home, — I am a strange old sinner."

EDINBURGH, *March* 16, 1802.

Lord Buchan's correspondence with distinguished persons was intimate and extensive, and the maxims contained in the following address to Americans resident in Edinburgh, on the 22d of February (1817), being "the anniversary of the birth of the virtuous and truly illustrious Washington," may be read and laid to heart with advantage at the present day by our cousins across the Atlantic : —

"GENTLEMEN, — My venerable ancestor, Henry Lord Cardross, having in times too similar to the present in Europe, formed an asylum for his distressed people in Carolina, from whence they were unfortunately driven by the Spaniards, I have felt a more than ordinary sympathy with everything relating to your country and nation, and did take accordingly, in conjunction with my excellent friend the first Earl of Chatham, a warm interest in behalf of the injured Americans then subject to mine, and although half a century has now elapsed since that memorable era it hath not ceased.

" I have therefore brought you together, Gentlemen, on this day, to commemorate the virtues of George Washington, the illustrious founder of your Republic, which I pray the Almighty Creator of the Universe to bless and preserve. That illustrious founder, Gentlemen, the truly excellent Washington, in one of his honored letters to me on the subject of his country, writes thus : ' To be little heard of in the great world of politics, in the words of your Lordship's letter, is expressive of my sentiments ; and I believe it is the sincere wish of United America to have nothing to do with the political intrigues or the squabbles of European nations, but on the contrary to exchange commodities and live in peace and harmony with all the inhabitants of the earth.' This, Gentlemen, I hope will continue to be the wish of your countrymen, and that you will treasure up in your memory the farewell advices and maxims of the glorious and virtuous President. ' Observe,' said he, ' a good faith and justice towards all nations ; cultivate peace and harmony with all. Religion and morality enjoin this conduct ; and can it be that good policy does not equally enjoin it? It will be worthy of a free enlightened nation, of a great nation, to give to mankind the magnanimous and too rare example of a people guided by an exalted justice and benevolence.

"'Can it be that Providence has connected the permanent felicity of nations with their virtues?

"'Promote, as an object of primary importance, institutions for the general diffusion of knowledge, etc.

"'I hold the maxim no less applicable to public than to private affairs, that *Honesty is always the best policy*.

"'Let us not indulge the supposition that morality can be maintained without religion.

"'In vain would that man claim the tribute of patriotism who should labor to subvert the pillars of religion and morality, the firmest props of the duties of men and citizens. A volume could not trace all their connections with private and public felicity!'

"I glory, Gentlemen, in having enjoyed the friendship and confidence of Washington; nor can I conclude this address, without quoting another maxim from his: —

"'The foundations of national policy must be laid in the pure and immutable principles of private morality; since there is no truth more thoroughly established, than that there exists in the economy and course of nature an indissoluble union between virtue and happiness, between duty and advantage, between the genuine maxims of an honest and magnanimous people, and the solid rewards of public prosperity and happiness, since we ought to be no less persuaded that the propitious smiles of Heaven can never be expected on a nation that disregards the eternal rules of order and right which Heaven itself has established.'

"Finally, Gentlemen, the learned and eminent President Jefferson has set forth the character of his illustrious predecessor to me in the following words: —

"'I feel,' writes he, 'a pride in the justice which your Lordship's sentiments render to the character of my illustrious countryman Washington. The moderation of his desires and the strength of his judgment enabled him to calculate correctly that the road to that glory which never dies is to use power for the support of the laws and liberties of our country, not for their destruction ; and his glory will accordingly survive the wreck of everything upon earth.'"

In this year also, on the occasion of my eldest brother setting out upon a Continental tour, Lord Buchan wrote a recommendatory letter to Lord Erskine, his distinguished brother, and sent besides a social and political passport, which he calls a "general letter of my approbation and good wishes. . . . . I flatter myself that this expression of my esteem and regard for you will prove useful, and that the Ministers and Consuls for Trade of my country, and the men of letters who have been formerly of my correspondence, will prove favorable to your views."

It has elsewhere been recorded, to the honor of Lord Buchan, that in his earlier years, while his income was scarcely adequate to the support of his position, he studiously limited his expenditure that he might be enabled to afford all desirable educational advantages to his two illustrious brothers. He was well repaid, not alone by their success, but by the grateful regard entertained for him throughout their lives ; and in estimating his character this evidence of his generosity ought not to be forgotten.

A letter from Benjamin West, *P. R. A.*, as being prophetic of the fame to be achieved by our Scottish school of Painting, may on that account be read with interest : —

"NEWMAN STREET, *January* 22, 1819.

"MY LORD, — Pray accept my sincere acknowledgment for your very friendly letter of the 17th ult., which I received through Mr. W. Donaldson, and allow me to express the satisfaction I feel in addressing your Lordship as one of my earliest and oldest friends.

"I am concerned to hear of Mr. Watson's misfortune in the bankruptcy of his son-in-law, though from your acknowledged

11

kindness in endeavoring to promote Mr. Watson's interest, I trust he will surmount any difficulty which may have occurred, as I think him a worthy man and an honor to his profession.

"The portrait which he painted of myself as President of the Royal Academy, I am highly gratified to find you intend placing in so honorable a station as your Lordship's collection, and adjoining to a picture from the pencil of Rafaelle, which circumstance, and in company too with the great Washington, I must ever consider as a most flattering testimony of your regard for the original. From your Lordship's attachment to the Fine Arts, and your liberality in promoting them, I am induced to mention the names of Wilkie, Allan, Geddes, and others, who have by their delineation of nature in the familiar occurrences of life, secured to themselves a lasting name in that country, so famed for its men of literature, science, and philosophy, and for its distinction in arms. These artists, combined with the talents of Raeburn and Watson in portrait-painting, and with those of Nasmyth for the truth and effect of his landscapes in portraying the romantic scenery of his country, will create a school for the Arts in Scotland, honorable in itself, and to the noblemen and gentlemen who have appreciated and encouraged the rising genius of that country.

I beg, my Lord, you will accept of the assurance of my sincere regard, and believe me your Lordship's obliged and obedient servant,   BENJAMIN WEST."

The regard entertained by Lord Buchan for my father was sincerely returned, and was shown by the gift of an admirable copy by Nicholson of Sir Joshua Reynolds's portrait of himself, and by giving him an antique ring, the device on which he himself so highly valued that he caused it to be carved upon his tomb at Dryburgh. The device is emblematic of immortality, containing the caterpillar, the chrysalis, and the butterfly, surmounted by the words Οὐκ ἔτι θνητός.

The Earl of Buchan died at Dryburgh in 1829.

Anna Seward

ANNA SEWARD.

All men are ready to make generous allowance for the un-graceful motions of one who has lost a limb — it may be in the service of his country — for in such a case the artificial member is a substitute, and not a voluntary addition ; but to walk by preference on stilts, from the cradle to the grave, how-ever easy the process may become, cannot be so comfortable for the elevated pilgrim as a more natural mode of progres-sion, nor will he long command the wondering admiration of spectators, however dexterous and surprising his performance. Walter Scott records in 1810, the year after her death, that "Anna Seward has for many years held a high rank in the an-nals of British literature,"[1] while Mr. Lockhart tells us that "Scott felt as acutely as any malevolent critic the pedantic affectations of Miss Seward's epistolary style," and that "in her case sound sense as well as vigorous ability had unfortu-nately condescended to an absurd disguise." "When she wrote upon subjects in which her feelings were deeply inter-ested, she forgot the 'tiara and glittering zone' of the priest-ess of Apollo in the more natural effusions of real passion. The song which begins —

> "'From thy waves, stormy Lannow, I fly,'

seems to have been composed under such influence."[2] Well

---

[1] See *Biographic Sketch* prefixed to edition of her *Poetical Works*, 1810. Miss Seward was born in 1747, and died on the 25th of March, 1809.

[2] *Biographic Sketch* by Walter Scott, p. 27, and vol. i. of *Poetical Works of Anna Seward*, p. 158 : —

> "From thy waves, stormy Lannow, I fly ;
> From the rocks that are lashed by their tide ;
> From the maid whose cold bosom, relentless as they,
> Has wrecked my warm hopes by her pride ! —
> Yet lonely and rude as the scene,
> Her smile to that scene could impart
> A charm that might rival the bloom of the vale —
> But away, thou fond dream of my heart !
> From thy rocks, stormy Lannow, I fly !

> "Now the blasts of the winter come on,
> And the waters grow dark as they rise !

had it been for herself and others had she been always under it.

Judging by the specimens of Miss Seward's earlier prose writing given by Sir Walter Scott in the extracts from her correspondence prefixed to his edition of her " Poems," her style appears to have been less artificial in youth than it afterwards became. In her later years she seldom condescended to use the language of ordinary life; instead of telling you that she had got a *frank*, she says, " I have succeeded in securing *senatorial freedom* for our correspondence," and a second marriage is thus described : " I hear with concern that Hymen is lighting his torch with the sprays of a cypress wreath." She was much admired by many of her contemporaries, — among others, it would appear, by my father and Sir Walter Scott, — but I suspect there are few among the notable writers of her day whose works are now permitted to rest more peacefully upon our shelves than those of Anna Seward.

My father owed his introduction to Miss Seward's notice to her relative and his kind friend Mr. Henry White, whose brother, Mr. Thomas White, was her residuary legatee. Miss Seward's earliest letter in my possession is dated Lichfield, September 18, 1807, and is as follows : —

" LICHFIELD, *September 18th,* 1807.

" DEAR SIR, —Though most extremely obliged, I am absolutely shocked to receive a present from you at once so expensive and so wholly unmerited. " The Life of Beattie " appears in a *formidably* elegant and costly dress. Pray, believe me *sighingly* grateful.

" I have possessed ' Bruce's Poems ' from the time they *first* appeared in 1770 ; the gift of one of his countrymen. He

> But 't is well ! — they resemble the sullen disdain
> That has lowered in those insolent eyes.
> Sincere were the sighs they repressed,
> But they rose in the days that are flown !
> Ah, nymph, unrelenting and cold as thou art,
> My spirit is proud as thine own.
> From thy rocks, stormy Lannow, I fly ! "

has always appeared to me no more than an elegant *versifier*. Not one bold, original passage have I met in his volume. The ' Ode to Spring,' so cried up in the Preface as not inferior to anything in our vernacular poetry, is all made up of *borrowed* ideas, which have met our attention from twenty pens, and several much *better* pens than Michael's. . . . . Macneill's and Jamieson's ' Poems ' I shall explore in my first leisure. They are new to me. The collection of ' Scotch Ballads ' is indeed a truly valuable book — too valuable for me, who, after all the best days of my long life had been devoted to harmony, now turn sickening from the sound — sad consequence of a sudden and dire fatality which from that hour, four years ago, in my heart, made *music* to awaken the nerves of anguish.

" If I should ever be able to obtain leisure to correct my ' Miscellany ' of published and unpublished poems, of prose and verse, and master courage enough to expose them, during my lifetime, to the oyster-knife dissection of reviewers (almost to a man of them unacquainted with the usages, the licenses, and indeed all that constitutes the *beauty* of poetry and eloquence), *you* shall have the first offer of the copyright ; and perhaps Mr. Scott will have the goodness to settle the terms. But you have no idea how my hours are ravished from me by the social claims.

" When you see Mr. Scott, have the goodness to thank him, in my name, for his late kind letter, and say that I purpose answering it the first opportunity.

" Mr. Murray sent me a valuable literary present. You are all but too good to me. Cousin White has already, he tells me, written to acknowledge your bounty to *him*.

" I remain, with great esteem and grateful regard, dear sir, your obliged friend and servant,   ANNA SEWARD."

In acknowledgment of a presentation copy of " Marmion," my father received the following : —

" *March 14th*, 1808.

" DEAR SIR, — Many and high are my obligations to you, this last far transcending all the former, and I am comparatively poor, even in thanks, poured forth as I desire them to be in all their ardor.

"Well might you add *great*, as an epithet to this poem. Great *indeed* it *is*, and adds new strength and accomplishment to my prediction that Scott and Southey were born for the poetic glory of the nineteenth century. Spenser and Dryden had great genius ; but what have they written that stands on any level with the three beautiful poems of these young eagles ?

"Amidst all the poetic charms of the 'Lay,' 'Marmion' is a strain of higher mood and dearer interest. Its grand and alternately beautiful pictures are of more frequent occurrence.

"Suffer me to assure you that this delay of acknowledgment did not spring from neglect, much less from ingratitude, for the delight I have received from your last priceless gift, which gold or diamonds should not purchase from me were the condition of not replacing it annexed to the offer. Many circumstances combined to produce this procrastination, and all which did not arise from my sedulous attention to the work itself were vexatious to me in the extreme.

"My friend Miss Fern, who since my cousin's marriage has lived with me, makes poetry *poetry indeed*, by her spiritual and harmonious recitation. She read 'Marmion' to me aloud in the scanty leisure we could obtain during the first six days after its arrival ; all which inextricable engagements left us in the ensuing week was devoted to re-reading the whole, with that discriminating and pausing eye which can only enable the mind most *used* to poetry to do entire justice to a long poem of distinguished excellence. That I might write to you, to the dear Bard himself, Miss White, and my other correspondents, on the subject, without the hazard of hasty and rash assertion, I made written remarks on every canto and every interlude, noting each passage of prominent beauty. So thickly sown, my pleasing task became an earnest and a *long* one. Last of all the causes of delay was the waiting to procure senatorial freedom for my packet.

"The rapid sale of 'Marmion' delights me, at once for your

profit and the fame of your author. Now, *this* is as it *should* be with great works ; though, alas ! the instance is perhaps unparalleled. Peculiar that it should have occurred in a period which has manifested stupid neglect of *other* first-rate poetry, and in which also the genuine unbiased taste for it seems extinct. The extreme both ways, in the fate of ' Marmion ' and ' Madoc,' where the merits are so high and so equal, may, I suppose, be fairly attributed, in this instance, to the generous national patronage of the Scotch nobility, and their wide influence in the higher ranks of English society, and to the incense offered to their sanguinary fallen idol in a poem much too noble for the effort of washing an *Ethiopian.* The reverse instance of molish-blindness and adder-deafness, is the result of tasteless stupidity, Review-injustice, and, as it was with *Milton,* of party-prejudice.

" I could not dream of being disobliged by your not answering my September acknowledgment of unmerited bounty, since do I not know how much your time is engrossed, that minutes are more to you than months to others ?

" Miss White speaks to me very thankfully of your attentions to *her.* You did right in not obeying her injunction to send me ' The Mountain Bard,' conscious as you were that our highsonged Bard of the Tweed had presented me with that volume. She was not aware that I not only *possessed,* but had reviewed it in the ' Critical Review ' for November last. If you have that Tract in your shop, you would still further oblige me by throwing your eye over the stricture, and by lending it for Miss White's perusal. Each of you will be pleased with the traces it bears of my admiration of Mr. Scott's poetic powers.

" That stricture is my *first,* and I mean it shall be my *last,* attempt to shoot forth my critical opinions beneath a *mask* battery. In former years I inserted letters of criticism in the ' Gentleman's Magazine,' in defense of poetic genius injured by the injustice of the Reviewers of those days ; but they had always my *own* signature, except in the strictures which I signed *Benvolio,* and sent to that publication, where they appeared in the numbers for February and April, 1786, and in that for Au-

gust, 1787. Their subject was the critical injustice of the des-
pot, Dr. Johnson, and his ingratitude to the Scotch professors.[1]

"I write to you on this shabby and crowded quarter of a
sheet, in apprehension that my packet will make its frank over
weight, should I be enabled to procure one, intending that it
shall contain a letter to Mr. Scott and to Miss White.

"Pardon this hurried and stained scroll from the most careless of all pens, believing me constantly, dear sir, with every
esteem, your obliged friend and obedient servant,

                                        "ANNA SEWARD."

Miss White, mentioned here by Miss Seward, was the celebrated Miss Lydia White, whom Walter Scott describes as
"what Oxonians call a lioness of the first order, with stockings
nineteen times nine dyed blue, very lively, very good-humored, and extremely absurd," and Mr. Lockhart, as "the in-
imitable Lydia White, who so long ruled with out a rival in the
soft realm of *blue* Mayfair." She also was a correspondent
of my father's, who appears to have been useful to her on the
occasion of her stay in Scotland in 1807 and 1808; and it may
be a relief to some of my readers to turn for a while from what
Mr. Carlyle might call the high-stepping of Miss Seward to
Miss White's somewhat less studied epistolary style, in returning an early copy of 'Marmion' lent to her for perusal : —

"MY DEAR SIR, — I return 'Marmion' with ten thousand
thanks. I would fain say something adequate to its merit.
There is an originality, a spirit, and a style of versification,
I must say, unequaled by any strains I know, except those
of Milton and Dryden. The various scenes are absolutely
brought before us 'in liveliest portraiture displayed,' and the
introductions to the cantos are glorious. I have seldom been
more touched than by the 'Lines on Mr. Pitt's Death,' together

---

[1] Should any readers desire evidence that Miss Seward *could* write unaffected
English, I commend the letters in the *Gentleman's Magazine,* under the masculine
signature of *Benvolio,* above alluded to. Her moral estimate of Dr. Johnson, if unfavorable, appears to be severely true, and she does ample justice to his genius and
his mighty intellect.

with the graceful commemoration of our other departed heroes;
I say *ours*, for surely we may claim our share of Brunswick.
I rejoice also in the animating praise bestowed on one of the
best and most early of my friends, Sir Sidney Smith, and I
never read a more beautiful compliment or finer lines than
those addressed to Miss Baillie. The convent scene is very
interesting ; but what is there in this poem that is not so ? I
am very impatient for the rest, and anxious that Mr. Scott
should be at work again, and stretch his eagle wing over some
new ground on those Parnassian summits so long unvisited by
mortal else. I cannot help applying Milton's beautiful description of Athens to Edinburgh, for here the Attic bird trills
her thick-warbled notes the summer long. How can I stoop
from such a subject as this to speak of the trash I returned
to you yesterday ? It must be very bad travelling where such
things prove recreations—sonnets on carriages breaking down,
and invoking the killing powers (in case there are such),
to say nothing of the effect of the poet's lamentations on
Thames's side, where the dire succession of *s's* fairly hiss the
reader off the stage, as I have often been chased by geese
upon a common in almost equal strains. I am indeed compelled to hope that these books will lie quietly on your shelves,
lest wicked wits should throw a cruel light on their deficiencies.

"Will you permit me to add to my numerous obligations to
you by requesting the favor of you to lend me the first volume
of the 'Spanish Don Quixote?' I wish also for 'Huddes-
ford's Poems' to give to a friend, 2 vols., 1801, and I am, dear
sir, your most obliged and faithful,   L. W."

In June of the following year, Miss White made a Highland tour, in which she was accompanied as far as Loch Ca-
trine by Mr. and Mrs. Scott. She writes to my father from
Inverary, *en route* for Oban and Staffa, and declares herself
much delighted with " the glorious place — indeed, with all
that we see, hear, feel, or understand in Scotland." Before
leaving Edinburgh she wrote her farewell, and was evidently

in high indignation at Mr. Jeffrey for the free manner in which he had dealt with ' Marmion ' in the ' Edinburgh Review ' : [1] —

"My dear Sir, — I very much regretted not having the pleasure of seeing you when I called this morning, and the more as I find you are going to town before I return from Ashestiel, and that it is uncertain whether we shall meet again, as I leave Edinburgh the 18th of May. I should have been glad personally to have thanked you for the numberless kind attentions shown to me since I have been at Edinburgh, and to have assured you how happy I should be to return them in any degree when you visit England in future. I trust you will not go thither without inquiring for me at my bankers, Messrs. Whitehead and Co., Cateaton Street, London, who will forward a note to me at any time. I am still much out of humor with your reviewers. I think you give these little shelties of yours too much corn, or they would not kick and fling at all the world as they do. Believe me, with much esteem, your most obliged and faithful, L. W."

Miss White lived and died "a lioness," and Sir Walter Scott in his Journal thus records her death : —

" *January* 28, 1827. — Hear of Miss White's death. Poor Lydia ! She gave a dinner on the Friday before, and had written with her own hand invitations for another party. Twenty years ago she used to tease me with her youthful affectations — her dressing like the Queen of Chimney-sweeps on May-day morning, etc. — and sometimes with letting her wit run wild. But she *was* a woman of wit, and had a feeling and kind heart ! "

On the 27th April, 1808, Miss Seward writes to my father, in reply to an offer made to her through Mr. Scott as follows : —

"Dear Sir, — Mr. Scott informs me that you prefer to purchasing the whole collection of my works, already arranged for publication, that of a single edition of two volumes, the

[1] See *Edinburgh Review*, No. xxiii., April, 1808.

size of Mr. Macneill's, to be filled by a republication of my
' Monodies,' together with a selection from my ' Sonnets ' and
other published poems, the said edition to consist of 1000
copies, for which you would give £130.

"My life is too far advanced to make the plan of selling a
single edition desirable to me. If I persuade myself to undergo the anxiety of republication, it must be with a copyright
sale either of a part or the whole of my collection.

"My published and unpublished works, already arranged
for the press, as observed above, would fill at least six volumes of verse and four of prose, besides thirteen half-bound
quarto volumes, closely written, of my own letters, selected
from my correspondence through the last twenty-two years,
with a variety of friends, some private and some public characters. The subjects of the said letters are critical, political,
moral, and characteristic, interspersed with incidental themes
of the day. Not one of them was written with a view of publication. But it is my custom to look over every letter I have
written. When such review teaches me to believe it worth
the attention of the public, I hastily, and too slovenly, transcribe it into these volumes. Not more than one in ten were
so transcribed, though the collection is so large. From each
epistle now in these repositories I weeded the passages of
trivial egotism and of tiresome enumeration of bodily maladies
either of my own or of my correspondents.

"However, these volumes are for future consideration, and
for appearance distant, probably posthumous.

"As to the present plan, I cannot consent to the mutilation
of anything I have published, not even of my one hundred
Sonnets ; since, though the themes of those Sonnets are
various, they form a sort of mirror, which reflects my poetical
mind, and the impressions it received through a course of
twenty-one years, in which period filial attentions, household
and passing cares, seldom allowed me leisure for compositions
of length. I should not like to see the number of these Sonnets abridged, neither to see detached from them the sub-
joined paraphrases of the most interesting of Horace's
Odes. . . . .

" For the entire copyright I shall expect six hundred guineas, and fifty copies to dispose of as presents to my friends ; to be paid according to Mr. Scott's statement, by bills, drawn at six or twelve months, date on the day of publication, which, by their discount, would make the immediate sum to me £600. The choice would be left to you to publish the four volumes at once, or two at first, and two the second year. This would be a much cheaper purchase to you than the Mountain Bard's volume, which Mr. Scott was so good to send, and for which he, to my best recollection, told me you gave the author £330, though his name was then unknown in the world of letters.

" But to this plan I should greatly prefer, as giving me infinitely less trouble, the sale of the entire copyright of all which I intended should form a complete edition of my works (the thirteen volumes of letters described in the first part of this letter only excepted). Their order of succession is already ascertained, and they would at least fill six, and probably eight, volumes of verse, and four of prose, the specified size. For them I shall expect one thousand guineas, and fifty copies for presents.

" Provided you and I agree upon terms, Mr. Scott most kindly offers his own and his friend Mr. Ballantyne's assistance in correcting the press of the poems of which I shall send you printed copies, and also in procuring franks for the manuscript poetry, that I may correct it myself. So swells he the large list of my obligations to his friendship.

" If you purchase the whole collection, which will, at 1000 guineas, be much cheaper to you than even the selection at 600 guineas, you will be at liberty to publish either at once or by portions, as you please, provided that you observe the marked order of succession, which my first proposal to you would perplex and disarrange.

" I hope the sale of Mr. Scott's late glorious poem slackens not its rapidity ; that it will prove to you and yours a golden and exhaustless mine. I remain, dear sir, your sincere and obliged friend and servant,   ANNA SEWARD."

My father's reply to this communication is not before me, but it is certain that Miss Seward's proposition had not been at once accepted, and also that he had avoided hurting her *amour propre* by its tone, for after her death, on March 25, 1809, the following letter, written on July 17, 1807, was found unrecalled : —

" In a will, made and executed since I had the pleasure of seeing you in April last, I have left you the exclusive copyright of twelve volumes quarto, half-bound. They contain copies of letters, or of parts of letters, that after I had written them, appeared to me worth the attention of the public. Voluminous as is the collection, it does not include a twelfth part of my epistolary writing from the time it commences, viz., from the year 1784 to the present day.

" I wish you to publish two volumes annually ; and by no means to follow the late absurd custom of classing letters to separate correspondents, but suffer them to succeed each other in the order of time, as you find them transcribed.

" When you shall receive this letter its writer will be no more. While she lives, she must wish Mr. Constable all manner of good, and that he may enjoy it to a late period of human life. ANNA SEWARD."

The bequest was gratefully accepted, the conditions faithfully observed. It is doubtful whether Miss Seward's liberality and that of her publisher, embodied in six 12mo volumes, has been duly appreciated by the public. Sir Walter Scott's edition of Miss Seward's poems was published in a uniform size by John Ballantyne and Co., in 1810. The manuscript letters, from which a printed selection has been made, contained many passages of interest which it was believed proper to suppress ; and I perceive, from the initials W. S. occurring frequently after deleted paragraphs in letters to Sir Walter Scott, that he had been permitted to exercise his own discretion on that portion of the correspondence. Some of the passages omitted are however so characteristic, and comparatively so free from affectation in style, that I now feel myself quite justified, in the interest of Miss Seward, in quoting them.

Considering the terms in which her " Life of Darwin " had been noticed in the " Edinburgh Review," [1] it is not wonderful that Miss Seward should owe a grudge to the editor of that Journal. That she had a right good-will to pay her debt, the following quotation from a letter to Sir Walter Scott will testify : —

"LICHFIELD, *June* 20, 1806.

" Not even you can teach me to esteem him whom you call 'your little friend *Jeffrey*', the Edinburgh Reviewer. *Jefferies* ought to have been his name, since so similar his nature. On his self-placed bench of decision on poetic works, he is all that Jefferies was when tyranny had thrown the judicial robe on his shoulder.

" Ignorance and envy are the only possible parents of such criticisms as disgrace the publication which assumes the name of your city. In putting them forth their author is baser than a thief, since to blight the early sale of an eminent work by unjust criticism is to rob the bard of his due remuneration, while the arrested progress of his fame must inflict severer mortification. Your poetic predecessor and namesake, the late Mr. Scott of Amwell, places amongst the Unhappy, —

" ' Him whom Envy robs of hard-earned fame.'

---

[1] " It has long been held, on high critical authority, that history must always please, independently of the particular mode, and even in spite of the defects of its execution : and unquestionably even that moderate portion of fact which may be reasonably expected in the life of every eminent individual, can scarcely be presented under any disguise so perversely absurd as entirely to divest it of interest. Under the influence of stubborn curiosity, we have been accordingly carried through a faithful perusal of these memoirs of the celebrated author of *The Botanic Garden* ; and . . . . Miss Seward must forgive us, if we add, that the most striking lesson we have derived from her volume has been the truly wonderful extent of that tolerant maxim to which we have alluded. The share which she appears to have long enjoyed of the intimate society of Dr. Darwin, ... had given to Miss Seward some peculiar advantages in becoming as she terms it, ' the recorder of vanished genius;' it is therefore the more to be regretted that she should not have been restrained, by some visitations of a better taste, from clothing her narrative in a garb so injudicious and fantastic." —*Edinburgh Review*, No. vii., April, 1804.

It cost Collins his reason, and Chatterton his life. No good man would hazard the inflicting such misery.

"Were it not that the generality of Review-readers are incapable of reflection, and disposed to take everything upon trust which depreciates rising genius, it would not be in Judge Jefferies' *power* (pray allow me to spell his name right) to injure the reputation of any poetic composition. They would, if they had an atom of discernment, see what sort of animal the lion's skin conceals, when, in his review of ' Madoc,' he recommends Racine and Pope as the best models for an English *epic poem* in *blank verse !*

"Sick of such nonsense, I have not since that Number was *sent* to me looked into an 'Edinburgh Review.' Indeed *that,* and the Number which contained observations on the 'Lay of the Last Minstrel,' which were partly as absurd, if not as *ma licious,* as those which sought to tear the immortal laurel from the brow of Southey, are the only ' Edinburgh Reviews' which I have seen or mean to see, infested as they are by this Zoilus, this Milbourne, this Dennis ! "

Mr. Scott and Miss Seward appear to have differed to some extent in their estimate of " Madoc," and Scott had objected to the introduction of *Mutiny* by Mr. Southey. In Miss Seward's printed letter of the 23d September, 1806, the following passage also has been omitted by the editor, which was a pity, as in it we see how easily she could write, when for a space she threw aside her stilts : —

" Plagiarism in one poet from another must doubtless lessen the merit of the work in which it abounds. Of that fault no man was ever more clear than Southey, no man more guilty than Virgil ; yet has not even that glaring fault eclipsed the fame of the Roman bard, or impeded its progress through the rounds of Time.

" Prose should not borrow from prose, except by citation, neither verse from verse ; but the poet has an established privilege of applying historic events and the records of discovery to the purposes of his Muse. *Mutiny* was so inevitable in the

traverse of unknown seas, extending in unexpected length ere
the limits of the earth had been ascertained, that the crew of
Columbus having mutinied seems to me no more a reason why
Southey should abstain from animating the voyage of *his* hero
by an event so probable and so interesting, than that he should
preclude himself from describing a fabulous siege and battle,
because sieges and battles have been recorded by historians.

"You ask me what I would say if an author should introduce into his poem the taking of another city by means of a
wooden horse? This I would say — 'Hang him up!' — for his
bad taste, much more than for his theft — far more inexcusable
than his from whom he might so steal, since Virgil's thefts
from Homer were engrafted beauties, while to steal the clumsy
and incredible wooden horse from the 'Æneid' would be such
felony as if a brother admiral had stolen Lord Nelson's work-
arm after his decease, and worn it dangling from his own
shoulder as an ornament.

"That unimaginable contrivance, or adoption of so mon-
strously fabulous tradition, always appeared to me a great blot
on the fair fabric of Virgil's epic. I admire the poetic powers
of that Roman bard, notorious plagiarist as he was, but I am
no 'fool to fame,' as Pope finely says of the blind idolaters of
the ancients. I cannot hallow gross defect and mistake it for
beauty; neither yet, like a modern reviewer, could I mistake
beauty for defect. A wooden horse, capacious of an host of
men, no combination of human strength with art could have
hoisted up the walls of Troy, or even have been able to push
it through the gates. Water is the only surface over which
such a machine could be made to pass. When human schemes
and events are described in verse, the poet should take care
that they be not incredible.

"We meet no such enormity in 'Madoc'; but that fault in
Virgil, together with his other imputed faults, is covered by
the blaze of his excellences. Southey has the same bright
shield for his violation of poetic justice in the fate of the sweet
Indian heroine and her Lyncoya; *you* have it for your dwarf,
and for the inadequate use made of the awfully mystic book

recovered from the tomb of Cornelius, which recovery intro-
duces a scene of never excelled sublimity."

Such as Miss Seward was, Walter Scott has recorded that
it was well worth a pilgrimage to Lichfield to enjoy the charm
of her society; and that "when young she must have been ex-
quisitely beautiful; for, even in advanced age, the regularity of
her features, the fire and expression of her countenance, gave
her the appearance of beauty, and almost of youth." This estimate of her personal appearance is quite borne out by the admirable portrait painted by Kettle in 1762, and also by a later
one from the pencil of Romney, referred to in the following sug-
gestive letter of her father : —

" November 20, 1748.

"DEAR SIR, —When I last wrote to my very worthy and
much loved friend, your brother Barker, I had but a melancholy account of his health, having been troubled with a bad
cough, which I hope is removed, or at least greatly alleviated;
but lest it should not, I shall avoid troubling him about the
favor which the Chatsworth family have so long conferred
upon me by sending me venison. I have not been able these
many years to pay my personal duty, and therefore fear that I
have lived to wear out all remembrance of me in that honorable family. But if I am so happy as not to be quite forgotten
as a contemporary with his Grace's grandfather, I then beg
the favor of your good brother or yourself to procure me the
usual warrant. The park-keeper, to whom they have been of
late directed has been very friendly to me, and tells me that
he always hopes to be so, if the warrant which I am favored
with is not so late in the season that the does have lost their
plumpness. My daughter has lately had the great honor of
having her picture drawn gratis by Mr. Romney, at the request of her great poetic friend, Mr. Hayley, who intends to
honor it with a place in his own library, just now most ele-
gantly fitted up in the South Downs of Sussex, on one of the
most beautiful and, in many respects, the most Parnassian hills
in the kingdom. The picture is finished, and is most highly

celebrated by all our acquaintance who have seen it in London. It is first to visit Lichfield, and then, I hope, to be copied by the same excellent painter before it becomes stationary in Mr. Hayley's library. I expect it very soon. I beg my most affectionate love to your brother, with a particular account of his health, for the establishment of which he has the most ardent wishes of your sincere friend,

" THOS. SEWARD."

" The picture is a very large one, and Mr. Romney grows so eminent, that his price for pictures of such large dimensions is fourscore guineas. We can make him no other return but a few eatables, when we can procure either game or venison."

JAMES GRAHAME.

The Rev. James Grahame, the amiable and sensitive author of " The Sabbath," had attained his fortieth year before the publication of that work, — which secured his reputation as a poet, and at length gave him courage to avow his title to that reputation. While still at Glasgow University he had printed privately, and given to his friends, some of his smaller poems, but the drama " Mary Queen of Scotland," appeared anonymously in 1801, and I have found in his correspondence with my father interesting reference to another work printed and *entered at Stationers' Hall* in 1799, though never published.

" Wallace, a Tragedy in five Acts," a copy of which now lies before me, has passages of considerable interest, but it does not appear to me that either the literary world or the author's reputation, has suffered injury by its having been strangled at the birth. Mr. Grahame's letters of the period are, however, so biographic that I shall give a few extracts from them. The following, to my father, dated " Saturday morning," is unsigned : —

" DEAR SIR, — You will receive herewith the Play which I spoke of last night. I send also the last half of the Preface, the first part of which does not quite please me. Whether the Play will do better with or without a Preface will be matter for after consideration.

"I have not a bit of india-rubber by me to rub out the scores of approbation on the margin. They are from the pencil of a too indulgent critic. You will not mind them. The Appendix, which will consist chiefly of extracts from Fordun, Major, Buchanan, Blind Harry, and Hume, will perhaps extend to ten or fifteen pages.

"Will you breakfast with me on Monday at half past nine, that we may concert measures in case we think it advisable to proceed?　　　Yours, etc."

"To proceed," must have been deemed "advisable," so far at least as the *printing* of the work was concerned, for on the 26th August, 1799, the author wrote as follows to his printer : —

MR. GRAHAME TO MR. WILLISON.

"DEAR SIR, — I sent the last proof-sheets directly to you. I now send the remainder. I am sorry that you should have thought any apology necessary for the suggestions which you make. You will see that I have not been inattentive to them.

"I rather incline not to add any notes. I have not now at hand the books from which I intended to make the quotations. The material facts are known to every one who is acquainted with Scotch history.

"Now that I am come to the point of publication, I again hesitate. I should like to be more assured than I at this moment feel myself, that the performance will please the public as much as it has pleased the individuals who have perused it. I beg it may not be advertised till I finally resolve. I presume you will immediately send a few copies to Mr. Constable in London. I am, dear sir, with many thanks for the very neat and accurate manner in which you have executed the work, and for the very great pains which you have taken in the revisal of it, your most obedient servant,　　　J. G."

"I should be happy to have a line from you mentioning what is done, or what you think ought to be done."

On September 2d he writes again, to my father, then in London : —

"DEAR SIR, — I am again shrinking. A deliberate perusal of the printed copy has opened my eyes to many faults, particularly in the conduct of the piece. Some of the scenes are not neatly connected together. These defects I could easily remedy, but it is now too late. I have enjoined Mr. W. not to advertise till I finally order it. Perhaps you have received a few copies. If anybody has seen them, let me know what is said. I beg you would immediately write to me what you think. I am, in great haste, yours truly,   J. G.

"Address to me at Gilsland, by Carlisle."

Again from Glasgow on October 11th : —

"DEAR SIR, — I wrote to you the day before I received your last letter, and if I recollect right I requested you to let me know what steps had been taken in London for keeping the publication completely in our power. I do not think that I shall come to a final resolution on this subject till I return to town. In the meantime, though I rather believe that I shall publish, I wish to have an option either to do so or not. I shall probably, too, make one or two alterations and add a few notes. I wish much to hear from you.

"The apology in your last letter was most unnecessary, and indeed was shown to be so by the letter itself, and by every one which preceded it. I am, dear sir, yours sincerely,

"J. G."

Nine of the copies that had been forwarded to London had meanwhile been deposited in Stationers' Hall, and to the infinite annoyance of the hesitating author, "Wallace" had been advertised by Messrs. Vernor and Hood for immediate publication. "I entreat that you will write to Vernor and Hood to strike 'Wallace' out of their future advertisements, and I wish every other possible step to be immediately taken for recalling what has been done."

By express desire of the author impartial criticism had been invited ; the opinion of a certain Mr. Wood had manifestly been unfavorable, and although not accepted as just by Mr. Grahame, may very likely have led to the withdrawal of the publication. Be that as it may, the nine copies sent to Stationers' Hall found their way to the privileged libraries, and my curiosity having been aroused by the correspondence just quoted, I have discovered and read that which belongs to the Faculty of Advocates. The following letter shows that Mr. Grahame was not devoid of parental affection for the child he had felt it prudent to disown : —

"DEAR SIR, — I was this morning favored with Mr. Willison's note accompanying 'Wallace.' Mr. Wood's slashing critiques leave it a mere *caput mortuum.* The quantity struck out was nothing. The judgment which he has displayed in *selecting* reconciled me entirely to the *extent* in which he has exercised his judicial powers. In my humble opinion he has struck out some of the passages which had a chance of rescuing the whole performance from condemnation. His mode of passing sentence in the form of lead-pencilled brackets I do not comprehend. I wish he had allowed some of his remarks or reasons to remain. You may easily perceive that I am irritated by his wholesale reprobation. I am open to conviction — I am not self-confident — but I am not to be intimidated by a solemn formal face, and a character for correctness of acting. Let any man read coolly the play, and consider what Mr. Wood has condemned compared with what he has left uncensured, and I am sure the critical powers of that gentleman will not be esteemed of the highest order. He may, however, be a judge of stage effect.

"You expected to be present at the Trial. I presume you were not. Will you let me know what has been done in the way of retracting ? I wish much to hear from you.

"Present my best compliments to Mr. Willison, and thanks for the trouble which he has taken. Yours most truly,

"J. G."

"The Sabbath," in spite of the faint praise of Mr. Jeffrey in the tenth number of the 'Edinburgh Review,' passed through three editions during the first year of its existence, and established the fame of its author, who lived to win loving commendation from the same incisive but not ungenerous pen.[1] In 1810, little more than a year before his death, Mr. Grahame invited my father to offer for the copyright of his poems, and proposed to pay him a friendly visit at Craigcrook. Whatever may have been the reply to the invitation, the offered visit would, I am assured, be with pleasure accepted, for the author of 'The Sabbath' was beloved by all who knew him, and the following lines from the monody by John Wilson on his death, are equally descriptive of the poem and the man : —

> "Methinks I see a fair and lovely child,
>   Sitting composed upon his mother's knee,
> And reading with a low and lisping voice
> Some passage from 'The Sabbath,' while the tears
> Stand in his little eyes so softly blue ;
> Till, quite o'ercome with pity, his white arms
> He twines around her neck, and hides his sighs
> Most infantine, within her gladdened breast, —
> Like a sweet lamb, half sportive, half afraid,
> Nestling one moment 'neath its bleating dam.
> And now the happy mother kisses oft
> The tender-hearted child, lays down the book,
> And asks him if he doth remember still
> The stranger who once gave him, long ago,
> A parting kiss, and blest his laughing eyes ! —
> His sobs speak fond remembrance, and he weeps
> To think so kind and good a man should die."

HECTOR MACNEILL.

The fame of this once popular Scottish poet must be allowed to rest upon "The History of Will and Jean : Owre True a Tale," "My boy Tammie," and a few other lyrics of considerable beauty. The sale of 10,000 copies of the larger poem within five months attests its popularity, and it is not

---

[1] Mr. Jeffrey did ample justice to the genius of Mr. Grahame in his notice of *The British Georgics*, in No. 31 of the same *Review*.

unnatural that the author's estimate of his own powers should have been elevated by so great success, though it is rather too much to find him quietly accepting and printing, as a sort of Preface to a collected edition of his works, a tribute from a contemporary poet, who consoles himself and the public for the loss of Robert Burns by the possession of Hector Macneill, whom he declares himself "Happy to see [thee] fill the place o' him awa." Porson said of some one that his works would be read when Homer and Virgil are forgotten, — *and not till then*. So may the fame of Macneill attain a resurrection when that of Burns has passed away.

The moral of "Will and Jean" was admirable, and in favor of temperance at a time when such advice was at a discount; but it is rather curious and somewhat inconsistent to find the author in the next poem of the series declaring —

> " I am resolved, be 't right or sinfu',
> To hae at least — a decent skinfu' "

of a large bottle of Jamaica rum, which accompanies a rhyming letter to his friend "Canty Chairlie." [1]

"The Pastoral or Lyric Muse of Scotland," published also by my father (in 1809), attracted comparatively little attention, and was not included in the collected edition of Mr. Macneill's works. In a letter dated 18th May, 1811, he intimates that he is engaged in writing a series of "stories or histories illustrative of the effects of improper instruction to youth," which he intends to be an improvement on Miss Edgeworth. His "Scotish Adventures, or the Way to Rise," published in the following year, were perhaps the first and only fruits of this project. More than the half of his long life was spent in Jamaica as a slave-driver, and he is said to have been a zealous advocate of the system of slavery. Mr. Macneill died in poverty, at the age of seventy-two years.

[1] The *Poetical Works of Hector Macneill, Esq.*, 3d edition, corrected and enlarged, 2 vols. 12mo., 1812.

AMELIA OPIE.

Miss Martineau, in announcing the death of Mrs. Opie, in 1853, says, "Another of that curious class of English people — the provincial literary lion — has left us. Mrs. Opie is dead. The young, and most of the middle-aged of our day will say, 'What of that?' or 'Who was Mrs. Opie?' or will think of her only as a beneficent Quaker lady, whose conversion to muslin caps and silent meetings made a noise some good many years ago. But the elderly generation are aware that a good deal more than that is connected with the name and fame of Amelia Opie." She early manifested a taste for literature, and we are told that she wrote a tragedy when not more than eighteen years of age ; but it was not till 1801, and in her thirty-third year, that she published her tale of " Father and Daughter," which, along with a volume of poems that appeared in 1802, was favorably noticed in the first number of the " Edinburgh Review " by Dr. Thomas Brown — no mean authority.

Mrs. Opie kept her place in public estimation as an author, and by her personal attractions, charm of manner, and great musical talent, became a distinguished favorite in society. In 1798 she had married John Opie, an eminent painter, and they rejoiced together for nine years, each in the success that crowned the efforts of the other, until their happy union was dissolved in 1807 by the death of Mr. Opie in that year. His widow then returned to Norwich, her early home, and devoted herself to the care of her father, Dr. Alderson, whose only child she was, and to whom she was tenderly attached.

In 1816, on the occasion of her first visit to Scotland, Mrs. Opie was my father's guest at Craigleith House, and although I was only at the time in my fifth year, I have a distinct remembrance of her bright and cheerful presence, and of the delight her singing seemed to give to others. In 1834 I saw her again, when under the attractive influence of the admirable Frys and Gurneys she had joined the Society of Friends. The lapse of eighteen years had carried her far beyond middle age, but her manner was cheerful as ever, and in her quaint and becoming attire of lavender and white she appeared to have gained instead of lost in personal comeliness. Her memory of 1816 was warm and fresh ; my father's hospitality and kindness had made a deep impression, though, as will appear from the correspondence I am about to quote, he had not been so careful as he ought to have been to retain the good opinion of his distinguished friend.

Mrs. Opie requested the exercise of my father's influence in procuring notice in the "Edinburgh Review" of two works lately published, written by persons in whom she is specially interested, and then proceeds as follows : —

"As you, my dear sir, are a man of business, and do not, *I am sure*, like writing letters, perhaps some one of your family would have the kindness to answer what requires answering in this one. Mrs. Johnson, who is, I trust, still with you, owes me a letter, and truly glad should I be to hear from her, and of you all.

"Dear Edinburgh ! how often have I been there in fancy this autumn. I go about in Scotch bonnets, and have lately purchased Albyn's 'Anthology,' which I first saw at your house. *Apropos*, pray thank Mr. G. Thomson for his present of 'Songs and Accompaniments.' I value them much. Don't forget this. And now for my own personal business — but I must take another sheet for it.

"I know not whether the 'Edinburgh Review' will think that very amusing work, the 'Sexagenarian,' by the late Mr. Beloe, worthy of its notice, nor, if it should do so, am I quite sure that the editor may think it advisable to redress an individual grievance at the representation of a complainant. Nor am I certain that it is ever right to notice and deny a calumnious report, because, as Lord Bacon somewhere says, a calumny is like a spark : if you attempt to tread it out it flies up in your face.

"Still, I wish to state, through your means, to Mr. Jeffrey, of whose good opinion I am, I trust, meritoriously ambitious, that Mr. Beloe in this posthumous publication has asserted of me a positive falsehood.

" I never saw Mr. Horne Tooke till I saw him on his trial, and the charge of my having scrambled over chairs and tables to get up to him on his acquittal, and then kissed him in public court, is as false as it is malignant.

" Such conduct not even my youth could have excused, and never at any period of my life could I, I trust, have been guilty of such an outrage on the delicacy of my sex, and such a violation of my respectability as a gentlewoman. My friend Helen Maria Williams I never saw till the year 1802 at Paris, and Mrs. Wollstonecraft I only knew first as Mrs. Imlay, when she seemed the deserted wife of Imlay, and subsequently as Mrs. Godwin.

" Now have patience with me while I tell you a plain and true tale, and one which I have often related to show Horne Tooke's self-possession at a moment of no small excitement and (one would have thought) of some considerable agitation.

" During his trial I was staying at the house of Mr. Boddington (a friend of his), and I used to accompany them every day to the Old Bailey.

" Mrs. Boddington (the frail and the beautiful) had then never been introduced to Mr. Tooke, and after the acquittal she was very angry with her husband for not finding out whither Mr. T. had retired, that she might be presented to him at once.

" This remonstrance induced Mr. Boddington to go in search of Mr. Tooke, and having discovered him in a small room waiting for his carriage, he took his wife and me into the apartment where he was.

" ' This is my wife, sir,' said Mr. B. Mr. Tooke saluted her and exclaimed, ' Madam, you have made me hate your husband.' ' Why, sir ? ' ' Because I always hate the husbands of pretty women.' Mrs. Coverdale was then led up to him ; she said, ' Sir, my father was one of your jurymen.' ' Then, madam,' replied he, ' you and I are brother and sister, for he gave you life and now he has given it to me.' [She meant her father-in-law, Mr. C. was her husband's father.] I was next presented, and having saluted me he said, 'I think, ma'am, I have seen you every day during my trial.' 'Yes, sir.' 'Then grant me one favor ; when I am tried for my life again, which I daresay I shall be six months hence, promise me to attend my trial again every day.'

" It was a justice I owed to Mr. Beloe to relate the above, as a proof that even the malignant lie in question was not without some foundation.

" Here ends my long epistle. AMELIA OPIE."

On the 9th of January, 1817, M. Louis Simond, for whom Constable and Company published in that year a second edition of his "Journal of a Tour and Residence in Great Britain," addressed the firm with reference to the publication in England of a work by Madame de Staël, to be entitled " Considérations sur les faits principaux de la Révolution de France," but which he suggested might with great propriety and more effect be called " Mémoires de mon Temps." The minimum asked for the English copyright was £2000, and this large sum, which it is believed had already been refused by Mr. Murray and the Messrs. Longman, my father's firm agreed to give ; but owing to what was probably a fortunate hitch in the negotiations the transaction was not completed.

Mr. Cadell, who happened to be in London about this time, writes as follows to my father : —

" While I was at Longman and Company's yesterday, Mr. Brougham came in. Mr. Orme introduced me, and I was much pleased with his manner and conversation. He had called to talk about Madame de Staël's work, he also being commissioned to sell it in this country. He thought her views quite extravagant, and her idea of getting anything like £2000 quite wild."

On the 30th January M. Simond writes : —

" I have not a word to say as to the terms ; you must judge for yourselves. It may seem strange that Madame de Staël should want money ; but she has married her daughter to a needy nobleman, the Duc de Broglie, and has two expensive establishments to support. She read a few pages of the manuscript to me; it was a spirited description of the first sitting of the *Etats-généraux*, and if the rest is like that, which I do not doubt, it will do, certainly."

To M. Simond Madame de Staël wrote as follows : —

" I feel myself much indebted to you, sir, for the trouble you have had the goodness to give yourself, and for the obliging answer of your correspondents, Messrs. Constable and Co. We are very near understanding each other, and I have only a few observations to make.

" My work is full of facts, and that part of it which particularly relates to Bonaparte's reign is in a great degree new. As to the title, I cannot agree to the addition proposed, as the one upon which I have fixed appears to me more suitable. A few days since, the Duke of Wellington, talking to me about this same title, advised me, on the contrary, to abridge it if I could, observing, with great reason, that the shortest titles were the most striking ; — a hero's opinion is entitled to some attention when the question is success.

" Respecting the pecuniary part of the business, which, as the mother of a family, I must not neglect. . . . . The first volume will be printed, I believe, on the 1st of April, the second by the 1st of May, and the third by the 1st of November : it is only at this last-mentioned period that I can allow the work to be published, but I require the first payment of £500 sterling to be made on the 15th day of April, on Messrs Constable receiving the first volume, the remaining £1500 sterling to be paid in three payments of £500 each at three months' interval. I publish on the same terms in Paris.

" I beg leave to propose, but without insisting upon it as a condition, that Messrs. Constable allow me for every subsequent edition of the work books chosen by me from their Catalogue to the amount of £100 sterling. If they are satisfied with the success of my work, they will, I hope, gladly contribute to the augmentation of my library.

" I think I may venture to say that Mr. Constable will find

this work sufficiently stored with curious and important facts, as well as speculative opinions, to insure a considerable degree of interest and extensive circulation, and that he will have no reason to regret his having formed so favorable an opinion of it. It includes the battle of Waterloo."

This book was published in 1818 by Messrs. Baldwin, Cradock, & Joy, on what terms I do not know, and my only reason for recording my father's correspondence with regard to it, and that with Lady Morgan respecting her first work on France, is that she and Madame de Staël were both remarkable women, who from the commercial value they attributed to their literary labor evidently knew the fact.

LADY MORGAN.

From Professor John Playfair my father received the following letter : —

"PARIS, 23d *July*, 1816.

"DEAR SIR, — Lady Morgan (formerly Miss Owenson), whom I have been so fortunate as to become acquainted with here, is engaged in a work that I am persuaded will be most highly valuable and interesting. It is on the present state of society, manners, and opinion in France, and I have no doubt that it will prove incomparably more just and impartial than any account of these matters that is yet before the public. She is a person of great observation ; she has been in the best society here, both fashionable and literary, and of her talent for elegant and spirited composition it is unnecessary to speak. She is quite above the prejudiced and morose views that have disgraced the descriptions of so many of our countrymen. Knowing this to be the case, I was glad to hear from herself that she had some thoughts of applying to you as her publisher. Though an introduction to such a person was unnecessary, I was very glad to offer to be instrumental in any degree in bringing about an acquaintance that may be so much for the benefit of all concerned. I am, dear sir, with very great regard, your obedient servant, JOHN PLAYFAIR."

The above was inclosed by Lady Morgan, with a few lines from herself, in which she says that " if her work is not curious from its originality, and interesting from its communications, the defect must lie in the inadequate ability of the author to the task she has assigned herself ; for her advantages during her residence in France were many and singular, and such, she has reason to believe, as few English subjects have enjoyed. Should Mr. Constable feel inclined to meet Lady M.'s proposals, she will have the pleasure of forwarding a *précis* of her work, which she thinks will make two or three volumes large octavo, and may be ready by February ; and she begs to add that she will feel particularly gratified by sending her work into the world from the Scotch press, the *foyer* which originates at this moment all that is most liberal and enlightened in Europe."

These communications having reached Edinburgh at a time when my father was absent in London, Mr. Cadell writes to him that after consulting Mr. Napier, Mr. Thomas Thomson, and Sir Walter Scott, who all approved of the new client — the latter saying "her last novel (' O'Donnell ') was excellent, and her book will be clever, but it depends a good deal on how long she was in Paris," — he had written cautiously but cordially in my father's name, inviting Lady Morgan to send the *précis,* which accordingly she sent. In it she gives a full detail of the subjects she intends to treat of, and tells that her views of " the general feelings of the higher orders towards the late and present order of things are chiefly illustrated by anecdotes collected during a residence in the châteaux of persons of rank, of the most opposite parties in politics, it being a singular thing that she went from the château of the republican La Fayette to that of the Marquis de Colbert, a decided ultra-royalist." Her *précis* concludes as follows : —

" Such is the roughest and simplest sketch of a work as yet but in progress, and whose interest after all rests chiefly in the nature and style of its details. Lady Morgan wishes that her plans ended here, and that the dignity of authorship was not of necessity sullied by paltry considerations of interest ; but it is long since the Muses disdained an alliance with Cocker, since numbers only served the purposes of poetry, and 'pounds, shillings, and pence' had no connection with the dreams of philosophy and the systems of science. These are days of mere calculation, and genius itself bows to the supremacy of the multiplication-table ! Lady M. will only add, after this humiliating confession, that she has refused a thousand pounds for her work on France from Mr. Colburn of London (the publisher of 'O'Donnell') this day, and that she hopes a more liberal offer from Mr. Constable will belie all the unfounded imputations against Scotch liberality in pecuniary interests, which those who hate Scotland for her liberality on all other subjects have uttered against her."

On December 6, 1816, I find the following passage in a letter from Edinburgh : " I shrewdly suspect that Lady Morgan's subject is beyond her powers, and her terms what I dare swear you will not give in to. I will act upon this supposition, and say nay. So much for Paddy Morgan ! " Her Ladyship had the good sense to close with Mr. Colburn, who published her work in 4to in 1817.

CHARLES KIRKPATRICK SHARPE.

Sir Walter Scott has been represented by Mr. Lockhart as looking with great lenity, if not with absolute approval, on the Chaldee Manuscript, where his patronage is described as a bone of contention between the rival publishers ; but the following letter from Charles Kirkpatrick Sharpe contradicts this view of the case. Mr. Sharpe, who is held forth to ridicule in verses 63 and 64 of the first chapter of the MS., had been offensively described in another part of the Number ; and the following letter, though less irate than others in my possession on the same subject from his pen, was evidently written in a mood far from complacency. Like many others of his letters, it is without a date.

MR. SHARPE TO MR. CONSTABLE.

"MY DEAR MR. CONSTABLE, — I had received a frank from Lord John Campbell yesterday, in order to write to you before the arrival of your letter ; and this I should have done sooner, had not rheumatism, after confining me to my bedchamber for about ten days, ripened into a swelled face of such extraordinary dimensions, that I resemble a figure of Fame with the trumpet broken off, or one of those bagpipe-cheeked Winds that you see in the front of the 'Tempest' in Dryden's Juvenal. However, I am resolved to make out my letter, though I am forced to write it put up against the wall, as my head will not permit me to stoop.

"To speak methodically, in the first place I did not deliver a certain letter, which you shall have as I received it when you return. I thought it quite needless to trouble Mr. G., after my mind remained satisfied that you had said nothing to Mr. Napier, whom I took to be the author of, etc., and who bears me no good-will, as we once had a *tiff*, as old maids speak, about the character of the Marquis of Montrose. Of your friendship I could scarcely doubt, for you have given me very good cause to think it sincere ; and the only reason I can have for dubiety is the regard I entertain for you, as you may have observed that friendship in this world of contradictions is very often like love — the more one cultivates a friend the more he dislikes you.

"Witness ——— ; but I am not come to him yet. I had a very long letter from Scott about the affair of the blackguard Magazine, of which this is the substance. He calls the thing a piece of impertinence, and says that he has no attachment to the work, but through a friend and bottleholder of his, a Mr. Laidlaw, who is engaged in it. He gives this person, of whom I never before heard, a long eulogium, and then proceeds to state, that when Blackwood applied to Laidlaw to write in his Magazine, the bargain was made under an understood condition that Scott would help him with a loose article now and then — 'But you may imagine,' he goes on, 'how I stared when I first saw what sort of company I had got into. I had immediately an apologetic letter from B., stating that the offensive article had been inserted against his will, and so forth, and offering all manner of excuses. I replied, that in addition to the general objection of personality (which is of itself sufficient to deter men of character and honor from meddling with any publication conducted on such principles), there were parts of this unprovoked attack which referred to particular friends of my own, who had a right to expect that I should resent the injury done to them by at least dropping all connection with a publication which had been the vehicle of such attacks upon them. When B. came to these parts he lodged at Mr. Laidlaw's, I myself being extremely unwell, and confined to my bed with a violent attack of my old enemy the cramp. I saw him for about half an hour only and gave him my opinion of the article in question, and of the impossibility of my giving any assistance to a work conducted on such principles. The consequence was a promise to republish the work, omitting the offensive article,[1] and offering an apology to the parties aggrieved, with a solemn engagement that no personalities should disgrace the work in future.' Scott then pays me some compliments respecting my opinion, etc., and with another allusion to the situation of Laidlaw, who is the tye here, the letter concludes. This, of course, dear Mr. C., is all between ourselves, but you will see by and by that Scott will be forced to detach himself entirely from this fellow B. Scott was to be in Edinburgh last night, and I should have put off writing to you till I had seen him, did not this tiresome swelled face forbid me hopes of getting abroad for some days.

"I am glad that Dalyell continues firm, but I confess I shall never be easy till you are safely here again. As to the authors,

---

[1] The following " Note from the Editor" was prefixed to the October Number of the Magazine: "The Editor has learned with regret, that an article in the first edition of last Number, which was intended merely as a *jeu d'esprit*, has been construed so as to give offense to individuals justly entitled to respect and regard; he has on that account withdrawn it in the second edition, and can only add, that if what has happened could have been anticipated, the article in question certainly never would have appeared."

etc., — from certain sly nods, winks, and whispers, I suspect this to be the true state of the case : Wilson wrote the letter to the High Constable, Lockhart the criticism on Hunt, somebody the groundwork of the other, but Wilson certainly made additions, perhaps Lockhart, ———, 'that fause loun', approved of all ; and as Candide was whipt in the Inquisition because he listened to Dr. Pangloss's philosophy with an approving face, so should he be treated. I was assured that B. erased much of what was afterwards printed by advice of the junto ; and this I have every reason to believe. Since you went, ——— called on me one morning, but when the name came up I said 'Not at home.' I then met him in Laing's shop, out of which he followed me and desired a conversation. I said I thought the less that was spoken of some things the better, but appointed next day. He came, and was beginning to give details in the matter so very marked, that I cut him short by reminding him that we might be examined on oath, etc. Of course he could not pretend that he made any efforts of consequence to prevent my portion of the abuse, and, after lingering a long while, and talking a deal of stuff that signified nothing, he wished me good morning ; and so exit a wretched character, the jackal of learned men, himself incapable of writing his mother-tongue — a sower of dissension, for the sake of strife — a would-be hypocrite, but no proficient in that contemptible trade. His sentiments are as mean as his pedigree, and his acquirements as empty as his title, and as he never read an English book in his life, so he thinks this Magazine in question the most delicate piece of satire that ever was penned.

"I think somebody, to mortify Lockhart in the tenderest point, should attack the criticism on Hunt *quoad* its own vulgarity, and the motto might be, 'Set a thief,' etc., for you will observe that the thing is written with an affectation of vast refinement. Now, in this tirade he talks of 'a man of fashion,' and 'people laboring to be genteel ; ' but in the London circle a man would be cut dead who used either of these phrases. The word 'genteel,' even *valets-de-chambre* sicken at. Again, he talks of '*My* Lord Holland !' No man of the world puts the *my* to a lordship nowadays ; moreover, his respect for lords is most vulgarly wonderful ! I wish some witty wag would do this ; it would have a very fine effect.

" I 'm told that Blackwood has engaged half a dozen boarding-school girls, with Mrs. Grant of Laggan at their head, or rather tail, to furnish his Magazine with poetry. Don't this remind you of the lines in Dryden's ' Mackflecknoe ' as descriptive of the work ? —

> " ' A nursery erects its head,
> Where queens are formed, and future heroes bred —
> Where infant punks their tender voices try,
> And little Maximins the gods defy.'

Apropos of lovely ladies, I think Lizars has done Lady Cassillis very prettily. I intend to give you a much prettier for your Magazine shortly.

" Many thanks for your kind offer respecting anything to be done in London. All I want is a cheap copy of ' Wodrow,' as I have that belonging to the Advocates' Library, per favor of Mr. Lockhart, and must return it very soon. Believe me ever, dear Mr. Constable, your truly faithful friend,

"C. K. S."

Mr. Sharpe, a " Memoir " of whom, with a selection from his writings in prose and verse, and illustrations from his wondrous pencil, has lately been published by the Messrs. Blackwood in a splendid 4to volume, was a man of marvelous versatility of talent, fastidious to an unusual degree, but in all æsthetic matters endowed with perfect taste — just, and even generous, in his dealings with his fellow-men.

I remember to have seen a recommendation in " The Times," with reference to a droll letter by Sydney Smith, on the locking of railway-carriages, that a paid public servant should be authorized to pinch that reverend gentleman occasionally, because he squeaked so amusingly on slight provocation. The operations of such a functionary on Mr. Sharpe would have amply repaid a liberal salary. His likings and dislikes were openly avowed, and his letters to my father in my possession bear evidence of the mutual appreciation entertained by them.

JAMES HOGG.

With the Ettrick Shepherd my father's correspondence began in 1804. In 1807 he published for him " The Mountain Bard " and the "Shepherd's Guide." [1] For 1000 copies of the former he paid the sum of £90, an arrangement with which, from the following extract, the poet would appear to have been well satisfied : —

" For this offer, sir, I thank you ; it proves itself to be that of a gentleman and a friend, or at least one who does not wish any great advantage over a ' Mountain Bard,' and I heartily accept of it. The copies are yours, only I expect that as my proportion of them will not supply all my subscribers, you will furnish me with such as I want at the lowest selling price."

The social deportment of the Shepherd has been severely depicted and commented on by Mr. Lockhart, but the absence of conventional good-breeding, at least in the earlier part of his life, is not to be wondered at, and the frankness of his confession and apology when made aware of any palpable transgression, more than atoned for such in the minds of his more generous friends. Take for example the following extract from a letter to my father : "*September* 26, 1808, — If you will be so kind as impute my behavior at this time to the effects of your own hospitality, and not to any natural bias, I promise — nay, I swear — never to offend you again in thought, word, or deed." This promise was not kept, but the failure was acknowledged and repented of, as we shall see.

---

[1] *The Mountain Bard*, consisting of Ballads and Songs, founded in facts and legendary tales. Archibald Constable and Co., Edinburgh, and John Murray, London.

The Shepherd's Guide ; being a Practical Treatise on the Diseases of Sheep, their causes, and the best means of preventing them, etc. Archibald Constable and Co., Edinburgh, and John Murray, London.

By these two works we are told by Hogg's biographer that he realized at this time £300.

When about to issue in 1810 the first number of " The Spy," a weekly journal of *belles-lettres*, morals, and criticism, Mr. Hogg wrote as follows : —

" Monday Morning.

" DEAR CONSTABLE, — I was so warmly solicited by my friends last night to procure your name as publisher of ' The Spy,' and there being nothing I have such a desire for, I haste to make our wishes known to you, for, cross as you sometimes are, experience is beginning to whisper to me that there is as little selfishness and as much of the gentleman in your character as in any man of my acquaintance in Edinburgh. Now, as you have no risk (profit from us I know you don't want), and as your name alone is very likely to save the poor ' Spy ' from public execution for a year or two, I beg you will not refuse it. A change next week, when the quarter is out, is absolutely necessary some way. I want your advice at any rate.

" THE SPY.

" P. S. — The above not to be inserted among the literary anecdotes in the Chapter for 1810. J. H."

This overture was rejected. " The Spy " appeared under other auspices, and soon died what was deemed a natural death. Two years later Mr. Hogg offered my father the first edition of " The Queen's Wake," in the following terms : —

" DEANAUGH, 24th September, 1812.

" MR. CONSTABLE : —

" Dear Sir, — Having now completed the ' Queen's Wake,' I must settle about the publication, for I am desirous that it should appear in January or February next. Of course, as your right, I give you the first offer of it. My terms are decisively as follows. The book shall be your property ; only on the publication of the first and all future editions, I shall receive a bill at six, nine, or twelve months for a certain proportion, which is all that we have now to settle about. In the meantime I engage to give you as many private subscribers as shall completely cover my quota of the first edition. You need not offer me below ten nor above twenty

pounds per hundred copies, for I will neither accept of the one nor the other, but if you desire it I will read the poem, or a part of it, to any literary gentleman on whose judgment you can depend. In one word, say that for every 1000 copies, as soon as printed, I receive a bill of £150, the copyright of the book and subscriptions to that amount to be yours. George Goldie requests a share of it ; that shall be as you please. I will expect an answer with your convenience.

" I am your obliged   JAMES HOGG."

This offer also, for some reason unknown to me, was rejected, and the exquisite poem on which the reputation of the Ettrick Shepherd mainly rests was first published by the George Goldie above mentioned. Mr. Hogg's desire that my father should introduce his works to public notice remained, however, unshaken, as the following extracts from letters written in 1813 and 1814 abundantly prove.

MR. HOGG TO MR. CONSTABLE.

" DEANHAUGH, *May* 20, 1813.

" DEAR SIR, — Exclusive of all other considerations than those connected with my own honor and final emolument, I have resolved to give you the first offer of every literary work which I venture to the public. I have for many years been collecting the rural and traditionary tales of Scotland, and I have of late been writing them over again, and new-modeling them, and have the vanity to suppose they will form a most interesting work. They will fill two large vols. 8vo, price £1, or 4 vols. 12mo, price the same. But as I think the Ettrick Shepherd is rather become a hackneyed name, and imagine that having gained a character as a bard is perhaps no commendation to a writer of prose tales, I am determined to publish them under a fictitious title. The title-page will consequently be to this purpose — 'The Rural and Traditional Tales of Scotland, by J. H. Craig of Douglas, Esq.' [1]

" With regard to pecuniary concerns I am not at all greedy

---

[1] In 1814 *The Hunting of Badelewe, a Dramatic Tale,* by J. H. Craig of Douglas, Esq., was published in 8vo.

that way, and have not the least doubt of our agreement, only I should like to bargain so that the work, or at least the edition, should belong exclusively to the publisher, that so he may have an interest in furthering it to the utmost of his power. As I really do intend to conceal the real author, that the critics may not suppose it is the work of a book-maker, and as no one in Edinburgh knows of it, save Mr. J. Grieve, you will easily see the propriety, my dear sir, of concealing this from all living. Send me your opinion in writing to his care, and believe me ever yours, JAMES HOGG."

THE SAME TO THE SAME.

" Monday, July 12.

"DEAR SIR,—I have never received any definite answer from you respecting the publication of my Scottish romances, for which I am still waiting before I mention them to any other. If you think the publication of the whole rather too high a venture at once, you may publish one tale in the first place as an experiment to sound the public, in a 6s. or 7s. volume,—for the truth is that I would rather give you a first edition almost on any conditions than intrust it with any other in Scotland. But I charge you, unless you think it a concern worth your while, not to let any regard for the author engage you in it.

"Do not send word for me to come and speak with you, for a quiet word with you is impossible, and I will not come nor attempt it, but write me your mind in a line or two frankly, as I do to you. I am your obliged JAMES HOGG."

THE SAME TO THE SAME.

"GRIEVE AND SCOTT'S, February 1, 1814.

"SIR,—Excepting a few notes, etc., I have finished a poem of 2200 lines, or thereabouts. I intend it to be such a volume as the 'Queen's Wake'—at least the same price, but not so thick; the number of pages, however, shall be at the publisher's option. Though I suppose it is in vain, yet, to save all reflections from my friends, and stings of my own conscience, I hereby make you the first offer of it. There is always one good thing attends our transactions, — When we don't agree about a book, we never cast out about it.

" As in reason this ought to be my best poem, so you may believe me, if I did not deem it so I would not publish it at this time ; yet, as calculation on such a thing is impossible, I think the fairest way is to agree on a certain sum for each 100 copies that are published, the number of the edition to be always what the publisher pleases. Say that £13 is allowed me for every 100 copies that are published, and on the day preceding the publication a bill granted for the total at eight or nine months. These are my ideas of the matter, and on these conditions I offer you the work, the copyright not removable without your consent as long as the conditions agreed on are faithfully fulfilled. Let me have your sentiments in answer to this, which I like as the most concise way. By the bye, as the only way left me of accomplishing a desired event, I should be very glad to bargain with you for a copyright of all my works hitherto published, but this must either be done instantly or never. I am, ever your obliged and most obedient servant, JAMES HOGG." [1]

MR. HOGG TO MR. CONSTABLE.

" EDINBURGH, *July* 25*th.*

" DEAR SIR, — I spoke to you some months ago about publishing a poem, price 12*s.*, about which, I believe, we were mostly agreed ; but, on mature calculation, I am resolved first to publish one not half so long, price 7*s.* 6*d.* This will be a less venture, and more will buy it ; and if it sell very rapidly I can the sooner add another, the same length and price, which will come to 15*s.*, whereas, were they both in one, they would be thought dear at 12*s.* The title of this will be ' The Pilgrims of the Sun,' a poem in four parts, by James Hogg,

---

[1] In the opening of this letter Mr. Hogg states that the poem of which it treats was almost finished, and in the following one he writes that he and my father were "mostly agreed" about the publication of it ; but I find no record of the appearance of the work, and do not even know its name. Probably it was *Madoc of the Moor*, published in 1816.

etc. It will not exceed ten sheets. I will give you an edition of 1000 copies for £70, at three months. As I want it put to press in a few days, before I leave town, I request your acceptance or non-acceptance of this by letter with your first convenience. I am, sir, yours ever most truly,

"JAMES HOGG."

R. H. CROMEK.

R. H. Cromek, a well-known engraver, and the editor of the " Reliques of Burns," and " Remains of Nithsdale and Galloway Song," [1] had done much work for my father, in illustrating Lady Stafford's edition of " The Genealogy of the Earls of Sutherland," and other books. He appears to have been highly esteemed by many of the distinguished literary men of his time, and had certainly won my father's warm regard, which he as cordially returned. In 1807, having collected a number of unpublished letters and poems of Robert Burns, he resolved to publish them as a supplementary volume to Dr. Currie's edition of the poet's works, and under the judicious supervision of Mr. Roscoe the volume appeared in 1808.

In the following extract from a letter of November 17, 1807, Mr. Cromek gives my father some details of the scheme : —

" MY EVER DEAR FRIEND, —. . . . I have as much manuscript as will make a fifth volume to Dr. Currie, even

---

[1] " You will rejoice with me that my volume of *Nithsdale Ballads* is on the verge of publication. I wish you had had it, because it ought to have issued from a Scotch house, and because it is a most curious and original book, and will most certainly have a very wide circulation. I have so high an opinion of it myself that I think Mr. Jeffrey will and must say it is the most valuable collection that ever yet appeared. I have now given — what I think was never given — the real *History of the Scotish Peasantry ;* and as far as relates to the twin districts of Nithsdale and Galloway, I have ventured to describe at some length their manners, attachments, games, superstitions, their traditional history of fairies, witchcraft, etc., etc., taken down fresh from the lips of old cottars. One of the most interesting and valuable of these was a Margaret Corson, an old woman aged ninety-seven. The title I send you ; the whole 1000 will be printed on India paper. Pray give one, with my kind respects, to Mr. Hunter, to add to his collection, as it is a wonderful group, drawn by Stothard from the peasantry."

Mr. Cromek inserted in this work, as genuine old ballads, some exquisite imitations and lyrics by Allan Cunningham, who also contributed most of the historical notes and illustrations.

after I have rejected what it would be improper to publish. It will be the most interesting volume you can imagine. One discovery I made, which is particularly interesting, of a MS. that contains observations on ' Scotish Ballads and Music.' I shall print it at the end of the volume as an appendix. It will bear this kind of title : ' Robert Burns's Remarks on Scotish Songs and Ballads, ancient and modern : containing Strictures on their Merits as Musical and Poetical Composi-tions ; and a great variety of Anecdotes of their Authors.' These remarks are written with great playfulness of fancy, and contain many lively, interesting anecdotes. They exist in the handwriting of Burns, in an interleaved copy, in four vols. octavo, of Johnson's ' Scots Musical Museum.' They were writ-ten by the poet for Captain Riddell of Glenriddell, one of the heroes of ' The Whistle,' whose autograph the volumes bear. These valuable volumes were left by Mrs. Riddell to her niece, by whose kindness I shall be enabled to give to the public transcripts of this amusing and miscellaneous collection. I shall now proceed to inform you of what I have done ; and I must beg, as the greatest kindness, you will immediately write me and give me your advice on the subject. In the first place, I read everything to Mr. Roscoe. He was highly delighted, and gave his opinion of the work in a letter to Cadell and Davies ; he advised me to sell the work, and edit it myself, as I have a number of valuable notes to add to it ; but he cau-tioned me against fixing a price, and to leave that to the book-sellers. I called at Cadell's ; they read Mr. Roscoe's letter, and asked me what I meant to sell it for. Of course I said that I could only judge of its *intrinsic* value, that to its com-mercial value I was quite a stranger. They candidly said that they *must* have it.

" I then proposed that a literary man should be sent to me to judge of the letters. Davies laid his hand on Roscoe's let-ter, and remarked : ' On the opinion and authority of this letter we would purchase MSS. to any amount, and no person shall be sent to you.' They then proposed that the price should be settled by Mr. Roscoe. To this I objected, as he is our common friend ; indeed, I knew he would not much like it. Davies then said, ‘ We can only say at present that, if you like to leave the price to us, you shall not only receive a proper price, but a liberal one — a price that will satisfy you and your friends.’ I told them that in time and money the collecting these materials had cost me near sixty guineas, which I believe to be not far from the mark. In this way the business rests. Dr. Aiken has been to me, and he is going to write something in the next ‘ Athenæum ’ about the discovery ; and, of course, Phillips will mention it. It will then be known ; and I hope something like a competition will be in the market. Davies told me I might expect a visit from the sheriff.[1] Now, my good friend, do tell me, for you can, how I am to act, and what value I am to place upon them. Certainly a volume of this interesting sort will be worth 250 guineas, including my expenses in collecting. I await your answer with great anxiety, because this is a work of moment. It is much talked of among the literati here. Walter Scott has a letter ; I trust to you to take an exact copy of it, and forward it to me by post. Also, for God’s sake, let me have Burns’s papers in your possession ; if you won’t look them out for his sake, will you for mine ? ”

On the death, in 1809, of Mr. Park, my father’s partner in London, Mr. Cromek offered his services as a successor. The offer was declined ; and the London firm almost immediately dissolved. Mr. Cromek was a man with many talents, and he was diligent in the employment of them. His engravings were highly esteemed ; but he seems to have lived and died in the midst of pecuniary difficulties, which the following letter, written five days before his death, proves that my father strove, as in many similar instances, to lighten.

MR. CROMEK TO MR. CONSTABLE.

“ LONDON, *March* 9, 1812.

“ MY VERY GOOD FRIEND, — Your letter and inclosure of Saturday relieved me from a pressure of anxiety almost insupportable.

[1] Sir Richard Phillips was at this time sheriff in London.

"On the generosity of your conduct on this occasion I am too poorly to-day to dwell. The last six days of March have been exceedingly trying; but I doubt not I shall yet weather the storm, in every sense of that emphatic metaphor.

"You promise me a letter. Inform me in it how I can serve you or your house here. My family are tremblingly alive to your goodness. God reward you!   R. H. CROMEK."

Mr. Cromek died on the 14th March, 1812.

WASHINGTON IRVING.

It was to Mr. John Miller that my father owed an introduction to Washington Irving.

MR. MILLER TO MR. CONSTABLE.

"BOW STREET, *August* 26, 1817.

"DEAR SIR, — I am glad to have an opportunity of introducing to your attention the gentleman who will put this into your hands. Mr. Washington Irving is a native of the country which gave birth to Washington and Franklin, and has contributed not a little to her literary stores. From his acquaintance you will receive both pleasure and information; and I know you will also be gratified to be serviceable to your friends, among whom you will, I hope, always think me worthy of a place, however humble that place may be. Mr. Irving is an entire stranger in Scotland, and any civilities you may show him will be the more gratifying to, dear sir, yours very truly,
                                                    "JOHN MILLER."

Mr. Irving met my father frequently while in Scotland, and appears to have been favorably impressed by him, for, after Mr. Murray had declined to undertake the publication of the "Sketch Book," we are told in the Memoir of his Life that the author applied to Sir Walter Scott to ascertain whether Mr. Constable would do so. He wrote as follows: "Should Mr. Constable feel inclined to make a bargain for the wares I at present have on hand, he will encourage me to further enterprise; and it will be something like bargaining with a gypsy, who may one time have but a wooden bowl to sell, and at another a silver tankard. "

To this Sir Walter replied, on December 4, 1819, that he had no doubt Constable would most willingly be Mr. Irving's publisher, and that he had always found him liberal in his dealings, but that until Mr. Irving had decided on what system he wished to base the transaction—whether to share profits or sell the copyright—he had done "no more than open the trenches."

Mr. Irving, in his Preface, says, "Before the receipt of this most obliging letter, I had determined to look to no leading bookseller for a launch, but to throw my work before the public at my own risk, and let it sink or swim according to its merits." He committed the "Sketch Book" to the care of Mr. John Miller, who, on the 5th February, 1820, wrote as follows to my father : —

"BURLINGTON ARCADE, *5th February*, 1820.

"DEAR SIR, — I am about to publish for Mr. Washington Irving (a gentleman who is known to you) the 'Sketch Book' a very clever little work lately printed in America, and very popular there. The English edition is very much altered and very much improved. It will form a handsome octavo volume of about twenty-four sheets, and I shall be much disappointed if it is not very successful here. The author has, I know, a strong wish that you should be the Edinburgh publisher, and I shall also be much gratified by it. Have you any objection to your name appearing in the title-page? And will you allow me to send you down twenty-five or fifty copies on sale or return — to be accounted for in six months at the London sale price? I think Mr. Scott has seen and spoken handsomely of the work. As it is just ready for publication, your immediate answer will very much oblige, dear sir, your obliged friend and servant,   JOHN MILLER."

Almost immediately after this Mr. Miller became bankrupt, and Mr. Irving tells us that "through the favorable representations of Mr. Scott, Murray was quickly induced to undertake the future publication of the work, which he had previously declined."

With the exception of a presentation copy of the "Sketch Book," inscribed " From the Author," I find no indication of correspondence between Mr. Irving and my father until July, 1825, when we are told, " Mr. Irving, still in Paris, received overtures from Constable for a ' Life of Washington,' " to which he wrote the following reply : —

MR. IRVING TO MR. CONSTABLE.

"PARIS, *August* 19, 1825.

" MY DEAR SIR, —Your letter having passed through two or three immediate hands, has been long in reaching me, otherwise you would have received a reply at an earlier date. I feel highly flattered by your thinking me worthy of contributing to your valuable ' Miscellany ' so important an article as the ' Life of Washington.'

" After the various works, however, which have appeared on the subject, it would be very difficult to treat it anew in a manner to challenge public attention, or to satisfy public expectation, if much excited. It would require a great deal of reading and research, and that, too, of a troublesome and irksome kind, among public documents and state papers, for Washington's life was more important as a statesman than even as general.

" The biographer should also be in America, where he could have access to all kinds of official papers and public records, and where he could have familiar and personal communication with the surviving companions and contemporaries of Washington. From them he might gather particulars of his private life, character, and conduct, which have hitherto been but scantily furnished by his biographers.

" Under the circumstances in which I am placed, I feel myself quite incapable of executing my idea of the task. It is one that I dare not attempt lightly. *I stand in too great awe of it.*

" In declining it, however, let me again express how much I feel flattered and obliged by your applying to me on the subject. Nothing would give me greater pride and delight than to be able to fulfill it in a manner satisfactory to you, the pub-

lic, and myself, but I shrink from the attempt. I am, my dear
sir, very sincerely and faithfully your obliged friend,

"WASHINGTON IRVING."

It is doubtless to my father's suggestion that we owe the
"Life of Washington," which appeared thirty years later si-
multaneously in England and America.

JAMES SHERIDAN KNOWLES.

James Sheridan Knowles possessed a joyous human nature
and a pure and lofty mind. He is described by a writer in
the "Athenæum" as the king of uneducated dramatists. A
great dramatist he certainly was, and not perhaps so highly
educated as some others of the fraternity, but his educational
advantages were surely as ample as those of Shakespeare, who
sits enthroned above them all. His father was a lecturer on
the English language, and the editor of an English dictionary,
as was also his uncle Mr. Sheridan, whose son, Richard Brins-
ley Sheridan, may fairly contest the palm as a dramatist with
his gifted cousin.

Sheridan Knowles, as he is always called, was a voluminous
and successful writer, though we are told that he had never
earned £200 in one year by his pen. He was perhaps too
rich in deeds of kindness to acquire more vulgar wealth, and
the following letter shows that he was quick to observe and to
appreciate a spirit kindred with his own. My father's name
had stood upon the title-page of "Caius Gracchus," and Mr.
Knowles's letter of the 9th March, 1825, suggests an offer to
him of the copyright of "The Elocutionist, a Collection in
Prose and Verse," published a few years earlier : —

MR. KNOWLES TO MR. CONSTABLE.

"GLASGOW.

"MY DEAR SIR, — Since I had the honor of speaking with
you I have received a proposal for my book. I stated to you
that £150 had been offered me before, and you approved of
my declining to accept that sum, as below its value. Will you

advise me as to the sum that I ought to take? The price of the book is 3s. 6d., and 4100 have been sold in three years and two months. If you can favor me with your answer by return, I shall esteem it a great kindness.

"And now, my dear sir, let me tell you that my last visit to Edinburgh was the happier on account of the few minutes I spent in your company, for, few as they were, they afforded me ample evidence that I had chanced to light upon a man who would do me a kindness if he could.

"My book you did not care about; it did not lie in your way; but I verily believe you would have become its purchaser, because you saw I was urgent to dispose of it, and I would stake my life against a pound that you mentioned Sir Walter Scott with the view of effecting an introduction to him in my favor, could it have been practicable. I left your shop, sir, with a glow of the heart with which I have not often left another man's table, and yet I have met with many a kind and worthy man.

"I state this by way of thanking you, which is all the poor return I can make for your most cordial reception of me, without the hand of a patron or a friend to lead me to your door. If you think there is any flattery in this, remember the advice you gave me, and you will change your mind. God bless you. Faithfully yours,   J. S. KNOWLES."

Hazlitt tells us that Mr. Knowles remained "unspoiled by success, unconscious of the wreath he had earned, and talked of his plays just as if they had been written by any one else." In later years religion was an all-pervading principle with him, and the inculcation of Christian truth the main object of his life. He became a preacher, and the writer of his obituary notice in the "Athenæum," December 6, 1862, says: —

"Knowles was an earnest man in his last as in his earlier vocation, but in his seriousness he lost none of his old cheerfulness of spirit. He was still a good man of this world, while busiest in showing the way to the next."

DR. WILLIAM KITCHINER.

The motto and creed, and probably — in his devouter moments — the prayer of Dr. William Kitchiner was ever *Dum vivimus vivamus;* and were man's body capable of immortality, the *peptic precepts* of this disciple of Epicurus, with his treatises on the art of invigorating, prolonging, and enjoying life, might have proved a veritable gospel to all who do not indorse the sentiment of Job, " I would not live alway."

Dr. Kitchiner's published utterances were frequent during the last ten years of his life, and for the most part *oracular*. His ex-cathedral injunctions and exhortations on every theme that can affect the health and worldly happiness of men were uttered with a dogmatic vigor that declare him to have been an incarnation of Gratiano's hitherto imaginary personage, who exclaims, " I am Sir Oracle, and when I ope my lips, let no dog bark." Witness " The Cook's Oracle " " The Housekeeper's Oracle," " The Traveller's Oracle," The " Horse and Carriage Oracle." He wrote also on " Telescopes," on the " Economy of the Eyes in the use of Spectacles," published a volume of " Observations on Vocal Music," edited a series of " Loyal and National Songs," composed some really good melodies for others, and, judging from his correspondence with my father, seemed ready on the shortest notice to undertake a manual on any non-medical subject, though as an M. D. of some repute in his day, one would have expected medicine to be his favorite science.

The kitchen, however, rather than the sick-room, was by preference his scene of action, and there he was thoroughly at home. This may account for and justify the success of his *chef-d'œuvre*, " The Cook's Oracle," which at once took rank, and has since kept its place for more than half a century, as one of the principal culinary authorities.[1] Sir Walter Scott

---

[1] With reference to a favorable bulletin from his publisher, Dr. Kitchiner writes in May, 1822 : "Your news about *The Oracle* is very flattering. When I first declared my intention of writing that book, all my old friends told me plainly that I was mad, and that the fame I had deservedly got for the book on *Telescopes* would

writes to my father: "I have heard of the fame of Dr. Kitchiner. . . . . What a singular correspondence the Doctor's name bears to the subject he has rendered so interesting! Somebody told me there was to be an edition in which all the fun was to be omitted ; I hope in that case that the Doctor will do as Mr. Hardcastle is asked to do in 'She Stoops to Conquer' — knock out the brains and serve them up by themselves."

The work is a quaint and amusing one, as well as practically useful, and the section of the Introduction that treats of Culinary Curiosities, including a leaf from the Devil's Cookery-Book, — which tells, among other things, "how to persuade a goose to roast *himselfe*" when you have not time to attend to him, — is really diverting reading. His advices to "Mrs. Cookey" and her mistress, or *lectures*, as he calls them in a letter to my father, are pithy and to the point.

Dr. Kitchiner was a severe student, and his kitchen was his "study," where he kept what he called his "Culinary Library, and grand Magazine of *Taste* of an hundred and fifty sauces !" and where every one of his receipts, as he tells us, was carefully proved before being submitted to that "enlightened and indefatigable Committee of Taste, composed of thoroughbred *grands gourmands* of the first magnitude, whose cordial co-operation I cannot too highly praise ; and here do I most gratefully record the unremitting zeal they manifested during the arduous process of proving the respective recipes ; they were so truly, philosophically, and disinterestedly regardless of the wear and tear of teeth and stomach, that their labor — appeared a pleasure to them. Their laudable perseverance has hardly been exceeded by those determined spirits who lately in the Polar expedition braved the other extreme of temperature, etc., in spite of whales, bears, icebergs, and starvation."

all be soon evaporated by the Cookery. I persevered, however, as I am doing with *The Bachelor's Oracle*, which I think may be as good a hit as the Cook's; but you are the commander of its destiny, and it will not pay a visit to friend Moyes (the printer) till you say ' Volo.' " I suppose that " Veto " must have been my father's utterance ; and that in consequence the Bachelor's may have merged in the *Traveller's Oracle*, published by Mr. Colburn in 2 vols. 12mo, in 1827.

My father had an unhappy tendency, whenever he felt unwell, to credit himself with all the ills that flesh is heir to, and was wont on such occasions to fly to Buchan's " Domestic Medicine " for general corroboration, or the compliance of his temporary symptoms with some malady therein described. Hence it was, probably, that when Dr. Kitchiner proposed to publish what he called " A Pandect of the Practice of Twenty-one celebrated Physicians and Surgeons " *in one or two special diseases,* while strongly dissuading him from the undertaking on prudential grounds, he suggested a more comprehensive work, where these, among others, might naturally find a place, and a volume be produced that should rival his favorite, Dr. Buchan.

Kitchiner, though a doctor, had no faith in medicine, and while manifestly unwilling to decline the task proposed to him, he delayed its execution on various pleas, — alleging at one time inability for any work whatever, at another that his head was too full of crotchets and quavers to attend to anything but music, — and finally abandoned the idea altogether. He had no inadequate estimate of his own powers, and his faculties were as versatile as those of most men ; pecuniary motives had also a strong influence, but conscientious scruples probably combined with the fear of failure to prevent his compilation of an Oracle of Medicine.

He wrote as follows in February, 1823 : —

" DEAR SIR, — I love money ; he must be a fool who does not. I love fame, so does every wise man ; but it must be that sterling, real claim to it which I have from the books Mr. Constable and yourselves have published for me.

" I have felt very uncomfortable ever since Mr. Constable mentioned the medical work, as I should be much hurt if he thought that I had not the highest respect for his universally acknowledged sound judgment on the subject of what will please the public ; but the mistake he has made is in extremely overrating my powers of authorship.

" I can only write on subjects on which I have a certain feeling, and a conviction that I can fearlessly enter the field

with an absolute certainty of eclipsing all who have previously
written on the subject. If Mr. Constable will give me a job
in the musical way, he shall have no reason to complain of my
want of diligence, and I hope not of my want of ability." [1]

To my father Dr. Kitchiner wrote on the 13th March, 1822:
" I grieve not to be able to begin the *medical work*. I am
afraid I can never do it. If I did, I must compromise that
—— ; in fact, my highly respected friend, Physic is nonsense,
—'throw it to the dogs,' as William Shakespeare says. I
could write honestly, and I think popularly, on the Eye and
Optics, — if I do will you take me under your wing ? "

With further reference to the " Domestic Medicine," my
father writes : —

" After all, this plan of mine may be worth little, and of
more difficulty in carrying into effect than I may be aware of.
Your callings, if I may so speak, are unquestionably various ;
but a bookseller, who must have his finger in every pie, has
subjects without number to engage his attention, and must
consequently be often wrong, as I have been to an extent
greater than I shall at present acknowledge. Still, I have

---

[1] Dr. Kitchiner here alludes to a project he appears to have had much at heart —
the publication, with appropriate musical accompaniment, of the *Songs in the
Novels and Tales of the Author of Waverley*, with reference to which my father
wrote, on January 24, 1822 : " I think such a publication, if properly executed,
would sell, but I cannot venture to say more on this subject. The author (*if he can
be found*) must be consulted, and his plans followed, whatever they may be."

So far as I know, this scheme was never carried out. Dr. Kitchiner was very
desirous that the words of the first Song in the Collection of *The Loyal and National Songs of England* — " God save great George the Fourth " — should be
written by Sir Walter Scott, who, in a letter to my father, replies as follows to the
invitation : " I am afraid I am not equal to do what Dr. Kitchiner requires of me,
and what I should have pride and pleasure in performing, could I do it well. But
the simplicity of the *old* anthem, like the old Psalter, will always carry it over
better poetry. The terminating on the *th* would be rather, I fear, harsh, both in
rhyme and music. Here is a stanza, however. Short as it is there is a false rhyme
in it, and I am not sure I could find a true one, unless I could bring in Craig
Geoth : —

" ' Winds, bear the accents forth,
East and west, and south and north,
Long live King George the Fourth,
God save the King ! ' "

done better by following my own plans than by adopting those of other people."

The variety of Dr. Kitchiner's "callings" was certainly great. In the month of December, 1822, he makes the following announcement : " I am busy about a new work, — 'Writing made Elegant and Easy to all.' Although I write badly enough now, writing was the hobby of my boyhood. . . . . I wish you and I could meet, as we did when you were here. I think I could build books tolerably well, with you for my architect." On 10th March, 1823, he announces that he is just commencing " The Invalid's Almanac, or Valetudinarian's Vade Mecum," and that he is also publishing " Dibdin's Sea-Songs, 100 for a guinea, with a Memoir of his Life and Writings."

Dr. Kitchiner never missed an opportunity of warning my father against his tendency to tamper medicinally with his system, and always gave him cheerful views of his natural constitution. In March, 1822, he writes : —

"I assure you that I am quite uncomfortable that you still persist in tampering with us doctors ! What does a man want with medicine who can ride ten miles without fatigue, eat plain food with an excellent appetite, has every domestic comfort to render the evenings delightful, and can sleep soundly from ten o'clock at night till four in the morning — aye, and all this in spite of the pains he takes to annoy his good and well-behaving stomach with *squills*, etc., etc. ? . . . . . You have a fullness in your head — and in your heart, forsooth, — well, nobody can deny that : the former is as full of good sense, and the latter of good nature, as any man's in Christendom. . . . . You are enjoying actually better health than almost any man of forty-five can boast, and will long continue to do so, if you do not undermine your excellent constitution by everlastingly bothering it with physic. I am ready to swear this before my Lord Mayor and the Court of Aldermen."

Again, — " I am sure intense exertion of mind has been the sole cause of your bodily complaints. Pray now, just consider Life as a plaything (!), and don't consume it uncomfortably in anxiety, that it does not deserve. . . . . . At our age we cannot expect to be long in this world, and as we wish to be here as long as we can, we must above all things avoid *Anxiety*, as the great enemy of *Age*, because *Hope*, the counteracting power which defeats it in youth, gets weaker as we get wiser, and every little care wears and worries us." "I have been hoping to have the pleasure of seeing you in London again ; the excursion always appears to be of great service to your health and spirits, — as indeed it must be, to meet so many who are heartily attached to you. Whenever you find the Blue Devils coming down upon you very fiercely, my prescription is, — Come to London !"

Dr. Kitchiner died on 26th February, 1827, five months before his correspondent.

CAPTAIN BASIL HALL.

There are some persons whose immediate business is so important and exacting, that if the working hours of life were doubled they might still seem insufficient for the discharge of duty — imminent from day to day, and who therefore hold themselves excusable for leaving what concerns their neighbors out of view. Some, again, whose spheres are more limited, and whose interests do not appear to need great personal attention, are yet so entirely engrossed by selfish aims that they find no time even to look upon the things of others. Besides these, there are idlers not a few, who yet may be called busybodies, and who, though conceiving the world to be entirely out of joint, are far from blaming as " cursed spite " the ordinance that seems to prompt at every turn that they were "born to set it right." These are ready to become directors-general to all mankind.

To neither of those classes did Captain Basil Hall belong. Sir Walter Scott, who, in his latest years, owed much to the Captain's active friendship, describes him as " that curious fellow, who takes charge of every one's business without neglecting his own." Of acute and wakeful intellect, of wide and varied experience and culture, the interest of Basil Hall was intense in all that concerned humanity, and it is sad that the sun of such a man should have set for others before his days on earth had ended. Ten years before his death, in 1834, he writes of himself : " I have enjoyed to the full each successive period of my life, as it has rolled over me. . . . . As a middy, I was happy — as a lieutenant, happier — as a captain, happiest."

His earliest correspondence with my father that was of any importance, had reference to a second edition, in octavo, of his account of Corea and Loo-Choo, which had been published originally in a quarto form. He writes, on 16th November, 1819, as follows : " Mr. Murray is very keen about it, and I confess that I myself am somewhat sanguine too. . . . . I hope to have your valuable aid in setting it about, and indeed, between ourselves, it has a *claim* on you, for without your counsel I do not believe it would ever have seen the light ! Will it be consistent with your plans and practice to let it be advertised on the envelopes of your wide-spreading books, — the ' Edinburgh Review,' the ' Magazine,' the new ' Journal,' and so on ? If so, I need not say how much obliged I shall feel for such an act of personal kindness to me."

This request must have been cordially granted, for I find Captain Hall writing some months later : " I have not forgot the *princely* manner in which you advertised my little book, and indeed I am disposed to ascribe much of its sale (I won't say *success*) to that act of kindness on your part. . . . . I don't know well how to thank you enough for your most obliging and friendly frankness with me on matters of business."

Shortly after this my father received from Captain Hall a special token of friendship and confidence, in being permitted to read a narrative that deeply interested all who were privileged to see it, but which, from feelings of delicacy, has hitherto been confined within a very narrow circle. After the lapse of more than half a century, it may be hoped that every motive for restriction may have been removed, and that a wider circulation may be given to what might still be interesting and profitable.

With reference to this Captain Hall writes : —

"I have a thing to show you, which is shown to very few people, but which I feel assured you will have pleasure in perusing. It is the narrative of my sister, Lady Delancy (now Mrs. Harvey), at Waterloo, from the time her husband was wounded till his death.

"I venture to offer you a sight of it, not only because I know that you are of a disposition to enter with full spirit into what comes fresh and warm from the heart, but from an idea that perhaps you might deem it worth your while to show your rising family so fine an example of the advantages which, at moments of severe trial, arise out of right principles and a well-regulated mind. I must make one condition — that you do not allow it to go beyond your own fireside."

This narrative, as had been anticipated, deeply interested my father — so deeply indeed that he proposed at a later period that it should be included in an edition of "Paul's Letters to his Kinsfolk," and, had the decision rested with Captain Hall, permission would certainly have been granted, for he writes : "I am equally desirous with you that it *should* be ; " but in spite of this, and of the following solicitation from Sir Walter Scott, it was withheld. Sir Walter wrote from Abbotsford to Captain Hall on 13th October, 1825 : —

" . . . . Constable proposed a thing to me which was of so much delicacy that I scarce know how to set about, and thought of reserving it till you and I meet. It relates to that most interesting and affecting Journal kept by my regretted and amiable friend Mrs. Harvey during poor Delancey's illness. He thought, with great truth, that it would add very great interest to the letters which I wrote from Paris soon after Waterloo, and certainly I should consider it as one of the most valuable and important documents which could be published as illustrative of the woes of war.

" Whether this could be done without injury to the feelings of survivors is a question not for me to decide, and indeed I feel unaffected pain in even submitting it to your friendly ear, who, I know, will put no harsh construction upon my motive, which can be no other than such as would do honor to the amiable and lamented authoress. I never read anything which affected my own feelings more strongly, or which, I am sure, would have a deeper interest on those of the public. Still the work is of a domestic nature, and its publication, however honorable to all concerned, might perhaps give pain where, God knows, I should be sorry any proposal of mine should awaken the distresses which time may have in some degree abated. You are the only person who can judge of this with any certainty, or who at least can easily gain the means of ascertaining it ; and as Constable seemed to think there was a possibility that, after the lapse of so much time, it might be regarded as a matter of history, and as a record of the amiable character of your accomplished sister, and seemed to suppose there was some possibility of such a favor being granted, you will consider me as putting the question on his suggestion. It could be printed as the journal of a lady during the last illness of a general officer of distinction, during her attendance upon his last illness, or something to that purpose. Perhaps it may be my own high estimation of the contents of the heart-rending diary which makes me suppose a possibility that, after such a lapse of years, the publication may possibly (as that which cannot but do the highest honor to the memory of the amiable authoress) not be judged altogether unadvisable. You may and will, of course, act in this matter with your natural feelings of propriety, and ascertain whether that which cannot but do honor to the memory of those who are gone can be made public with the sacred regard due to the feelings of survivors."

On December 6th, 1825, Captain Hall makes a final allusion to the subject in a letter to my father : —

"I am extremely sorry to tell you, that after using every proper argument with the person chiefly concerned, I have totally failed in obtaining leave to print the Narrative which you were so anxious to obtain, and which I was equally anxious should see the light. I regret much that it is totally out of the question. There can be no more done or said on that point, and I have only to assure you that I did all I could."

ROBERT PEARSE GILLIES.

ROBERT PEARSE GILLIES.

JAMES HOGG.

OST truly, if Burns was deservedly considered a wonder on account of the disadvantages which he surmounted in early life, Hogg was, by parity of reasoning, a supernatural wonder, seeing that, up to the age of twenty, he could scarcely read his Bible, and at that epoch first taught himself writing, by copying with great effort from printed books. From this date onwards, I believe his literary career to have been *sui generis*, and altogether unexampled! I never forget a remark of Mr. Southey's, when he honored me with a visit at a time of year when Edinburgh was deserted, namely, that among all our literary characters the only one whom he then felt particularly desirous to meet again was the Ettrick Shepherd. With very pardonable vanity, Hogg repeatedly wrote memoirs of himself. He has recorded the feelings of surprise, delight, and triumph with which he heard one of his own ballads chanted by a country girl, who had no suspicion that the Shepherd, whom she met daily, was its author. But it may be noted as a yet more remarkable instance of his unexpected influence, that long before James Hogg was generally known, my learned uncle, Dr. Gillies, who had never even heard of his name, nevertheless got hold in London of his afterwards well-known stanzas, commencing —

> "My name it is Donald Macdonald,
> I live in the Hielands sae grand," etc.

and these he treasured in memory, and sang as often as he felt himself in jovial or patriotic mood.

I don't think that any two poets could be more unlike in disposition and temperament than Burns and Hogg. The former was from youth to manhood a prey to alternating fits of excitement and despondency; he wrote for the most part with care and difficulty, and in his productions there was condensed force. Hogg, on the contrary, had his joyous moods, seemingly without any reaction of gloom; with the help of "the sclate," he composed with great facility, and had a dislike to corrections afterwards ; his temper was sustained and equable ; his ambition, though steadfast, was of a quiet character, and though baffled, as it often happened, in his purpose, he was never for a moment cast down.

Surely there never has been any instance of the pursuit of literature under circumstances more untoward than those which the Shepherd so cheerfully encountered. Take, for example, the difficulties attending his first attempt at publication. Being appointed to the vastly pleasant and poetical task of driving a herd of cattle from Ettrick to Edinburgh (for All Hallow Fair) in the dreary month of November, he suddenly conceived the notion of getting a volume into print, but having no manuscript in hand, he tried during his walks to remember the verses, and as often as they recurred ran into a shop to borrow a stump of pen and morsel of paper to note them down. In this way copy was provided ; luckily for his purpose, he found a good-natured printer, and an octavo volume, or pamphlet, was produced in a week, with which he returned in triumph to the Forest.

Walter Scott could not persuade himself that the author of this *brochure* could ever live by mere verse-making, and as a better speculation, recommended that the author should turn his thorough knowledge of sheep-farming to account in districts where it was not so well understood as in Ettrick and Yarrow. In furtherance of this plan Hogg took a walk from Ettrick, across hill and dale, into Argyleshire, whence he embarked for the island of Harris, intending, if he met with en couragement, to take a farm there, but nothing came of it. The next we hear of him is that he had found some kindly disposed though humble friends, at Edinburgh, and had with their help put together a volume of poetry, entitled the "Forest Minstrel," moreover that, to the utter amazement of the said friends, he had set up a new weekly paper, entitled "The Spy," consisting of strictures on the state of manners, morals, and literary taste in the modern Athens, and varied by original stories and poems. Wonderful to tell, this work, written by himself alone (in large quarto sheets with double columns), went on regularly for a year or more. A new weekly journal, to be penned exclusively by one and the same hand, would have been a stout undertaking for any literary man ; it was altogether marvelous on the part of a lonely, illiterate shepherd.

About this time James Hogg tenanted a room at a suburban residence near Stockbridge. It was a weather-beaten, rather ghostly, solitary-looking domicile, like an old farm-house in the country. At this tranquil abode he finished, within an incredibly short time, the "Queen's Wake," which, as he said, when once begun, "went on of itself." Indeed, he always ascribed a separate vitality and *volonté* to his compositions, so that it was not his business to carry them on ; on the contrary, they carried on their author, and carried him away, till at last he wondered even more than others did, at his own work ! "Aye, ye 're a learned man," he sometimes said to me in after years ; "there 's nae doubt about that, wi' your Virgils and Homers and Dantés and Petrarchs. But aiblins ye mind yon fragment upon the sclate that ye despised t'ither morning. Eh, man, sin syne, it 's ettling to turn out the vera best thing I ever composed ; and that 's no saying little, ye ken ! "

The "Queen's Wake," when completed, was so extraordinary that it soon found a publisher. It appeared in 1813, just after I had migrated from Castle Street to Northumberland Street, and I shall never forget the impression it made on my mind at the first perusal. Till then Hogg had only been talked of as an eccentric being, uncouth and rude in manners, who had written divers clever songs and ballads, which appeared in magazines and newspapers. But the " Queen's Wake " instantly lifted him up to an entirely new and unexpected grade on the Scottish Parnassus. Almost every poem of length which came out in those days, was less or more an imitation of Scott or Byron. But Hogg decidedly struck a key-note of his own. There was a freshness, a vigor and variety, a bold and joyous spirit in the long ballads here strung together, which riveted the attention of every one not impassive to poetical impressions. I treasured up this volume, and watched for an opportunity to make the author's acquaintance personally, which did not present itself till the following summer.

As I had little or no acquaintance with the select society which the Ettrick Shepherd frequented at Edinburgh, I followed Professor Wilson's advice, and called on him without ceremony at an apartment which, having left Stockbridge, he then rented from a hackney coachman under the North Bridge. To my agreeable surprise, I was received as cordially, and with as little ceremony, as if there had been a previous acquaintance betwixt us of many years. I found with him his publisher, Mr. Goldie, who soon took his leave ; and on my surmising that my visit had interrupted business, he desired me to be quiet on that score, as no visits could be more unimportant to him than those of his publisher. " I have been trying this half hour," said he " to bring him to business, but ye micht as weel try to grip an eel by the tail."

" But the ' Queen's Wake ' ought to be a fortune to its author, " said I ; " and it will not always do for a poet to rest content with deserving reward which he never gains."

" The fortune will no come oot o' Goldie then," said the Shepherd ; " he has never paid saxpence yet, unless it be to the printer, and even that 's no settled. But aiblins ye think owre muckle o' the ' Queen's Wake.' It 's tolerably gude, I 'll no deny that ; but, eh man, that 's naething compared wi' what I am able to do ! I hae a grand poyem upon the sclate yenoo, that fashes me rather, for it wants to rin on faster than I can copy with the pen. Ye 'll think but little o' the ' Queen's Wake ' when ye come to see that ! "

The "sclate" was before him, covered with very close writing, and I naturally expressed a wish to hear some portion of what must be so extraordinary, to which he responded briskly, "Na, na, fules and bairns should never see wark half done!" I insisted that Voltaire had his old woman, and that Scott had been in the habit of consulting with William Erskine and other friends on his poems as they advanced. "That's vera like a man that's frighted to gang by himsel, and needs some body to lead him! Eh man, neither William Erskine, nor ony critic beneath the sun shall ever lead *mei !* If I hae na sense eneuch to mak and mend my ain wark, no other hands or heads shall meddle wi' it ; I want nae help, thank God, neither from books nor men."

Be it here observed once for all, that the good Shepherd's vanity differed from that of all other authors, inasmuch as it was avowed and undisguised, and he himself laughed at it objectively as such. It never for one instant appeared to me as arrogance or self-conceit ; on the contrary, it was mere native eccentricity, or, in better words, decision of character. He had great power and facility of composition after his own manner ; was naturally conscious of this power, and of course placed reliance on himself. As to Fortune's smiles or frowns, he little needed to care. Every day he was sure of being hospitably received somewhere or another at dinner, after which came unfailingly the Glenlivat punch ; and as for his house-rent and all expenses of living in other respects, I suppose £25 per annum (perhaps less) would have been ample.

We might have talked for hours, but having an engagement, I said my object in coming was not merely to make, but pave the way for improving our acquaintance, and I wished to know whether and when he would favor me with his company at dinner.

"Eh man, I'll come at your kale-time, whenever ye 're sure o' being at hame and I 'm no engaged ; but this day, aiblins, ye 'll tak your denner wi' *mei*, at Wullie Young's. He 's a border man, and will be richt glad to see yow, or ony ither freend o' mine. The morn I 'm engaged for a grand music

15

party at Grieve's, and the next day at James Gray's, but after that I 'm at your service."

The acquaintance thus begun was kept up uninterruptedly and cordially from 1813 till my departure from Edinburgh for London in 1827. I believe no member of the "learned" faculty of advocates saw so much of James Hogg as I did; also that I was the first who brought him into repute as a welcome guest among what are called the upper classes of society, meaning by such the better and more artificially educated classes; in which purpose of mine the late Lady Williamson (widow of Sir Hedworth) aided me by her dinner parties. On the first of those occasions, during dessert, the Shepherd was painfully puzzled, for not having till then met with ice-cream in the shape (as he said) of a "fine het sweet puddin," he took, incautiously, a large spoonful, whereupon with much anxiety and tearful eyes, he appealed to me, "Eh man, d' ye think that Lady Williamson keeps ony whuskey?" to which I replied instantly, that I did not think but was quite certain upon that point; accordingly the butler, at my request, brought him a *petit verre*, by which he was restored to entire comfort and well-being.

Hogg came punctually on the day fixed for his first visit at my house, and found Mr. William Erskine and Mr. Pinkerton in the library. Then occurred one of those exhibitions of captious temper in which "Pinkie" was apt to indulge, and to which James Hogg led most unwittingly. Playfully, and in the spirit of perfect good-humor, the Shepherd rallied me on having such unlimited store of books, insisting that the number of volumes that lay on the table alone, were more than any ordinary man would read in a year; and, finally, demanding whether I thought really that book-learning could be of any use to a veritable poet?

This was like a direct attack on one of "Pinkie's" favorite crotchets, for he maintained that a poet, in order to be deserving of notice, required book-learning most especially, and ought to have all Dante and Petrarch, and countless others, at his fingers' ends, before he presumed to walk alone, as Hogg expressed it, even so far as to compose a single sonnet.

The Shepherd's leading crotchet was, that by keeping clear of books, he did very effectually guard against the risk of becoming an imitator. In his own words, he "made sure of perfect originality in his own compositions" (though whether of *novelty* is another question). Pinkerton, on the contrary, opined that Hogg, since he learned to read, had got a little book-learning, of which he had become conceited, believing that there was no need for any more, and so he tried to nettle him with the hackneyed quotation, "A little learning is a dangerous thing," etc. The Shepherd maintained his ground with imperturbable good-humor, having indeed far the best of the argument, while Pinkie became cross and sarcastic, in which mood he remained for some time afterwards. At dinner that day, he must needs introduce, *en passant*, some sneers against religion, thereby exciting instantaneous wrath on the part of good old Mrs. Grant of Laggan, who gave battle immediately. By ill luck, she made it a point of duty to assume an angry tone, and very soon lost temper utterly, whilst her tormentor, sipping his *œil de perdrix*, was jocose and sardonic. Evidently, the Shepherd was amazed and vexed at this. It argued a want of tact on both sides, not reconcilable to *his* notions of good breeding. The dispute would have grown tiresome, had it not been for the excellent management of my late sister-in-law, Mrs. Arthur Clifford, who strenuously claimed Pinkie's attention on account of a promise he had made of going with her to see the Duke of Hamilton's pictures at Holyrood (though she had no intention of accepting his services). The wicked antiquary saw through the *ruse*, and thankfully acquiesced in changing the subject. With great vivacity, Mrs. Clifford then implored Mrs. Grant to settle some doubts she had long entertained as to the meaning of a certain passage in "Temora." So the discord was quashed, and when Pinkie had *cottoned* to a bottle of curious old Hermitage, and the Shepherd received materials for brewing his first jug of toddy (after which he volunteered a song), of course all was well, and we spent a jovial evening.

To some readers this notice of a family dinner-party will, no doubt, seem the quintessence of twaddle ; yet, according to my notions, this one infinitesimal incident, like the pebble thrown into the lake, producing its endless circles, was the commencement of an epoch. In plainer terms, I think the appearance of the good honest Shepherd in our Edinburgh society, acquired by degrees a marked influence on the tone of that society, and even gave a new impetus to our literature. Numberless were the convivial parties at dinner and supper which, but for him, would never have taken place at all, and but for his quaint originality of manners and inexhaustible store of good songs, would have been comparatively so *fade* and lifeless, that no one would have desired a repetition. Further, I am thoroughly convinced that his example gave a new impulse to literature. There were individuals who, observing with wonder the facility and pertinacity with which he composed, and the undeniable merit of his productions, became ashamed that with all their book knowledge they should allow themselves to be outdone and cast utterly into shade by an illiterate shepherd, a man also who seemed to give himself no thought nor care about his own works, but to be engaged day after day, or rather night after night, in scraping on the fiddle, singing his own ballads, and, with the help of Glenlivat, making himself and others uproariously merry! In truth, after his appearance, the number of aspirant authors increased wonderfully; and as Hogg insisted that no one deserved the name of poet, whose writings were not perfectly original, so every such aspirant began very resolutely to aim at somewhat entirely new in matter and, if possible, in form. Hogg all the while went his own way, perfectly unconscious and regardless of the influence which he exercised, and for which no one had the civility to thank him. Amongst other effects of his eccentric example, I may notice, that but for his suggestions, although he never in his life could write a page in prose that was fit to be read, Blackwood's far-famed " Magazine " would probably not have come into existence. The Shepherd was snubbed for saying so in his autobiography, but it was nevertheless true.

Towards the month of September that year (1814), Edin-

burgh, as usual, became deserted. Even the Ettrick Shepherd disappeared for some weeks, having taken a walk across
the border to visit Mr. Wilson at Elleray, in Westmoreland,
and to improve his acquaintance with Wordsworth. As it was
not entirely suitable for one in the Shepherd's circumstances
to be contented with praise alone, and (with a slight change)
to adopt Sir Egerton Brydges's line, —

> " Careless of gaining *cash* if I deserve,"

he had taken up the notion, from a scrap book which lay on
my table, of borrowing an original poem from every author of
the day, and publishing the collection on his own account.
" Annuals " and " Souvenirs " were not known then ; and truly
if every poet had composed with as much facility as James
Hogg, and thought as little as he did about his productions
afterwards, the plan might have been realized. One of the first
promises he received was from Lord Byron, who often favored
him with long letters, which Hogg usually lost in a day or two
after their arrival. From other quarters, promises or hopes
were held out, but in no instance came to fulfillment, except in
that of Mr. Wordsworth, whose poem, however, could not be
available by itself alone, and was therefore included by the
author in his next publication.

This plan being rather inconsistent with Hogg's usual notions of independence, I doubt not he had all along in the
background the quizzical plot which he afterwards carried out,
namely, that when every brother of the quill failed him, he
would keep his own counsel, and would himself quietly compose a poem for every one of the authors who had made half
or whole promises and broken them ! Accordingly, he began
with Byron, writing the " Guerrilla Chief "— a story in the Spen-
serian stanza, and followed it by specimens of Scott, Southey,
Wordsworth, Wilson, and I forget who more, till at last he
made up a volume, which was published under the title of the
" Poetic Mirror." John Ballantyne, who not only loved a joke,
but delighted in mystification, made the most of this notable
jeu d'esprit, bringing his customers into the dilemma of ad-
mitting either that the poems were genuine, or else that James

Hogg, having produced the whole alone and unassisted, must be the most wonderful shepherd that ever tended a flock. And he managed so well, that within six weeks he handed over thirty pounds to the author (far more, I suppose, than he ever gained by the first edition of the "Queen's Wake").

I cannot forget that the ballad allotted to himself in this volume, namely, "The Gude Grey Catte," was in its own way super-excellent. This with the "Witch of Fyfe," in the "Queen's Wake," are, according to my humble notions, enough by themselves to immortalize the Shepherd, from whose works a judicious selection, accompanied by a memoir, is surely a *desideratum;* but in our enlightened era he seems nearly forgotten.

It was in the year 1816, I think, that he received from that most amiable and exemplary of noblemen, the late Duke of Buccleugh, a lease, *rent free,* of Altrive Lake, a farm in Ettrick, near St. Mary's Loch. I feel very sure that on this occasion it was the Duke's intention to provide permanently for Hogg's well-being and stability in the world. He believed that Altrive farm, properly managed, would yield quite enough for the necessary expenses of a man so easily contented as his friend the Shepherd (for after their first meeting, the kind-hearted Duke ever named him as his friend, and delighted in his company at convivial hours). Alas! that noble heart, though unchangeable in its active benevolence, had sustained wounds for which this world admitted no cure ; too visibly the Duke's health declined, and his once buoyant spirit, though it might flicker up for a while at the festive board, was rapidly on the wane. By his deeply-lamented death, our Shepherd lost the best of patrons, who would never have deserted him, and who took a more lively interest in his fate than his no less kind, charitable, and munificent successor could be expected to do. For this there were some obvious reasons. The Shepherd's lines on the death of the Countess of Dalkeith, did honor to his head and heart ; there are also some very beautiful verses in his address to Lady Anne Scott, prefixed to a most unreadable prose work, called the "Brownie of Bodsbeck." I would gladly transcribe both poems if I had them within reach.

No poet was ever more grateful to a patron than our worthy Shepherd to the Duke of Buccleugh. He took possession of Altrive with the determination to be wise, knowing that a small but sure income could be made of it; and that by care and judicious improvements it might yield more. But for such improvements capital would have been needed, which he did not possess; and as the matter stood, a new house was required, a very small one it is true, which was soon finished, and all might have gone well. But in his convivial hours at Edinburgh, the Shepherd had made many acquaintances, not all of them advantageous or well chosen. In town this was of no consequence; it mattered not much, in his estimation, how the evening hours were whiled away, and during the daytime his landlady could, upon occasion, enact the part of Cerberus, and indicate that Mr. Hogg was busy or not at home. Unfortunately, however, when such friends knew that he was quietly established in the country, one after another they took up the notion that it would be vastly pleasant to visit him there, and "see how he got on." They might arrive when he was not at home, it is true; he might be looking after the sheep, or catching fish for dinner, or enjoying a lonely walk to meditate a "grand new article for next number of Maga." But this availed him not; either they took possession of the cottage on pretext of being tired, or they mounted the nearest hilltop to look for him, and tracked him out in his solitude. An invitation to dinner followed of course; they usually arrived towards dinner time, after a very long walk; thereafter, in the words of Burns, "the night drave on wi' sangs and clatter," and as the nearest town was far far away, they must needs remain and bivouac at Altrive, feeling themselves extremely comfortable under the influence of the Shepherd's "whuskey toddy," which of course they did not spare. Such a mode of life would never do. These kind friends had no doubt the best possible intentions, but Hogg, unluckily, had too many such "well-wishers." The cottage was too small for him and them together; inevitably they robbed him of his time; they would not allow him his peaceful mornings to work out his poems

on his old broken "sclate." Instead of living on £50 or £60
a year, which Altrive might yield, he would have needed a
separate annuity to support the expense of entertaining his
guests.

For my own part, I was selfish enough not to be altogether
sorry at this, for as I never went to Altrive, I feared we should
have lost sight of the Shepherd altogether. The result, however, was very different, for he soon found himself under the
necessity of looking to Edinburgh as a place of retirement
and refuge. There he was cordially welcomed as a resident
in the house of his very sincere friend, John Grieve of Teviot Row, George Square, and as business every day called his
host abroad, he had the entire house to himself, with store of
books and music, from the breakfast hour till dinner time.
He was then more with us than ever, having found out by experience who were his most steadfast friends.

I think that era of his residence in Teviot Row was about the
happiest of his life, and he revolved numberless literary plans,
including the "Jacobite Relics," beginning to collect materials, though the volume was not talked of or published till long
afterwards. There was no house, as he averred (not even his
"crony" Grieve's), where he felt so much at home as in ours.
His habits and fancies were understood and provided for
there, and his originalities were occasionally a source of wonder as well as entertainment to those who met him for the
first time. He planned music-parties after his own fancy, and
tried again and again the notes for his "Border Garland," a
collection of his own songs with the music, which was afterwards revised by Nathaniel Gow, and published. It was un-
justly neglected; but of that the author recked not. I believe
he had no great respect (perhaps none at all) for the judgment
of our wise world, and thought the best practical rule for a
shepherd-poet was to keep on his way rejoicing, as long as he
could, regardless of praise or blame.

I have said that James Hogg was an object of some wonder
to those who met him for the first time; *exempli gratia* to
our kind friends the late Lord and Lady Macdonald, Sir John

Trevelyan, John Kemble, and divers others "from the South," who were habituated to life in London, where such a phenomenon as the Shepherd certainly had never appeared ; but where he was flattered and invited *partout,* during a short visit (his first and last), some fourteen years afterwards. Among all our visitors, however, no one so thoroughly appreciated the originality of his character as our ever-respected and unalterable friend, Mrs. Brooke Richmond, in her early years celebrated as the first horse-woman and fox-huntress in England ; or, I should say, in the world. On the same principle of active benevolence, and with the same buoyant spirit which would lead her to take the part of any friend fallen in the world, and to assist in the hour of adversity, she delighted in promoting the hilarity of social circles. Three words from *her* voice would at any time rouse the Shepherd to sing the most uproarious of his festive songs. At the risk of being blamed for truism or tautology, I must say again, that Hogg was a character *bien prononcé,* and in his way matchless. Of longer works, he had written and published the "Forest Minstrel," the "Queen's Wake," "Madoc of the Moor," the "Pilgrims of the Sun," "Queen Hynde," "Dramatic Tales," and the "Poetic Mirror," besides countless minor poems and ballads ; in prose were to be reckoned, the "Shepherd's Calendar," the "Brownie of Bodsbeck," the "Three Perils of Man," and "Three Perils of Woman ; " besides "Jacobite Relics," with music, and various contributions to "Blackwood's Magazine ; " yet after all these extraordinary performances, he remained in his demeanor, appearance, and manner of speech, *integer purus,* the same unalterable Ettrick Shepherd who but a few years ago had driven his herd of "*nowte*" to All Hallow Fair, and borrowed scraps of paper in the shops to write his first pastorals for the printer. For this genuine decision of character, it is needless to say how much I honored him.

SIR WALTER SCOTT.

Sir Walter Scott being from infancy addicted to literary pursuits, also having a fondness for antiquities, and having collected old ballads before he heard the name of Bürger, would in all probability have contributed to the literature of his country, without any incitement or inspiration from foreign sources. Yet I have always been persuaded, that had he not chanced (and in those days it was a rare chance) to get some German lessons from a competent professor, and had he not also chanced to have "Lenora" and the "Wild Huntsman," placed before him as exercises, we should never have had the "Lay of the Last Minstrel," or the "Lady of the Lake." The keynote was struck, the innate powers of the young student responded, he translated those two ballads *con amore*, and they were so much wondered at for their novelty of feeling and expression, that the translator's character was at once established as an extraordinary person. He had done what no one before him had accomplished ; and, moreover, there was no one in all Scotland who could do the like. Consequently, the attention excited by those versions of "Lenora" and the "Wild Huntsman," printed in quarto, by Ballantyne, at Kelso, insignificant as the matter was in itself, formed in great measure the basis of all Sir Walter Scott's future achievements as a poet.

But, although he succeeded, most assuredly the literary revolution in Scotland was not accomplished without a struggle. We were disposed to be quite as obstinate against improvements in this respect as in others. Lavater's Aphorism was very applicable in the case of Sir Walter Scott, who never lacked detractors and enemies. Notwithstanding private friendship, Edinburgh critics sneered at his poems as often as they conveniently durst. Yet divers circumstances favored his career, and he triumphed. In other instances we did not fail to mark our critical acumen, and our extreme abhorrence of innovations.

It is true that by no efforts of criticism could we "put down" the "Lay of the Last Minstrel." Even the ballad of "Rosabelle," and the description of Melrose, by moonlight, were alone enough to keep it buoyant, notwithstanding that the poem was decidedly at variance with all our acknowledged models. The author had begun humbly by translating from

Bürger, and by imitating old ballads, but progressing, he had achieved a work such as was till then unexampled, and purely original. Moreover, the patronage of the Buccleugh family attended it, so that the author had influence political as well as poetical, and consequently the publisher did not hesitate to pay £600 for the copyright; an event such as had never happened before to any poet within the enlightened realm of Scotland, where Burns, after devoting his attention for years to a series of lyrical compositions which will never die, and which became afterwards a fortune to his patron, did from the said patron receive as recompense for all his productions — the handsome sum of £5 ! ! !

To Sir Walter Scott I shall have frequent occasions to allude in the course of these records. He was not only among the earliest, but most persevering of my friends ; persevering in spite of my own waywardness, and latterly of the *mauvaises langues* of pretended friends, who did what they could, but without success, to sow discord betwixt us. In the year after his death, I contributed (anonymously as usual) my humble homage to his memory in the shape of " Recollections." The first edition appeared in " Fraser's Magazine." The second, with considerable improvements, was published by Mr. Fraser, in 1837. Availing myself of my *anonyme*, and being under the necessity of making my work applicable to Sir Walter's whole life, I introduced into the first part certain conversations and occurrences not less true than characteristic, which did not take place until a later period of my own life. The cottage at Lasswade was well known to me, for I have spent many happy hours under its roof when rented by Captain Hamilton. The dog's manner of welcoming his master's guest, the conversations with Lord Kinnedder, the accident suffered by Sir Walter, and his disregard of it, the family dinner — all these were taken from vivid remembrance. Mr. Lockhart appreciated my correctness, and has quoted part of that first section. But as above said, I introduced the passages at an epoch in the story, when, if a visitor to the poet at Lasswade, I must necessarily have attained by this time the age of at least seventy-three.

Any farther reference to my former " Recollections of Scott" is at present impossible, for I have no copy left. My last was presented to Lady Stratheden and Campbell during my residence in France, several years ago, and I could not now get another.

Perhaps at no period did Sir Walter feel more buoyant in spirits than whilst inventing and recording the fortunes of " Marmion." It was his second great work, and with the melody of the " Last Minstrel " still on their minds, the public watched with the most eager expectation for the moment when this unequaled musician would commence again. Wonderful to tell, in this instance, as in almost every other, he began to print his work before it was even half written. I have never heard of this method being adopted by any other author, unless by one very impatient or very needy; whereas, in Sir Walter Scott's case it was a self-imposed difficulty, for which there seemed no assignable reason, except that he " required the spur of the press." Delays arose in the publication of " Marmion," which had been promised for Christmas and was not then ready. Inquiries were made daily at the publisher's ; and wherever the author went, he also was liable to be assailed by questions. This gossiping talk and solicitude about a work whilst it was still on the anvil, I believe disgusted him, and contributed afterwards to his plan of secrecy in regard to the authorship of the " Waverley Novels."

He was entreated, as a great favor, to read portions of " Marmion " at the Duchess of Gordon's *soirées*, and on one of these occasions, Mr. William Erskine (Lord Kinnedder) was his representative, and did read a canto. The author was a most inadequate reader of his own compositions. He would recite ballads and poems of others with great animation and *onction*, but could scarcely recite his own at all ; and when he read them, it was in a cold, monotonous manner, as if he were all the while putting his verses to the proof, and questioning about their faults, rather than desirous to make a favorable impression on his audience.

One point respecting " Marmion " was especially gratifying to the author, namely, that by means of it he could place £1000 at the command of a relation who much required aid, whilst he himself had the salary of two public offices to recline upon. This allusion to pecuniary matters reminds me of a favorite aphorism of Sir Walter Scott's, namely, that the " literary character with all its duties was perfectly reconcilable with the habits of a man of business and man of the world ; " thus making into a general rule a *dictum* which the experience of many (and at last his own) imperatively contradicted, and for which his premises were certainly inadequate. It was quite true that he himself could manage the irksome duties of a clerk of session, and those of a county sheriff, and could also mingle in society, without on that account renouncing his literary pursuits. These facts, drawn from experience, were his premises, and how inadequate to bear out the complexive conclusion, I need scarcely say.

It is, moreover, most true that he himself had the disposition and courage to contend with difficulties and to surmount them. He looked the demons of adverse chance in the face so quietly and steadfastly that they recoiled from his glance. And this courage no doubt would have distinguished him had he followed his natural inclinations of entering the army, from which only his lameness and the slowness of promotion withheld him. But if employed as a general officer, or even if in full employment at the Scotch bar, most assuredly he would not have written " Marmion ; " for his professional duties in either case would not have allowed him that command of time and attention which poetry requires. And though he did look difficulties in the face, he did so from a quiet and comfortable home, the sanctity of which could not be invaded. How much he appreciated that tranquillity which the literary character requires, might be guessed at from his extreme dislike of controversial squabbles, his wish to avoid notice personally, and allow his works to make their way without a name, his aversion to general society, and divers other symptoms. In truth he cleaved to the *sanctum* of home, as much as Dugald Stewart or any other metaphysician could have done, " Old

John " and Peter the coachman being both instructed that at certain times (especially Sundays and Mondays) they were to act the part of Cerberus against all visitors, excepting two or three, who having the *entrée* would not be put back, and who when admitted would not attempt to stay long.

The sanctity of that home, I mean the house in North Castle Street, was indeed profaned at last, and the blow thus inflicted was not unfelt, though he had Abbotsford for his retreat and stronghold. Some time afterwards there was, moreover, an unexpected enemy, a certain Mr. Abudd of London (no doubt vastly respectable there), for whom he was unprepared. This worthy chose to assume the amiable position of being the only creditor who would not accept the terms Sir Walter had so nobly proffered for the liquidation of debts which in equity and justice were not his own. Mr. Abudd preferred the London practice, and, like Shylock, would " have his bond," or *contrainte par corps.* The mere apprehension of such an event as a compulsory removal from home, as he has himself recorded, did entirely unhinge and disable him for ten days. Sir Walter could contend nobly with difficulties, and look them in the face, but he never was pitted against the veritable demons that follow in the train of poverty. If so inclined, he might at any time have laid down his pen and retired on a competent income, instead of which the tasks that he voluntarily undertook were indeed Herculean, so that he might be said to realize in another phasis his early intention of becoming a soldier. In order to maintain his position without compromise, the latter years of his life were spent in unremitting warfare in which he signally triumphed ; but the battle was won at the expense of health and life, in other words, the fatigue and the wounds proved mortal.

Soon after my return to the country occurred an event which, in my estimation, made a distinguished era or epoch, namely, the publication of Sir Walter Scott's " Lady of the Lake." John Ballantyne dispatched my copy per mail, along with some choice old tracts, which he rightly thought would be acceptable. It is impossible to express what importance I attached to this quarto volume, with its resplendent fragrant leaves and matchless type ; the finest specimen that had yet been seen of the Ballantyne press. The author was then in the very zenith of his poetical powers, for surely " the Lady " was the very best among his longer and more sustained efforts. As a long ballad, or lay of the Minstrel, it remains, and probably will forever remain, unequaled. The work evinces so much of natural and vivid feelings, and such perfect adherence to truth and life in the delineation both of scenes and characters, that the reader is more than compensated for absence of that superior guise of mystery which attends the " Lay of the Last Minstrel," or of the more complicated web of plot in " Marmion." I wrote at this time two or three stanzas as a humble tribute of admiration, which I believe were often reprinted ; but though I could still write other verses with similar intent, I could not recall those to memory *now*, if for so doing I were promised a crown and kingdom.

The copyright of this poem was estimated at £4000, and in truth its success was unprecedented. The necessity of having it to read for fashion's sake precluded borrowing in many instances. It was a kind of disgrace, a losing of *caste*, not to possess it. But it found numberless intelligent, as well as fashionable readers. More especially were young hearts gained by this metrical story, for in it there was nothing which they could not understand. On the contrary, there was much which they had themselves perceived and felt, yet were not able to express, nor had heard expressed before. Of this I remember one very remarkable instance, but time presses and I must not dwell on it.

In the autumn of that year a degree of homage was paid to the poet, such as has never been manifested before nor since. All the world, rich and poor, including crown-princes and *noblesse*, crowded to visit the scenery which he had depicted. Instead of being, as usual, a dull, stupid village, whose inhabitants were all in a state of *cabbageism*, Callander of Monteith became a rallying point for all classes, a place wherein to study varieties of character. Truly *that* study was not very consolatory or edifying. Owing to accidental circumstances, I spent three months of the year 1810 in the neighborhood of Loch Katrine, but of society or characters noticed there, have little or nothing to record. Certain portions of the scenery remain ever vivid in my remembrance, especially Loch Vennachar, Benvoirlich, with its gray rocks fringed with birch and hazel, the heights immediately above Callander, and the view therefrom ; these are pleasant recollections, the rest fades away like a dream, and my *precious* verses belonging to the period (unless it be " Glenfinlas," in the " Edinburgh Annual Register "), are all lost.

At this time I met Sir Walter Scott almost daily at Ballantyne's, or elsewhere. He invited me again and again to dinner, which (excepting once) I declined on the score of ill health ; and he dined more than once *chez nous*, to meet Sir Brooke Boothby and other friends. This I mention only to show how kindly disposed he was towards any literary aspirant, however unmanageable and wayward such aspirant might be. In truth, his good-will was not easily to be alienated by eccentricities. I remember his complaining this year that on his list of incipient poets, he had one so incurably shy that attention and encouragement were thrown away on him ; he would not, properly speaking, accept of either. This was Mr. W. Howison, afterwards well known as " M. de Peu de Mots," a man of real genius, as I believe, but whose excessive fastidiousness prevented him from ever attaining that literary rank to which his talents would otherwise have been entitled. In 1811, Scott was not only employed in writing the poem of " Don Roderick," but on divers other tasks, to all of which he buckled with the utmost zeal and cheerfulness. As I have elsewhere remarked, he seemed even to enjoy the difficulties of his position : he could look them in the face and laugh them to scorn. I was often at his house, and was always kindly received, because I came with this or that old book, which I thought might be acceptable, and because I never stayed long. To say little and retire quickly, was what he most desiderated in a chance visitor. But he had then begun to cherish the plan of early rising, which he afterwards kept up systematically, and which enabled him to complete his long compositions unobserved : so that in after years an entire Waverley Novel was finished in a time incredibly short ; and the Ettrick Shepherd averred : "He was vera sure that Walter Scott could write a three volume novel within, at the outside, ten days." Jesting apart, I believe that with the help of a sufficiently clever amanuensis, the realization of Hogg's assertion would have been by no means impossible. To his present favorite Wallace (a wiry-haired terrier), he gave the credit of introducing this early system, inasmuch as the said Wallace was of a restless temper, and loved to see his master up and at work, taking his place very regularly on a chair beside him, with a piece of paper clinched in his mouth.

Out of many letters with which I was honored by Sir Walter Scott, some few remain to me, among which two or three are dated this year. They are hastily written, and are not long, but, nevertheless, will afford very sufficient evidence to bear out my previous assertions, how willingly and kindly he encouraged the literary attempts of aspirants, however whimsical and unmanageable they might be.

"ASHESTIEL, *26th April*, 1812.

"MY DEAR SIR — Upon receiving your letter, the date of which ought to make me ashamed, I applied to John Ballantyne for the account of Carey's poems, but found it was set up for the 'Register.' I dare say I shall find some other scrap for the 'Bibliographer,' although I shall hardly venture to enter into a personal correspondence with Sir S. E. Brydges, because I am certain, from a consciousness of my own infirmity in such cases, that I should let it drop awkwardly ; in which case, you know, it is better not commenced. Few people are worse at sustaining a literary correspondence than I am, for which I have only the apology which the Neapolitan lazarone pleaded when asked why he did not work instead of begging. 'Did you but know,' said he, in a most piteous tone of voice, 'how lazy I am!'

"This same vice of laziness has made your letter lie too long in my desk unanswered, and perhaps you will think I had better let it so remain than take the privilege of an older man to give you a gentle scolding for some expressions in your last. In truth, it gives me great pain to think that a young gentleman at your time of life, with such favorable prospects, and a disposition so amiable, should give way to that state of depression which your letter announces. Believe me, it is not right to do so, and it is very possible to avoid it. The fiend which haunts you, if resisted, will flee from you. Plunge into active study, diversified by agreeable company, and regular exercise ; ride, walk, dance or shoot, or hunt, or break stones on the highway rather than despond about your health, which is the surest way in the world to bring about the catastrophe which you are apprehensive of. An untaught philosopher, my neighbor in this place, had the misfortune to lose an only son, at an age when the parent's heart is chiefly wrapt up in his offspring. He used always to be of my fishing parties, but within a day or two after the funeral, I was surprised at his joining me with his spear in his hand. 'I see you are surprised,' he said, with the tears in his eyes, 'and undoubtedly I have sustained the severest wound which fate could have inflicted ; but were I to sit down to muse over it, my heart would break, or I should go mad, and I judge it more like a man who has duties left to perform, to resume my active occupations of business and of pastime.' Go you, my dear sir, and do likewise. If you would not laugh at me, I should recommend you to fall heartily in love with the best and prettiest girl in your neighborhood. The committing the power of teasing us to another, is very apt to prevent us from exercising that irritability of feeling on ourselves.

"I don't apologize for these observations because I am sure you will ascribe them to a sincere interest in your welfare. I trust your law studies will bring you soon to town, when I shall have the pleasure to see you. Meanwhile, believe me, yours very faithfully,   W. S."

"EDINBURGH, 12*th May*, 1812.

"MY DEAR SIR, — I am greatly to blame for not sooner acknowledging the receipt of your letter with the verses, which I think very pretty ; indeed, I have little doubt that by giving your mind occasionally to literary and poetical composition, you will alleviate, and in time conquer the nervous feelings which you entertain, and which are really to be conquered by exertion, and by exertion alone. My present situation is a very hurried one, as I am on the point of leaving Ashestiel, long my summer cabin, and occupying a very small tenement upon my late purchase of Abbotsford, until leisure, which the learned define as implying time and money, will permit me to begin a more convenient one. Meanwhile, the change, though not much more important than from the brown room to the green, as was the Vicar of Wakefield's great revolution, fails not to require some superintendence and to make a great deal of bustle. So this must be my excuse for not writing to Sir Egerton Brydges at present, with whose domestic calamity I sincerely sympathize. I have the clamor of about twenty people, with twenty different demands, all of the most trifling nature, still stunning my ears ; and I begin to think that what the Scotch call a *flitting* may be so effectual a mode for giving scope for your exertion, and exercise for your patience as any of the prescriptions I formerly took the freedom to send you. I return to all this confusion in the course of this week or the next, when I hope to end it.

"I should have liked to have said more about your verses, which I really think very elegant. I am sorry the conclusion has a melancholy turn, and I must beg you, my dear young friend, for the sake of all that is dear to you, to recollect that active exertion is peremptorily imposed upon us as a law of our nature ; and as the price of that degree of happiness, which our present state of existence admits of. You see the rich and the proud reduced to purchase contentment and their night's rest by the hardest bodily labor. Those to whom nature has kindly indulged the power of literary labor, occupying the higher, instead of their mere corporeal functions, ought not surely to be less active in their pursuits than mere fishers or fox-hunters. Crabbe says somewhere, 'As labor lets, we live.' It is really the charter by which we hold existence, and be it in picking straws, or legislating for empires, we must labor or die of *ennui*. I hope, therefore, to hear that you are forming some literary plan, with the determination of carrying it through, and depend upon it, you will learn to defy the foul fiend. I have got a present of a handsome little copy of Douce's unique romance of 'Vergilius.' Do you know who edited it? Yours ever, W. S.

"I have managed this so awkwardly that it will cost you double postage, M. P.'s being now scarce here. What do you think of trying your hand on a dilettante edition of something that is rare and curious?"

The following note would seem too trifling for transcription, were it not that it serves also to corroborate some of my previous records, and shows that Sir Walter would not write to postpone a convivial meeting, without adding some kind words of advice and encouragement.

"EDINBURGH, *Monday* (1813).

"MY DEAR SIR, — I am very sorry it will not be in my power to wait upon you again at kale-time, till I return from Abbotsford, my time being already occupied by far too much of engagements abroad, and too much to do at home. When I return, I shall be happy to meet Sir Brooke in Heriot Row.

"Pray don't talk of yourself in the way you do. Your health, it is true, is not such as I sincerely wish it to be, but then you have many means of alleviating the tedium of indisposition, both by your pleasure in perusing the works of others, and your own

"'Skill to soothe the lagging hour,
With no inglorious song.'

You must not, therefore, allow yourself to be depressed by your complaints, but seek amusement in those harmless and elegant pursuits, which will best divert your mind from dwelling upon them. I am sensible that it is more easy to recommend than to practice that command of spirit which abstracts us from the immediate source of pain or languor. But it is no less necessary that this exertion should be made, and really in this world the lots of men are so variously assigned to them, that each may find in his own case, circumstances of pleasure as well as points of pain unknown to others.

" Excuse the freedom I use, and believe me, with every kind wish, very much yours,   W. S.

" Many thanks for the novels. I will take care of them, and safely return them."

Insensibly, whilst writing about the year 1817, I have run on to events (if studies can be called such) which did not take place till two years later, an anachronism very natural from association of ideas, and for which I need scarcely apologize. As little need my reader murmur if I should pass over the years 1818 and 1819 without much of comment, seeing that I then rather avoided society, and did not make many new acquaintances. One event during that epoch made too deep an impression to be left unnoticed, namely, the sudden and severe illness of Sir Walter Scott, whose constitution for the preceding twenty years had seemed invulnerable. Without any premonitory symptoms, the first attack took place when he had a dinner and evening party, to which he had kindly invited me, but that same day I had company at home. My brother-in-law, Colonel George Macdonell, and the Ettrick Shepherd left us at ten o'clock for Sir Walter's house. During dinner, and afterwards, he had appeared in his usual health and spirits, but towards eleven o'clock, greatly to the alarm of Lady Scott, he retired to his room laboring under the first onset of that spasmodic disorder, of which he observed to me afterwards, that in his own belief no one else could have survived pain so great and so frequently recurring. From the beginning to the end of that long battle, though too often physically prostrate, he never once quailed in spirit. Dr. Ross, I think, was either of the party that evening, or came immediately, and by him he sent down a message that nothing would tend more to keep him ill, than to think that his friends were not merry at supper, and it would promote his recovery if Mrs. Henry Siddons would sing another song.

I have said long before, that a man's worth may be tested by the question how much he is missed and mourned after his death ; in like manner it may be tried by the degree of anxiety expressed for his recovery while ill. It was on this occasion, as I have elsewhere mentioned, that the Ettrick Shepherd, in walking home that night with James Ballantyne, gave way to a paroxysm of wrath, and threatened to fling his companion on the pavement for daring to betray his fears that Scott's illness was very serious. Too truly it proved so. Three or four months afterwards, judging by his changed appearance, few among his friends could repress the darkest forebodings. But his tranquil submission to all, *except one*, of the prescribed remedies or cautions, and his indomitable spirit, saved him. He thought not about his illness, but followed implicitly the advice of the medical men on all points, except that of total abstinence from literary labor. The habit of composition had become to him so natural, that he could not abandon it. In every intermission of the disorder, even during its paroxysms, he would keep hold of the thread of the story, making illegible scrawls with a pencil, or dictating, when at the worst, and still resuming the pen at brief intervals. In this way, according to his own avowal, nearly the whole of " Ivanhoe " was composed. I have also heard from John Ballantyne, that the best jokes about Caleb Balderston and the *ménage* at Wolf's Crag, were interrupted in dictation by the most acute sufferings. It was not till the following autumn at Abbotsford, during the long vacation, that by the late Dr. Dick's entirely new mode of treatment, the disorder began to abate. Exercise being allowed as usual, he was daily assisted to mount his pony, and then moved along supported by a servant on each side. In this melancholy state, his strength exhausted by constantly recurring pain, he persevered for many a day, till at length (in his own words) he "felt very proud" when he was able once more to ride out with no other companionship but that of the pony, Maida, Mustard, and Ourisk.

About the year 1822, as is well known, the influence of Sir Walter Scott as a romance writer was so great, that any one of his productions in that department realized in one sense, though not in another, a sum so large, that by itself alone, the produce of a single work would have been fortune enough for any prudent family ! But, as is equally well known, the publisher, instead of cash payments, gave only long-dated bills. On the author's side, all the gains were invested on Abbotsford ; on the bookseller's, all were pledged on grand speculations which were to realize enormous wealth one day or another, but which required expensive nursing at present. At last the supposed realities were utterly gone, and nothing remained but bills to an amount of £120,000, which, the bookseller having become bankrupt, Sir Walter Scott was called upon to pay ; that very fortune for which he had labored being thus wrested from him, and his work, like Penelope's web, having to begin anew. In 1822 the fortunes of literary men from high to low, wore *couleur de rose,* but the desire of pecuniary profit degenerated into self-imposed *necessity,* under which evil influence talents might still be shown, but the natural emanations of genius declined and faded away. Even in 1822, how different were the romances of Sir Walter Scott from those of earlier date !

The towers of Abbotsford, its pleasure grounds and woods, had been costly, not to speak of hospitality and keeping almost open house. *Per contra,* novels could be produced without cessation ; but alas, the paralyzing effects of adventitious necessity became always more and more apparent ! As in the case of "Redgauntlet," "Peveril of the Peak," and some others, four volumes instead of three were brought out, not because the story required it, but because the profits on the sale would be so much greater. And these are the *only* works of this admirable author, which up to the present hour I have not been able to peruse, inasmuch, as the contrast betwixt them and their precursors is too painfully apparent. Compare for example, "Redgauntlet" with "Guy Mannering," or, shifting to another epoch, I might say, compare the "Lord of the Isles" with the "Lay of the Last Minstrel." On the latter occasions, the object was not so much to achieve a work which deserved to live, as to gain £10,000 for a living! Unrivaled talents, artistical skill, learning, labor, and unwearying patience were visible. But the *naïveté*, the freshness, the buoyancy, the unaffected humor, or heartfelt pathos of genius, delighting in its own peculiar realities, irrespective of realizing thereby even a single guinea, were comparatively wanting.

I have written diffusely about the facilities afforded to authors, especially the *guerdon* allowed even to "supernumeraries" in those days. But towards the close of 1825, after a tranquil summer, a cloud began to lower upon their fortunes, and a change generally came over the spirit of this dreamy world. In plain terms, "the panic" approached; thereby the supplies of ready money were at once cut off, and without the slightest regard to that awkward circumstance, every one holding the position of an unsatisfied creditor was prepared to enforce his claim without mercy.

By a strange coincidence, it was about this time that Sir Walter Scott first began to keep a diary. But it was begun in a gay spirit, before the lingering sunshine of autumn had departed, and before the clouds of "the panic" had appeared at Abbotsford. Within less than a month, the storm had commenced at Edinburgh, and thereafter he recorded its effects on himself and others minutely and from day to day.

I need not dwell upon this epoch, otherwise the "city in the panic" might make a fitting subject for a volume, either in verse or prose, quite as well as the "city in the plague." My family were living in a hired cottage on the sea-shore near Edinburgh, when the storm loomed visibly, and I had too much reason to apprehend that pecuniary difficulties would soon interrupt the current of my employments. I do not intend filling this chapter with egotism. I wish only to afford a few hints, which perhaps may still be useful, respecting the phases of the said panic, as indicated by its effects on various characters, myself not quite excluded. I speak of events "quorum pars *minima* fui," and I would wish to record them (though as briefly as possible) "non meâ causâ sed aliorum."

From Sir Walter Scott's diary above mentioned, which has always appeared to me a model of autobiography, I shall take the liberty of extracting one passage, which, as preëminently characteristic, dwells on my remembrance : —

"*Dec.* 18. — Poor T. S. called again yesterday. Through his incoherent, miserable tale, I could see that he had exhausted each access to credit, and yet fondly imagines that, bereft of all his accustomed indulgences, he can work with a literary zeal unknown to his happier days. I hope he may labor enough to gain the mere support of his family. For myself, if things go badly in London, the magic wand of the Unknown will be shivered in his grasp. He must then, faith, be termed the Too-well-known. The feast of fancy will be over with the feeling of independence. He shall no longer have the delight of waking in the morning with bright ideas in his mind, hasten to commit them to paper, and count them monthly as the means of planting such scaurs and purchasing such wastes ; replacing dreams of fiction, by other prospective visions of walks by

> ' Fountain heads and pathless groves,
> Places which pale passion loves.'

This cannot be ; but I may work substantial husbandry, that is, write history and such concerns. They will not be received with the same enthusiasm ; at least I much doubt the general knowledge that an author must write for his bread, at least for improving his pittance, degrades him and his productions in the public eye. He falls into the second rate rank of estimation : —

> ' When the harness sore galls, and the spurs his sides goad,
> The high-mettled racer's a hack on the road ! '

It is a bitter thought; but if tears start at it let them flow. My heart clings to the place I have created. There is scarce a tree upon it that does not owe its being to me.

"What a life mine has been! Half-educated, almost wholly neglected or left to myself; stuffing my head with most nonsensical trash, and undervalued by most of my companions for a time: then getting forward, and held a bold and clever fellow, contrary to the opinion of all who thought me a mere dreamer; broken-hearted for two years; my heart handsomely pieced again, but the crack will remain till my dying day. Rich and poor four or five times; once on the verge of ruin, yet opened a new source of wealth almost overflowing. Now to be broken in my pitch of pride, and nearly winged (unless good news should come), because London chooses to be in an uproar, and in the tumult of bulls and bears, a poor inoffensive lion like myself is pushed to the wall. But what is to be the end of it? God knows; and so ends the catechism.

"Nobody in the end can lose a penny by me; that is one comfort. Men will think pride has had a fall. Let them indulge their own pride in thinking that my fall will make them higher, or seem so at least. I have the satisfaction to recollect that my prosperity has been of advantage to many, and to hope that some at least will forgive my transient wealth, on account of the innocence of my intentions, and my real wish to do good to the poor. Sad hearts, too, at Darnick, and in the cottages of Abbotsford! I have half resolved never to see the place again. How could I tread my hall with a diminished crest? How live a poor, indebted man, where I was once the wealthy — the honored? I was to have gone there in joy and prosperity to receive my friends. My dogs will wait for me in vain. It is foolish, but the thoughts of parting from these dumb creatures have moved me more than any of the painful reflections I have put down. Poor things, I must get them kind masters! There may be yet those who, loving me, will love my dog, because it has been mine. I must end these gloomy forebodings, or I shall lose the tone of mind with which men should meet distress. I feel my dogs' feet on my knees. I hear them whining and seeking me everywhere. This is nonsense, but it is what they would do, could they know how things may be. An odd thought strikes me — When I die, will the journal of these days be taken out of the ebony cabinet at Abbotsford, and read with wonder, that the well-seeming baronet should ever have experienced the risk of such a hitch? Or will it be found in some obscure lodging-house, where the decayed son of chivalry had hung up his scutcheon, and where one or two old friends will look grave, and whisper to each other, 'Poor gentleman'—'a well-meaning man'—'nobody's enemy but his own'—'thought his parts would never wear out'—'pity he took that foolish title.' Who can answer this question?"

The mournful pages which I have extracted from Sir Walter Scott's Diary, were written under gloomy forebodings. When the storm had been matured and came in very truth, he stood up against it cheerfully and calmly. But on reflection, is it not perfectly clear that in his case there *ought not* to have been one moment's gloom or perturbation, and that they did not arise from necessity, properly so called, but from the wildness and madness of the uproar which our amiable world of London then engendered and fostered? for in regard to his situation, is it possible to deny the following premises? Firstly, his official income was not menaced, it amounted to £1400 per annum, and this alone was surely enough to supply the necessary requisites of life; secondly, he had the power of immediately raising £10,000 on valid security, and did raise it; thirdly, his health at that time was good, and so great was his popularity, that by writing at his ordinary rate he could gain £24,000 per annum! With such indisputable points in his favor, *why* should Sir Walter have been disturbed and tormented at all? To this there is but one answer, "The panic" did it, and we made "the panic." Our excellent world would have it, and then it stalked and *rampaged* about like a Frankenstein, alarming everybody and upsetting everything. Moral courage and self-possession might exist, but the individual gifted therewith was not for that reason protected against pressure or danger from the wild changes and commotions by which he was environed.

When misfortune lowers — when the waves of chance and

change are adverse, and the poor man is not allowed to steer
according to his own will and conscience, — it is natural to
seek for advice and coöperation from the best and wisest of
his friends. In the world of Edinburgh, there was one individual preëminent, and by that preëminence insulated —
nearly the last in some respects, from whom I could expect
sympathy or counsel, and yet the first to whom I applied for
it ; and this was Sir Walter Scott. From the commencement
of that epoch, when he seemed unavoidably carried away by
the tide and vortex of his own popularity, when his engagements of all kinds multiplied, when he lived in gothic halls of
his own building, dined *en petit comité* with George IV., received a title and kept open house, though he remained in
heart and mind unchanged, and though now and then he dined
with us, as in days of yore, yet our intercourse had retrograded
rather than advanced. But on his part, sincere good-will
towards the poor wayward supernumerary, remained immutable, and this he very soon proved. Sir Walter was not num-
bered among those exemplary men of the world whose friendship or good-will would evaporate in mere words, and fail to
kythe in actions.

At that time (towards the end of 1825), in common with all
the world, I felt assured that Sir Walter's own position was on
a rock of strength ; I believed that let the panic rage as it
might, its performances could not interfere with his domestic
tranquillity. But the purposes of my application to him were
very limited. At first I depicted my predicament in the black-
est possible shades, rather going beyond the mark in this respect, but not forgetting to place *en couleur de rose* my schemes
for its amelioration ; and in seeking his advice I was prepossessed by the notion that he would apply the maxim, "tu ne
cede malis," and would, accordingly, approve my plans. In
that case, all I desired was the interposition of his opinions
and influence against those kind friends who recommended a
smash as the best thing that could happen ; a remedy which
I then thought equally absurd and eccentric, but which, from
subsequent experience, I recognized to be an established and
unalterable *formula* of practice on every such occasion.

How changed was the well-known old house in Castle Street then ! It was the same, and yet in aspect how different ! For a long series of years this had been the great author's home and principal stronghold — there were kept his books and so-called museum. The cottage at Lasswade, and afterwards the house at Ashestiel, were but summer *shielings*, where the reception of many guests was out of the question. If only his ambition had been prudent, and stopped there ! Now, the old favorite library, the scene of so many invocations of the Muse, was dismantled and abandoned. All that remained of its furniture was the cumbrous writing-table, which had been transplaced into a back drawing-room on the first floor, where he wrote and received visitors, — a cheerless, gloomy apartment, as I thought, and rendered more so by a cast from the skull of Robert the Bruce, recently exhumed at Dunfermline, which came in lieu of *ci-devant* scutcheons and trophies, and formed the only remarkable object.

But though the house was thus changed (and having neglected many of his former counsels, I had little right to trouble him again) the manners and conduct of its owner were as kind and cordial as in days of yore. During that winter I had divers conversations with him in that gloomy study ; for as I came late in the afternoon, and did not stay long, his concluding words usually were, that he would think more about it, and in a day or two we should meet again.

Unluckily, as I then thought, there were but few points on which we could entirely agree, and one of these few was the reality of existing difficulties. According to my notions, he drew an exaggerated picture of the storm that was approaching, and against which, as he averred, every one who had wife and children should seek shelter before it was too late. He did not forget the maxim "tu ne cede malis," but with regard to the "contra audentior ito," he maintained that there were cases in which the duty of a good general was to arrange an orderly and honorable retreat. In plainer terms, he thought my plans very intelligible as to their drift, but rather incoherent and irreconcilable in practice. For example, I determined to retain the possession and management of my own property, cleaving to my present home, and to continue my literary pursuits unmolested. "You will find," said he, "that these are practically imcompatible with each other, and even were it not so, the struggle to unite them will be more trouble than the matter is worth. If the storm comes in earnest and no adequate provision is made against it, your first postulate will be disputed, and you will be put to so much inconvenience that the second will become quite hopeless and impracticable. I have thought anxiously on the subject, and such, at all events, is my conviction. Besides, I do not find that you are sufficiently true to your old principle — that poets and men of business are characters dissimilar and irreconcilable. I wish now that you would abide by your own *dictum* — leave these troublesome affairs to mere men of business ; place heritable property under their exclusive control, so that they may adjust all claims on it ; stick to your poems and translations ; retain your working tools, especially your German books, and such other personal property as is needful for family comfort and well-being.

"Now listen and perpend ! You have often told me about your partiality for a country life. Some years ago you asked my advice about taking the old house at Athestiel, which I told you was grown crazy. Now Chiefswood is untenanted and is likely to be so.[1] It is heartily at your service. The coal-cellar, I know, is well-stocked for the winter ; the furniture will be enough for the wants of your family ; of the wine-cellar I need not boast, for you have your own binns of Hock and Rüdisheimer. After arranging most of my year's end accounts in advance, I have fifty pounds in my desk ready to cover all your expenses of removal. One carrier's load, and your own carriage will, I suppose, do for all. My best advice, after matured reflection, is to retire with your books to Chiefswood, where, possibly, I shall not be the worst of neighbors ; and henceforward let us see what we can make of the world together !"

I could not leave out this anecdote, first, because it made an

---

[1] Mr. Lockhart's residence, forming part of the estate of Abbotsford.

indelible impression on my mind, and secondly, because it serves so amply to illustrate and prove what I have said elsewhere of Sir Walter Scott's benevolence. Avowedly, he aimed at being a man of business and man of the world, yet never adopted our most Christian world's amiable maxim, "Every man for himself *alone.*" Prudence and wisdom, — his own experience of the wayward supernumerary's conduct, perhaps forbade the kind offer he then made to me ; but he flung these overboard, and so thoroughly sincere were his intentions that on the departure of Mr. R. S. Wilson, in whose presence the conversation occurred, he took the unusual trouble of leaving his room, and coming down-stairs into the lobby, to add a few parting words. "You have refused my offer wholly and unconditionally," said he, "but to own the truth, I am not quite satisfied with your assigned reasons. Suppose they were ever so good and cogent, a man with wife and children should think less of his own feelings than of their safety and welfare. I am almost sure there is a storm coming ; take them out of harm's way ; at least, make me one promise, that before dismissing my proposal entirely from your thoughts, you will consult about it with your wife, and take her opinion ; let her have a fair and unbiased vote."

I met Sir Walter Scott soon after the opening of the Court of Session, when he said I should find him at his new quarters, and more busy than ever heretofore. I went and found him domiciled precisely as my early friend, the Rev. Mr. Mullens, used to be in days of yore, namely, in a third-rate lodging, in North St. David's Street, where, under a load of other cares, he was every day progressing with the "Life of Napoleon." It appeared to me too evident that no constitution could remain uninjured by the trials, self-imposed, which he then underwent. He fixed his attention on his employments without the slightest consideration for his own feelings of whatever kind, either in regard to state of health or domestic sorrows. He had undertaken certain tasks, and whether *invitâ Minervâ* or otherwise, these were to be, and *must* be accomplished.

On the 16th May, Lady Scott died at Abbotsford. Ten or twelve days after that melancholy event, he returned to town, took his place as usual in the Court of Session, and resumed his tasks. It seemed to me, that from this date onwards his literary undertakings were comparatively all forced work. He sustained outwardly an aspect of entire tranquillity, but was not in a natural state. Formerly, Sir Walter used to insist that three hours per day of application to literary composition was as much as any brain could safely bear. Now this kind of caution seemed to have been quite laid aside ; he rather argued that fatigue was a needless weakness, and that the best way was not to allow the existence of such a bugbear. I can imagine that during that year, 1826, he wrote on an average ten or twelve hours per day, yet was all the while haunted by the conviction that he could not by possibility render justice to the enormous and bewildering mass of materials which crowded on him.

I had refused his kind offer of a tranquil asylum in the country, and having prepared for strife with adverse circumstances, did not grumble about the trouble ; my ground of complaint was, that I did not meet with fair play. Cleaving to home, and desiring to work there unmolested, I found myself constantly threatened with the loss both of liberty and property : according to the wise law of the land and fashion of the times, I was again and again proclaimed a rebel, and Sir Walter officially had occasion to sign the warrants for these very proclamations, so that my condition, in that respect, was forced on his attention. I had wife and children to support, and if this *mauvaise plaisanterie* of a continued civil war were kept up at such rate, it was very clear that all means of providing for them would be annihilated. My income was consumed in law-costs, my time occupied in useless negotiations, and valuable property was by degrees frittered away. In the beginning of June, Sir Walter Scott wrote to me as follows. It was a letter intended to be shown as indicating his notions what might be done even by a humble supernumerary, in order to realize some permanent income.

"St. David's Street, Thursday night.

" MY DEAR SIR, — I have been thinking with some anxiety on the subject of our conversation to-day. It is needless to say how much I wish that matters were otherwise. The business is, if possible, to help them as they are. It has often struck me that a quarterly account of foreign literature, mixed with good translations, and spirited views of the progress of knowledge on the Continent might make a regular and reasonable, though not a large income for a man who was disposed to work regularly and to confine himself within limits as to expense. Germany, in particular, affords a fund of information to which each Leipsig fair is adding much that is good, bad, and indifferent. The difficulty would be to find a publisher, as times go, for such a work ; but if it could be assisted in the beginning by a handsome subscription, the obstacles would be much diminished. You are eminently qualified, in many respects for such a task. Whether you could bind yourself to the drudgery of it — for daily and constant drudgery you must look for — you only can judge, and I will make no apology for recommending any honorable labor, however severe, as I am myself a hard-working man.

" It is true that no great result could be expected from such a plan at the commencement, but it might afford support, and might, if steadily followed out, secure independence.

" I have little time to write, but will be happy to explain my ideas more at large, if you will call any day at three o'clock, when I am rarely abroad. I forgot, that Lord Gillies is absent from Edinburgh just now about some family illness, I believe. But I would much rather speak to him when something like a plan was fixed upon than otherwise, since I fear if I had not something to propose, our conversation would be very vague and useless. Observe, my dear sir, all I can promise from such a plan in the beginning would be a very small matter ; but industry and exertion might make it a great one. I think, in the mean time, you should abstain from printing or publishing anything which malignity, however injustly, might interpret as reflecting on any of your connections. It can in no

17

circumstance do good, and may do a great deal of harm. Excuse my writing abruptly and to the point, for I was born and bred a man of business, and therefore am in the habit of writing little more than the needful. I am, dear sir,

" Your most obedient servant,   WALTER SCOTT."

THE LAIRD OF BONNYMUNE.

One of the most illiterate, *obdurately* illiterate and obtuse, of the old-fashioned grandees, has already had his name in print. He has figured more than once in magazines, and been commemorated by autobiographers ! And at the time when Carlton House was in its so-styled glory, the late amiable and facetious Mr. M. Harris was specially invited thither, in order that he might recite to his Royal Highness the Prince Regent, his far-famed anecdotes of the Laird of Balnamoon, pronounced Bonnymune, or rather Bonnymœne. In this gentleman's mode of telling the stories, no doubt there must have been considerable comic force, otherwise a critic so fastidious and acute as his Royal Highness would not have felt interested. But as to the substance of those *historiettes*, independently of the narrator's comic manner, sure enough there was little that merits preservation.

I have, however, been repeatedly desired to resuscitate the Laird of Bonnymune, who happened to be my neighbor in early days ; and if I am to attempt this at all, it may as well be done in my first or second chapter as elsewhere. (Indeed, twaddling stories suit best with the epoch of childhood.) As already said, the traditionary anecdotes of this worthy are meagre, but the Laird himself, contemplated on his own paternal acres, I think did form an object of some interest to those who are fond of observing eccentric characters in odd situations. I have a dim, dreamy apprehension of having once seen the veritable man ; but all that remains of him in my mind consists of boot-hose, a coat with great square pockets and flaps, a periwig and cocked hat. His visage, demeanor, and style of conversation, have all faded away. Perhaps I never did meet the man at all, for at the period now referred to, if still alive, he was very old and infirm ; but I have had letters in his own hand, bearing date 1790–91. However, I knew his place of residence vastly well.

At a "convenient distance," that is, four or five long miles from the nearest market town, on the border of the Grampians, but on level, marshy ground, under the black and bleak hill of Catterthun, stood, and no doubt still stands, his an-cestral mansion. Environed and sheltered was it by stunted woods, principally of dark Scotch firs, and from the character of the scene altogether it might seem to rash and inexperienced observers a most gloomy abode. It was like the whole world, however, to the Laird of Bonnymune. It was his own domain, where he ruled like a petty sovereign, and in comparison with which the rest of the so-called world afforded but mere subsidiary adjuncts.

Among the old Laird's numerous peculiarities was this, that he would not use a carriage, but always travelled on horse-back ; and it is to be supposed that he never travelled very far, because he had made it a rule absolute that he would not retire to rest at night in any house under the moon except in his own paternal stronghold. His ancestors had all lived contentedly there, and so did he. Strange to say, some of them must have been *literati*, therefore very different from our venerable friend, for in a certain old tower they had preserved a valuable family library, of which more hereafter.

For the vicinity of the market-town, unless it were to gossip, to sell cattle, or to dine with his friend the provost, the Laird cared not a rush, for he never lacked provisions. According to ancient usage, his rents from petty tenants were in great part paid in *kain* hens, and he had always poultry enough, including geese, ducks, and turkeys to supply a garrison. The Grampian Hills, swarthy as they looked, afforded herbage for numberless sheep. Beeves, too, and game, partridges, hares, and grouse, he had in abundance. He brewed his own ale, and baked his own bread. His wine-merchant would have honored his order for twelve pipes as confidingly as for twelve dozens of wine. In Scotch phraseology, he

might be called " self-contained," self-subsistent, this Laird, or
in less metaphysical terms, he had all resources and appliances of comfort within his own paternal estate, and thither
he allured many friends by dint of hospitality ; for in so far as
concerns providing and proffering great stores of food and
drink, such means of becoming popular and praiseworthy
were never wanting at Bonnymune. Arrive there on any day
of the year, provided you did not forget the dinner hour —
for he would not wait even for an invited guest — you were
sure of a hearty welcome and ample cheer.

There was not merely enough, but superabundance. Six or
eight *kain* hens in one dish formed a not unusual *entrée ;* on
gala days these were responded to by six or eight more at
the other end of the table. In like manner it might happen
that two gigots of mutton or two roast pigs were paraded.
But let it not be inferred that there was any deficiency of miscellaneous *entrées* or elegant *hors d'œuvres.* On the contrary, the *cuisine* at Bonnymune was famed for a multiplicity
of productions, curious and *recherchés*, particularly ancient
Scotch inventions now almost forgotten, though an ingenious
attempt to revive them is sometimes made at the anniversary
dinners of the Edinburgh Antiquarian Society. It is almost
needless to add, that the wines, ale, and whiskey, " the
drinks," as dear amiable Mrs. Gamp would have said, " *was*
all good ; " and I think the old Laird of Bonnymune would
scarcely have found it in his heart to withhold a welcome even
from his inveterate enemy if he had ventured to present himself at dinner-time.

And in the drawing-room, moreover, there were always
" nice conversible young leddies," some of whom could perform on the spinet, the celestina, or harpsichord ; and there
were whist-tables, loo-tables, faro-tables, according to fashion
in those most enlightened times. In short, there was to be
found at Bonnymune all that can solace and gladden the heart
of convivial man. But, as a matter of course, the old Laird,
like all his fraternity of lairds, loved drinking, hearty, convivial, uproarious drinking, and would have thought it impos-

sible to live without that resource. Moreover, in all scholastic acquirements he was dolefully deficient : wrote (when forced to write) with much labor and many growls, an awfully cramp and precise hand, very legible, however ; detested books, and despised their authors. Lastly, and as aforesaid, he travelled always on horseback, would not go to sleep in any house but his own, and was attended in all his excursions by a confidential servant, whose name, by some singular chance, was not Saunders, but Peter.

On these elementary principles (negations rather) in Bonnymune's character, were founded Mr. Harris's facetious anecdotes, which, I have already said, amount in substance to woefully little ; but as I have been particularly requested to repeat them, here they come !

The good old magnifico's taste in drinking became at length obtuse, so that one evening after dinner, at a friend's house, he very willingly drank cherry-bounce, mistaking it for port, and declaring that it was a " pleasant, pure, fruity, and generous wine, and very old in bottle. " As a matter of course, when the midnight hour approached, the Laird wished to ride home, and the horses were ordered. But Peter had never in his life seen his venerable master "so far gone ; " besides, they had a long way to ride, and the night was both dark and gusty.

After some consultation with the kind host and his family, it was agreed that Bonnymune could not, and must not attempt to ride home. But as any proposition for his going to bed or staying in the house after twelve o'clock would be resisted and resented with obduracy, stratagem was used.

They led him out of doors with a light, which the wind instantly extinguished. Then, in the pitchy darkness, they assisted him to mount, not upon horseback, but upon a *fail* dyke, *Anglice*, turf-wall, a common kind of fence in the far North Here Peter had cleverly attached the bridle to the stump of an elder-bush ; he put the reins and the whip into his master's hands, and then retired with the words, " Noo, your honor, the road 's straight afore ye ! "

Away went the laird, as he supposed whipping and spurring to his heart's content, till he arrived at the land of dreams and utter oblivion, when wearied of his exertions he tumbled off. Now Peter ventured to advance. " Eh, sirs ! Hech me, to think o' the like o' that ! " Then, raising his voice, " We 're at hame noo, sir ! We 're at hame, I 'm tellin' ye ! Your honour's just fa'en off at our ain stable door ! "

But stratagem was no longer needed. The Laird persisted most comfortably in his profound sleep, and was carried to bed without a murmur. Next morning, however, no sooner did he awake to consciousness, than he vowed vengeance for the trick that had been played on him ; declaring, moreover, that had he been allowed his own way, he could have ridden home as well as ever he did in his life. He departed at day-break in huge wrath, and would not by any persuasions be induced to visit at the same house again. It is, I must own, but a meagre story this ; nevertheless it was no doubt considered a " right merry jest " in the year 1794, on the Grampian Hills, and it always formed one among Mr. Harris's comic recitations.

Thus having illustrated, by anecdote, the Laird's propensities for conviviality and riding home at midnight, I shall only repeat one more, which refers to his dislike of books and contempt for their authors. This, I believe, was his Majesty King George the Fourth's favorite story, for which reason I am admonished that it deserves being once more recorded. I say once more, although current and common as it used to be in the far north, I am not aware that it ever appeared in print. As a conscientious chronicler, however, I may observe that the facetious Mr. Harris, in arranging this anecdote, availed himself of one event respecting the family library, which did not take place till the reign of the old Laird's next heir and successor ; *mais, c'est égal cela.*

Be it declared, then, that once upon a time, a good friend of the old Laird's came by chance to dinner — of course was hospitably entertained — and the weather being tremendous, was consequently invited to stay all night. Next morning the storm had increased. This Peter averred when he came to awake his master : " Catterthun had on his nicht-cap ; the

rain blattered on the windows ; the fords were impassable ;
't was an awfu' morning for baith man and beast ! "

"Harken, Peter, ye villain ! " said the Laird. " Is Sandie
Hunter come doon the stair for his breakfast yet ? "

" No, your honor."

" It 's an awfu' mornin', ye say ? Then, ye 'll gang direct
to the parlor ; see that the fire 's blazin', licht the cawnels, set
the punch-bowl filled wi' plottie on the breakfast-table, steek
the shutters, and we 'se try what kind of a nicht it will mak ! "
(In plainer language, what sort of a night we can make of it.)

Now it so happened that this visitor, in comparison with the
Laird, might be reckoned a *savant.* He was at least an ama-
teur of old books, and he by no means loved inordinate drinking. On his descent into the banqueting-room, therefore, he
was not a little alarmed and amazed at the effect of the Laird's
orders, which had been obeyed to the letter. Instead of ad-
miring·such proceedings, he would have opened the shutters
if he durst. Steadfastly he refused to accept even one glass
from the punch-bowl, and restricted himself to tea, with eggs,
grouse-pie, mutton-ham, kippered salmon, rolls, bannocks, and
marmalade.

" Weel, every man to his taste, and do as ye like, Sandie,"
said the Laird ; "but I think ye 'll no be for facing the road
this day, and ye 'll no venture far at the pootin' ! " (*Anglice,*
shooting.)

" In troth, no," replied Sandie ; " it 's a day for keeping
cosey at the ingle-neuk. But if I dared mak sae free, Bonnymune, have ye nae auld buiks aboot the house, that micht
help to keep a boddie out o' languor in a weety mornin' like
this ? "

" Buiks, man ? " repeated the Laird ; "ten cart-loads o'
them, gin ye like ; and what 's mair, ye 're welcome to tak'
them hame to your ain house, if ye think siccan rubbish worth
the expense o' cartage ! "

As might be supposed, the intelligent visitor felt attracted
by this, and desired to examine the neglected repertories, to
which the Laird assented ; and in the course of the morning,

Peter was employed to open the window-shutters in the library room of the old tower, now seldom visited. Arrived there, the *connoisseur* began eagerly to scrutinize the contents of the shelves, Bonnymune all the while peering over his shoulder, and accompanying his proceedings with a continued verbal commentary, which Mr. Harris used to recite as a kind of running bass, or series of contemptuous grunts, varied by Sandie's exclamations of delight or admiration.

" Beautiful Elzevirs ! " exclaimed the latter. " And here, on my conscience, editions *in Usum Delphini*, with uncut edges, that look as if they had never been opened ! "

" Them 's Laytin buiks, I see," interposed the Laird. " Heathen trash ! Hech, hech ! What the callants are garr'd work at in the schule, when they 're done with their arithmetic, just to keep them frae stealing apples, or playing at pitch and toss. Wha the deevil was ever the better for being able to read Laytin, I wad be glad to ken ? Is na' our dominie just the stupidest boddie in a' the parish ? " (A pause, till the *savant* changed his position.)

" And noo, Sandie, ye 're delvin' and houkin' amang that rubbish o' Greek. There 's no muckle there that ye can translate better than me, I 'm thinking. Weel, I never got owre muckle Laytin, and I never could *Greek it* ava, that 's gospel truth ; but I ken the buiks, because the vera printed letters is no' readable." (Another pause.)

" Them 's English history buiks," resumed the Laird ; " ilk ane telling the tale his ain gait and contradictin' his neebor ; as if we needed to care what the chaps did and said in days o' lang syne. Will *that* pit siller in our purses, or smeddum into your brains or mine ? "

" And noo' ye 're pokin' in a heap o' auld trash, poycms and plays and novels, deevil's buiks, I reckon ; contrivances just for diverting idle loons, and helping them to turn young limmers' heads ! "

" Bonnymune," said the *connoisseur*, " here 's an auld folio — it 's a play-book — that I wad like to borrow for a while, if there 's nae objection ? "

" Borrow ! " replied the Laird ; " the chap 's doitit, I think. Didna' I tell ye to cart awa' the hale lot o' them ! Pit the folio in your saddle-bags, man ; mak' a kirk and a mill o't, or licht your pipe with the paper."

Par parenthèse, this despised volume happened to be the veritable *first* edition of " Shakespeare," a rarity now almost unattainable by collectors, at any price ; and which afterwards, flanked by the second and third editions, all richly and uniformly bound in Russia leather, was sold to the late Mr. James Roche, of Castle Granagh, for £500. So much for the Laird of Bonnymune's worldly prudence in regard to his estimation of old books.[1]

" Foreign clanjamphry, I see," continued the wise man ; " that 's whaur ye 're delvin' the noo. Outlandish mixtry-maxtry, indeed, as if we had na' buiks in plenty o' our ain, without seeking help frae the Pope o' Rome, or the munti-banks in Spain or France."

" Hah ! " suddenly screeched the Laird, as if stung by a viper, " Sandie, let them buiks alane ! I redde ye, let sleepin' dogs lie ! Them 's *law* buiks. D—n them and the writers awthegither ! I hae had, and I have it yet, a ganging plea in the Court of Session ; five-and-twenty years the villains hae been at it ; fifteen hundred pounds sterling wad na' pay their charges, and at this day I 'm no farrer ben than when I set out. D—n the law buiks, Sandie, and gif I could see them and their authors burning at the stake, wadna' I poke the fire, d'ye think ? "

Lastly, and to wind up this long yarn of twaddle, the curious inspector came to a compartment of the library which excited his no little surprise. The books were veritable certainly, but they had an odd appearance, and by no efforts could he extract one volume from its resting-place. Hereupon the magnifico said not one word, but began to chuckle.

" Ye 've said owre muckle about the de'il, I 'm thinking,"

---

[1] Respecting the purchase, Mr. Roche acted as agent only. He was a banker, and so good an economist, that I doubt whether he would have parted with £500 to restore William Shakespeare himself to life !

exclaimed Sandie, "for he's been amang the buiks here. I never saw the like!"

"Then the de'il was just John, the wricht" (*Anglice*, carpenter), quoth the Laird; "and a clever callant he is. Noo, Sandie man, ye're a guid bairn, and I'll tell ye how it happened. The skelves here was auld and worm-eaten, and yae stormy nicht the buiks and skelves thegither fell on the floor wi' a blatter like thunder. Then the greive he wantit the floor for an extraordinar' crap o' blue potatoes, and John cam to mend up the skelves, and like an honest lad *that* he did. But when the job was done, and he tried the buiks, d—n them, they wad na' fit! So he ranged them regular on the floor, measured them with his ruler, and then measured the skelves."

"John and me communed thegither, and I garr'd him tak' the *saw* to the biggest volumes, and he sawed off an inch here and half an inch there, till we made *snod* wark. Then the buiks fitted, and John packit them and drove them in wi' his mell. Ye need na' think to poke there, Sandie; it wad tak' the deil's ain fingers to draw them out again!"

LORD ARBUTHNOT.

Like the old Laird of Bonnymune, distinguished, as we have seen, for having once rode upon a *fail* dyke, a certain old Lord Arbuthnot was in those days also reckoned excessively droll, though the phasis of his lordship's pleasantry was altogether different. According to prevalent belief, this nobleman's principal crotchet was parsimony (or penury); yet, in his capacity of miser, he nevertheless helped me, in a rather absurd argumentation, to prove that the Scotch are not avaricious. I contended that his lordship, at all events, ought not to be classed as a miser, but rather as an eccentric humorist, who purposely turned avarice into ridicule whilst he seemed to practice it; and, possibly, the notion was in some respects correct enough. Lord Arbuthnot *caricatured* the part.

His lordship, however, had been bred up and educated in a humble sphere; and his habits were formed before he was

called on to don the family coronet. Instead of his habits
being changed on the acquisition of that new dignity, his character seemed only to become more stubborn and *prononcé*. I
presume the family estate was not then entailed, for the new
incumbent inherited along with it a great load of debt, accu-
mulated by his predecessors ; and with fierce oaths he declared
he would liquidate them to the uttermost farthing. Such an
undertaking as this, it may be imagined, served him as a very
sufficient excuse for a mode of life not otherwise quite consistent with baronial or comitial dignity. Like that of Bonnymune,
his lordship's will was law ; and, although twice married and
twice left a widower, his habits were like those of an old bachelor : and he would not allow any relation to interfere with, or
venture near him. Now nothing can be more clear than that
in cherishing decision of character and unity of purpose, a
share of oddity may well be excused : in truth, it is often inevitable.

In this respect the Lord Arbuthnot of those days (he died
before 1794), certainly merited respect instead of ridicule. He
persisted, with inflexible resolution, in his purpose aforesaid ;
and I do not know that the opprobrious term of miser ought
ever to have been applied to one who did not aim at hoarding
large sums in secret repositories ; who neither rack-rented his
tenants nor practiced usury ; but who pinched, pared, and skill-
fully calculated in order to pay off incumbrances on hereditary
acres, and to liquidate even the personal obligations of his
careless predecessors.

Lord Arbuthnot's humor, as I have heard, consisted chiefly
in this, that he actually made a parade and boast of his own
excessive frugality, therefore might expect to be stared at, and
in this way his penurious habits and stratagems might be carried *à l'outrance*. Obliged by his station to retain some household servants, he himself personally was almost independent of
their attentions ; their appearance was seldom needed, unless
when he had visitors, and then, truly, the fare produced, unlike
that at Bonnymune, was by no means profuse or sumptuous.

Par parenthèse, I may notice that his lordship's old valet,

having much time at his own disposal, was not invariably a
model of sobriety, and though never pardoned for infraction of
that virtue, was yet never turned out of doors. One afternoon,
however, his lordship in great wrath, and with many oaths, declared that such conduct was no longer endurable. "Either
you shall quit the house directly, you scoundrel, or *I* must!"
(So the viscount wound up his complaint.)

"Hech me!" replied Saunders; "and *whaur* dis your lordship think to gang, whaur ye 'll be sae weel?" In plainer
terms, his lordship might leave the house, but the notion of
his own exile therefrom was perfectly inadmissible.

In his ordinary *ménage*, Lord Arbuthnot was, like Bonnymune, "self-contained," as well as self-willed, but in a very
different style. In one mysterious closet, *sanctum* or study, he
kept all the means and appliances of his own domestic life.
Herein he might seem even to be his own cook and valet. A
shrewd man he was, thoroughly versed in what is called "business," and not quite ignorant of books; but as to his fair
estate, his broad meadows, heath-clad hills, or cornfields, by
all accounts, he never once thought of them but as means of
reaping money; he had no eye for the romantic or picturesque.
The beauties of the finest landscape, whether in its natural
wildness, or adorned by the artistical operations of a Repton,
White, Brown, or Marshall, would have been lost on him. He
had some taste, however, for Archæology, or at least for old
family archives : and when allusion was made to that edifying
event, the "boiling of the sheriff," which took place divers
centuries ago, in a royal forest, some ten miles distant from
Arbuthnot, his lordship swore with great *gusto*, "By G—, sir,
we were there!" Indeed, he had at his own command documents commemorating this event, and the names (Arbuthnot
included) of those who claimed the king's pardon for the
murder.

In the closet or *sanctum* above-mentioned, during his old
age, he secluded himself voluntarily, as a poor man has often
done by compulsion in the dreary cell of a prison. In this
mysterious apartment he conserved not only his books and

papers, but coals, turf, wood, candles, oatmeal, eggs, butter, cheese, and other stores. Hardly any mortal was permitted to enter this private room, and, when entered, it exhibited the most complicated disorder, though it was remarked that if any written document or other article was wanted, his lordship could always discover it at a moment's warning.

If a guest arrived on a winter's day, and complained of cold in the reception-room, where perhaps there was only a smouldering peat in the grate, his lordship would trot back into the closet, and reappear, carrying a ration of coals on a broken plate. Possibly, he weighed out his own daily portions of food and drink, drove hard bargains with himself, and tried the question on how little he could subsist. This, however improbable, need not be incredible, for, some thirty years later, I knew an instance of a London merchant, a very independent and wealthy man, who scrupulously persisted in the weighing system, screwing himself down at last to a regular expenditure of only one shilling and sevenpence per day, and all for the sake of exhibiting an example of prudence and economy to his two sons, both of whom, naturally enough, became spendthrifts and devotees to the bottle.

Lord Arbuthnot's decision of character was unalterably marked even in his demeanor and tone of voice. The former was energetic and abrupt; the latter, to say the truth, was habitually the tone of wrath or sarcasm, from which he rarely swerved even in his convivial moments. Perpetually at war with creditors, whose claims he did not pay so fast as they expected; also at war with habits and manners of the times, which he thought finical and extravagant, he yet had his jocose moods, when he could laugh heartily (though sarcastically), and make others laugh. And to his honor be it recorded, that he lived to realize in great measure what he had undertaken, rectifying the blunders of his ancestors, and leaving the family estates in a comparatively manageable and prosperous condition.

The Laird of Brucks.

Brucks, as far as I know, had never been incommoded with any debts ; he had extensive though not fertile lands, and was what the world calls independent ; neither was he deficient in such educational acquirements as usually fell to the lot of Scotch lairds during the eighteenth century. But notwithstanding all this, he cherished a very eccentric fancy, namely, that he would lead the life of a common laborer, nay, would labor harder than any of his own paid workmen were willing to do.

In one respect this might no doubt be considered a very exemplary notion. If the now rich proprietor of a great factory or coal mine would go into it for a month or two, and work there like one of his own poor hirelings, without allowing himself one pennyworth more of better food or other comforts than they have, it might perhaps enlighten his mind somewhat, and modify his conclusions respecting the condition of the working classes. However, it may be doubted whether Brucks derived any such enlightenment from his experiments. He was, of course, his own taskmaster ; could regulate his own time, feed luxuriously if he pleased, and choose his own kind of work. The sort of labor, which in his wisdom he preferred, was that of building stone dykes, and his leading principle to try how many miles in length of those fences he could swear to having completed with his own hands.

The said stone dykes were structures of a peculiar and capricious character. They were built either of freestone, with the help of hammer, pick-axe, and wedge, or of unbroken " whinstones," as the case might be ; but there existed an indefeasible rule, that the mason must neither use mud nor mortar. How the walls could stand without it was the wonder, but they did stand, with gaps, no doubt, here and there, and were detestable eyesores to every lover of the picturesque. Of such dykes it is said that Brucks lived to build some scores of miles' length, *manibus propriis*, and when he had fenced all his own fields, he offered a demonstration of his expansive energy and benevolence in behalf of his neighbors.

But in one respect, that of restricting himself to privations and hard fare, he did by no means conform to the model of his own laborers. Unlike Bonnymune, who always rode, Brucks performed his various journeys, whether long or short, on foot. In this way he not unfrequently crossed the Grampian Hills to visit his friend, the Laird of Morphie, who then resided in a sheltered situation of the Lowlands, on the banks of the beautiful river Northesk. On the day of his arrival, he was contented with any sort of fare, were it but kailbrose and bread and cheese, and the never-failing whiskey-punch ; but next morning, the preparation for breakfast made a kind of revolution in the house.

A large salmon, newly caught from the river, a gigot of mutton roasted, were *entrées* not unusual on those occasions. Brucks had been known to devour nearly an entire salmon for breakfast, then attack the gigot, and complacently finish his repast with half a pint of undiluted whiskey, after which he would address his friend in these words : " And noo, Wullie, man, I think I 'll *sey* the Cairn ! " In plain English, *essay* to get across the Grampians, of which the highest that lay in the Laird's homeward route was called the Cairn, or " Cairn-a-mount." I believe the distance he had to walk was about thirty miles ; a mere trifle for Brucks, who, it is almost needless to add, possessed Herculean strength.

PROFESSOR THOMAS BROWNE.

Among the literary friends who honored me with confidence or kind condescension, the late Professor Thomas Browne holds a distinguished place in my remembrance. The world, I believe, recognizes him only as a metaphysician, but with the most perfect decision of character as a laborious and indefatigable student, he had versatility of talents such as have rarely been equaled. At this time Dr. Browne held the very responsible situation of Dugald Stewart's chosen representative and successor, and consequently was every day occupied less or more in improving those popular lectures which, since his death, have gone through seventeen editions, and immortalized his name. But instead of adhering to this employment alone their author might, to a superficial observer, have seemed quite sufficiently occupied with the pursuits of poetry and romance, and (as he did not shun the social circles) with conviviality. Like President Blair, Henry Mackenzie, and Henry Erskine, he never lost his juvenile interest for even the lightest literature of the day, not rejecting even *mediocre* novels and poems, provided they were not altogether stupid, but looking upon them as useful in their degree, and contributing advantageously to a great whole. Dr. Browne published volume after volume of his own original poetry in a great variety of styles, but (excepting two volumes in 1804) always anonymously, nor would he acknowledge the paternity in conversation, but if they were mentioned, forthwith changed the subject. As he resolutely denied himself any personal repute for these productions, it may be naturally supposed that, like St. Chrysostom, he wrote in verse, " because it was more difficult than prose." In truth, he delighted in grappling with literary difficulties, which seemed to dissolve utterly before his quiet resolution and imperturbable amenity of temper. How often during our afternoon walks in vacation time, have I heard from him such expressions as the following : " More than half the difficulties in this world are of our own making ; you imagine them to be far greater than they are. It is like as if a child held out a drawn sword, and a foolish giant ran right against it, instead of waving it gently aside."

Among Dr. Browne's minor poems were occasionally passages of great beauty. I remember one (though I cannot repeat it), addressed " To a Withered Leaf," which I treasured for many a year ; but like thousands of other literary leaves, it is beyond my reach now, and I do not know that it was included in any of his printed volumes. On his lectures, luckily, no comments of mine are needed, for since that era in my own life, when metaphysics became my favorite study, the book, like his treatise on " Cause and Effect," has never fallen in my way. But I feel very sure, that if, instead of studying in the school of Dugald Stewart (much as he differed from him) Browne had given his attention fairly and sufficiently to the works of Immanuel Kant, he could have conquered their difficulties and rendered justice to an author, who, up to the present hour, in his own country and elsewhere (even by his admirers) has been so woefully misrepresented. Dr. Browne was a most valuable and steadfast friend, ever willing to prescribe benevolently for infirmities, either of mind or body, and if he detected good points in any character, he weighed them scrupulously, and would not easily be shaken by defects or aberrations. I have repeatedly said that the utter absence of affectation or pretense of any kind is a distinguishing mark of real genius, and it is not likely that I shall ever withdraw that assertion. In convivial circles, however, and for ordinary observers, Dr. Browne's demeanor and conversation were for ordinary observers deceptive, though without the remotest intention on his own part to deceive. The contrast betwixt those pale study-worn features, and his playful gayety of manners was indeed very striking, and under the disguise of the latter, a stranger would not easily detect the deeply-reflecting metaphysician or the deeply-feeling poet. But I do not allow that in this there was one particle of affectation. It indicated merely a duality of the phasis of action. His proper sphere as a philosopher was in his own retired study (a gloomy backroom of a *rez de chaussée* in Prince's Street); but he moved in society unscathed, assuming, of course, a manner, for the occasion, in which, properly speaking, there was no affectation. One might quite as well have accused John Kemble of pretense and affectation if, for some reason or another, he had taken it into his head to act Tony Lumpkin!

Henry Mackenzie.

The first time I met him was at a jovial dinner-party, in 1810. During the next three years, before I settled in Great King Street, where he not unfrequently honored me with kind visits, I used to look on the venerable " Man of Feeling " with

18

an indefinable sentiment of awe and wonder. As he used much exercise, I had the luck to meet him often in the streets; occasionally, too, he looked in at John Ballantyne's, where he was received with profound respect and obeisance, as befitted the steadfast friend of Scott, and the patriarch of our northern literature.

No weather daunted him. During squalls, not uncommon at Edinburgh, such as I would not *willingly* have encountered, I have observed him both early and late (often attended by a favorite pointer) drifting along with the tempest, or tottering beneath its attacks, yet by inflexible resolution bidding defiance to both wind and rain. Considering his advanced age, his attenuated form, wrapped in a long, dark *surtout*, which always seemed too wide, as if only a skeleton were under it, and his countenance, then worn away and sharpened, like that of Voltaire in his very last days, and yet capable at all times of the most animated expression, he appeared to me in the same light as Goethe afterwards did in the year 1821 ; that is to say, he was like a *revenant* from another epoch, at which time *our* world was not in being. After better acquaintance, and not till then, did I become convinced that the title of *revenant*, in its French meaning of *ghost*, could only have been applied to him by a very absurd blunder, seeing that our authenticated visitors under that name have almost invariably turned out to be very stupid, wayward, and unprofitable affixes to society, whereas Mackenzie did most cordially contribute to the well-being and improvement of our present world, and although he had seen more than three-score and ten winters, could participate in its goings-on as cheerfully as he did in those of society fifty years ago.

Mackenzie affords me an illustrious example in support of another favorite aphorism, namely, that men of real genius are always the most simple and unaffected in manners. Some readers will look upon this as no better than a *truism* ; others may dispute it, and bring example to the contrary, which I am very sure would, upon due examination turn out fallacious.

The " Man of Feeling " did not exactly keep the table on a

roar with quaint old stories, like Sir Walter Scott, but I have known him do nearly the same thing, and he was quite as much a foe to *starch* or pretension, as the "Great Unknown" or anybody else could be. There was one special character-istic of his table-talk which dwells in my remembrance, namely the aptitude and inexhaustible store of his references to Shakespeare. If the whole of Ayscough's laborious "Con-cordance" had been engraven on the tablets of his mind, he could not have been better prepared than he was with appro-priate quotations for every occasion. By one lucky trait re-vived from "Falstaff," I have known him give not only new zest to the *Châteaux Margout*, but a new and genial tone to the conversation of an entire evening.

Mr. Mackenzie, it is true, had ceased to write, or at least to publish books, but his interest in literature never abated. When the first sheets of "Waverley" were given to the printer, it was supposed to be the work of an author not merely name-less by choice, but hitherto unknown ; and the wise publisher doubted whether he should venture to take off even one thou-sand copies of such a thing ! In order to forward matters, James Ballantyne intrusted the opening chapters to a few lit-erary friends, whose judgment, he thought, was rather more to be relied on than that of any bookseller. I remember with what fervent zeal the pariarchal critic hurried and drifted along the streets at his fleetest pace, to express his conviction that this would turn out to be no ordinary novel, and, whatsoever the publisher might think, was "not the work of any ordinary man." Mackenzie was indeed always ready to manifest his activity, and interpose his influence, where good could be done in any shape or way. One of the last interviews I had with him was, when he desired my humble coöperation in muster-ing pupils for a foreign lady of noble birth and excellent tal-ents, who had come to Edinburgh with her husband and family, in order to live there by teaching languages, in which purpose she afterwards fully succeeded.

John Pinkerton.

This winter, after I had brought my books from the country and arranged them in a large room, Sir Walter Scott not unfrequently wandered down to Northumberland Street, whence he would sometimes walk away with a load of books, stowing three or four volumes into each capacious pocket, and carrying others on his arm. On one of these occasions, he prepared me for a visit, at his suggestion, from the well-known John Pinkerton, then a visitor at Edinburgh, who, for his forthcoming tragedy of the "Countess of Strathearn," desiderated an epilogue, which he had requested of Scott in vain. As it was impossible on my part to plead any great pressure of business, I readily agreed to read the tragedy, and to write the epilogue, with which, when achieved, Mr. Pinkerton was entirely satisfied, saying that it "glowed with genuine poetry." It turned out, however, that an epilogue was not required, for the "Countess of Strathearn," when tried upon the Edinburgh stage, was decisively condemned — a result which Sir Walter had no doubt foreseen.

Perhaps the less that I say of John Pinkerton the better, inasmuch as my notice of him cannot be very favorable. He became afterwards my frequent guest, and in the autumn of that year spent three months with us in the country. He had figured in the world as a poet, a bibliographer, historian, archæologist, geographer, and geologist. It was by his two volumes of early Scottish poems, published from MSS. in the library of Magdalene College, Cambridge, that he was best known to me; and for the merits of this production alone I should have been willing to bear with or overlook his overweening egoism and numberless eccentricities, in consequence of which, when he left Edinburgh in 1814, there were but three individuals in the whole community with whom he remained on speaking terms, namely, Sir Walter Scott, Mr. Thomas Thomson, and my obscure self. He had ample worldly shrewdness (in pecuniary matters at least), great perseverance and power of research, was a fierce and uncompromising critic of all works, either in prose or verse, excepting his own ; and for one who did not feel disposed to quarrel with his dictatorial manner and *bizarre* notions, his conversation, from its variety, afforded an inexhaustible stock of amusement.

In his capacity of critic sometimes he did not spare even himself, as when he remarked that at one period of his youth he had wished only to live so long as to complete and publish his volume entitled " Rhymes, by Mr. Pinkerton," which he then thought a grand poetical achievement, but which he now regarded with contempt or pity. He had special notions about the perfection of art, and the duty which devolves on a poet in that particular. According to him, it was quite enough, in order to merit immortal honor, if an author, during his whole life-time, produced only one solitary sonnet deserving to be called good and perfect of its kind. As such, it must be moulded strictly on the Petrarchan model as to rhymes ; for otherwise it was no sonnet at all, but merely a " quatuorzain."

" Pinkie Winkie " and I had differences of opinion, and arguments grounded thereon every day, yet we never quarreled. Our mode of life in the country was regularly and pleasantly arranged. In the mornings we seldom met at all, his hour of breakfast being later than mine ; but usually about twelve or one o'clock, at his suggestion, the carriage was brought to the door for an excursion to pay visits, or search after antiquities and geologistic specimens. I often found time to compose a sonnet whilst my venerable Mentor's thoughts were engrossed with Roman camps, Caledonian stations, green earth, plum-pudding, agate, jasper, quartz, and hornblende. Some few of those sonnets he thought tolerable ; but I cannot refer to any one, for they have all perished.

I remember divers pleasant afternoons spent in this manner, cheered by autumnal sunshine, especially one at Finella's Castle (or rather the foundations thereof), near to Fettrcairn House, where we were hospitably received by my friends Sir John and Lady Jane Stewart. My learned companion was stoutly provided with anecdotes of this eccentric lady (Finella, I mean), and sedulously pointed out to me how far the building had extended originally, and how very strong a fortress it must have been. In the same neighborhood is a Roman camp, which, of course, engaged his especial veneration. Another ruin of a different kind (for its lofty towers were still standing) dwells on my recollection — I mean Edzel, one of the many possessions of Lord Panmure. Here " Pinkie " found less of interest than I did, because the castle happens not to figure prominently in Scottish history. No sorceress, like Finella, was remembered here, and we could only conjecture what sort of beings its inhabitants once were. At Edzel, the most remarkable trait, in my estimation, was the remains of a large pleasure garden adjoining the walls, with terraces and such like, in which no baronial owner had taken his pleasure for at least two centuries, and in which, strange to tell, perennial flowers yet sprung up and bloomed here and there, of a race belonging to that epoch when the castle was in its glory. But of all our haunts, that which best pleased my eccentric guest was the agate quarry, near the town of Montrose, where he would work with his hammer for hours together among the green earth and plum-pudding blocks ; indeed, would not have come away till dusk, if I had not reminded him that dinner would be spoiled. On his departure in November, his room was lumbered by specimens, a selection from which I afterwards sent to him by a Montrose vessel.

CHARLES KIRKPATRICK SHARPE.

In all Edinburgh surely there could not be found two literary men more utterly dissimilar than Mr. Sharpe, the fastidious Oxonian, seated in his tapestried chamber, stored with ancestral reliques, and James Hogg in his den under the North Bridge, with the old broken " sclate " always before him, the very sight of which made one shudder with remembrances of intricate problems in arithmetic. Yet with hearty enthusiasm did Mr. Sharpe enter into the humors of Hogg's witches ; and the design by which he manifested his sympathy is worthy of the artist whose " Queen Elizabeth dancing " was such a favorite with Sir Walter Scott, that, in his own words, he

" could laugh as heartily when looking at it after ten years' acquaintance as he did the first day."

If one happens to possess a good house and well-appointed *ménage* in the best part of Edinburgh, I must admit that the notion of going farther into the country for the love of land-scape scenery, may be dispensed with. From the year 1815 till 1827, I regarded the modern Athens as my home, and have never seen more beautiful autumns than there. During one season I made it my habit every day before dinner to walk by St. Leonard's to Duddingston Loch, thence to climb right up and athwart Arthur's Seat, and so return home. My next favor-ite resort was Corstorphin Hill, especially in the spring season, when the first leaves were on the larch trees, and the first *gowans* came out in the sun shine. Another resort was to Braid Hill, taking the route thereto across the meadows and Bruntisfield links ; and I made light of the walk to and from Roslin and Hawthornden in fine weather. By all this twaddle I mean only that Edinburgh may be a pleasant residence all the year round, even for one who loves the country.

Mr. C. K. Sharpe, who inclined to this opinion, was one of my frequent visitors in 1814. He did not quite approve my long pedestrian excursions, but oftentimes during the golden light of the autumnal sun, we had protracted rambles through the old town ; not rambles, exactly speaking, for we went al-ways in quest of houses haunted, where ghosts either had been or might be expected ; or to search after the remains of such mansions as had actually been inhabited by the so-called great and powerful in days of lang syne. I have met with few lit-erary characters, if any, so thoroughly versed as Mr. Sharpe in the history and antiquities of Scotland and England, in which respect he sometimes proved a valuable auxiliary to Scott, by giving him the required evidence *viva voce,* and at once ; so saving the trouble of opening even a single volume.

It was then, and I suppose is, Mr. Sharpe's peculiar fancy that every object around him (in his own house I mean) should remind of past ages, and of those only. His favorite room was fitted up with tapestry in the style of the sixteenth century, leaving, however, one compartment for miniature paintings, each of which had its appropriate legend. The chairs, the tables, and every article on the latter were in keeping. The last visiting cards, the last letters arrived by post, or last notes of invitation to dinner were not to be seen. Any missives, or other manuscripts, mixed with the antique pocket-books and snuff-boxes had all been traced by fingers long since mouldering in the grave. His own handwriting was like an autograph from the days of George Buchanan. With these appliances, and his very sincere love of legendary lore, Mr. Sharpe's own views were very peculiar. At all times he delighted most in the ludicrous, the grotesque, and sarcastic ; seemingly his leading drift was to prove how completely the world was made up of ridiculous humbug in former ages, also that radically speaking it was not one jot better now. But of course he could move with more alacrity and freedom on the former tack than the latter, and his conversation afforded an infinite fund of entertainment, portrait succeeding to portrait, the quaintest revivals from the *soumités* of society, long passed away into the realm of shadows. To one who wished to banish cares and escape from himself, Mr. Sharpe was consequently an inestimable companion, and as such, he has my gratitude for many cheerful hours.

" BLACKWOOD'S MAGAZINE."

Literary men are apt to mark epochs in their lives by the appearance of this or that remarkable publication, just as a politician dates from the occurrence of some desperate cabal in the House, or from the outbreak of a war. I think it was towards the close of the year 1817 that a sort of warfare did break out at Edinburgh, in a very whimsical manner, having for its indirect cause the emergence of the first number of " Blackwood's Magazine." And truly this afforded, in its way, as notable an illustration of our then existing state of society, as any that I have yet adduced in these memoranda. My good friend, the Ettrick Shepherd, had often talked to me on the propriety and duty of establishing a new monthly miscellany to supersede that of Constable, which dragged on a sort of dead and alive existence, having no attractions for any class of readers under the sun. And he very properly insisted that the new journal ought to be a "bold, uncompromising, *out-spoken* work, having on all points originality, freedom, and freshness of style to recommend it." Among the Shepherd's acquaintances and cronies from the Forest was the late Thomas Pringle, author of divers meritorious poems, a young man of excellent literary tact, and of most amiable disposition, mild, persevering, patient, and industrious, who, on the strength principally of his own patience — fortitude without fortune — determined to establish a new Edinburgh magazine. Too truly, he could not manage this alone, but he was on good terms with divers brethren of the quill ; moreover, he had a colleague whose name I think (but am not sure) was Cleghorn ; a burly man, with a strong voice and very dictatorial manner, who was, or had been, editor of the "Farmer's Magazine." [Both of them had the misfortune to be incurably lame, Pringle skipping about briskly on crutches ; his friend, I think, seldom moved from his chair.] The former was of course to represent the "Dichter," the latter the "Weltmann" of the plot. At my friend Hogg's suggestion, I had some interviews with these worthies, at which Pringle, with great complacency, pointed to a large square box as the treasury, into which, from time to time, he had been depositing materials.

I wrote for them a long paper which was forthwith printed, namely, a review in favor of Hogg's "Dramatic Tales," just then published, and which, with all their faults, I thought and still think, a very marvelous demonstration of the Shepherd's powers. I believe the new magazine went so far as two numbers under the management of Messrs. Pringle and Cleghorn, without making any great sensation, Mr. Blackwood having all the while been hatching his own notions about a magazine, and quietly taking measures to realize them. In his views and plans, whatsoever they were, the two editors did by no means agree. The burly man could dictate willingly enough, but would not submit to dictatorship of the bookseller, in consequence of which a quarrel very naturally arose, and Mr. Blackwood suddenly announced his own " Edinburgh Magazine," to be managed of course according to his own judgment, with a determination that he would declare war against the principles of the " Edinburgh Review, ' indeed against the whole race of Edinburgh Whigs ; moreover, that he would treat with sarcasm and contempt not only the defeated editors, but every author, or authorling, who had presumed to offer him advice or contributions without being competent thereto ; contempt, in short, for all except the chosen few with whom he had privately concerted his plans.

The privacy was kept up for some time, though little or no precaution was used for that purpose. People wondered where the pens had so long lain inert which were now used all of a sudden with such vivacity and acrimony. Where, indeed, were his authors ? Visibly and personally they made no manifestations, for the young men who frequented his readingroom did nothing there but, as Cowper said of himself and Thurlow, "giggle, or make giggle." They came seemingly to toss about the newspapers, and pass their jokes on the magazine, its publisher, and on all the world. In this pleasant vein was jotted down a certain "fragment from an ancient Chaldee manuscript" of which Hogg used to claim the paternity ; a production now as utterly forgotten, I suppose, as if it really belonged to the Chaldean repertories, but which (no doubt to the amazement of its facetious authors) raised such a commotion at Edinburgh, that nothing like it was on record in our literary annals. This notable fragment was a kind of allegory than which, in all ages, no style of composition has been found more forcible and *frappant*. The unfortunate editors " skipping upon staves," also Mr. Constable and the Whigs were sascastically indicated ; and the rejected advisers and contributors were all designated as " beasts," who came one after another like a series of monsters *a la* Teniers, clamoring and babbling round a " man in plain apparel," namely, William Blackwood, who at last addressed them in a speech commencing, "O ye beasts!" of which I forget the substance. It was truly a most laughable *jeu d'esprit*, every hit being intelligible to a select few, whilst the portraits were nevertheless so grotesque and shadowy, and the whole so evidently intended for a harmless joke, that the worthies indicated, had they been wise, might either have joined in the laugh, or treated the matter with silent contempt; but on the contrary, all without exception took offense, and some commenced actions in the Court of Session, and got judgments in their favor for injuries done to their reputation!

Meanwhile the new magazine flourished beyond all precedent, and beyond expectation. Every one talked of it, from the wise and learned judges on the bench, who gave their decisions in defense of "the beasts," down to shopkeepers and other people who had never read a new book till then. For in those days, literary journals published as now at a penny a week, and yet supported by men of genius, were not even dreamt of. (Alas! we may well say in England, *die kunst nach brod geht*, in plain language, genius starves.) Blackwood's first number was immediately bought up, and a new edition issued, from which, however, the fire-brand "Chaldee" was prudentially excluded. But by this exclusion the prevalent taste of our amiable public was put to the test. Every purchaser expected to have his copy of the far-famed satire, and every one growled at its absence. Copies of the original number were handed about with manuscript notes, identifying the principal characters, and high prices were occasionally offered for a copy which the fortunate possessor had read and could dispense with. Never, in short, had there been such an uproar made about a scrap of literary *babillage* since the days of Jonathan Swift, and scarcely then.

That this was a lucky and unexpected mode of getting notoriety, a proof also by what means an enlightened public might in future be attracted, is very obvious. It is equally obvious, however, that the Chaldean Shepherd was but the Merry Andrew of the plot; and without originality, strength, vivacity, and freshness in the serious contributions, the un-

precedented success of this new journal would have been impossible. It told best of all with discriminating readers who
cared not a rush about the "Chaldee Manuscript," though
those of course were few in number; but Mr. Blackwood was
thus "*utrumque paratus*" for the gossiping majority and the
rational minority of readers. By whom were such various and
unexpected productions written? The mystification about unknown authors and a "veiled editor" was for some time very
easily kept up; and as Mr. Blackwood ostensibly managed
everything, and was his own Coryphæus, the editor might
wear the mask as long as he thought proper. Mr. John Wilson and Mr. J. G. Lockhart were on amicable terms with the
publisher; but seemingly they had no leisure to write, being
otherwise employed. It is very needless to add that eventually the mystification, accidental at first, was, like that of the
Waverley authorship, abandoned.

Mr. Wilson, however, complained from the outset that the
new magazine, notwithstanding its double columns, allowed
no sufficient space for authors to develop their thoughts.
Either the articles must be left imperfect, or there would be
a want of variety; and instead of desiderating good Mr. Pringle's stores of reserved *copy*, he very decisively maintained
that any man in a state of tolerable health, and disposed for
literary amusement, might write an entire number in the course
of two days! He it was who recommended carrying on the
same article in chapters from one month to another, and would
print all poetical extracts in diamond type (against which Mr.
Mackenzie vehemently protested), and occasionally would
have a double number when the stores of unused materials became too cumbersome and extensive. Moreover, Mr. Wilson
ab initio took possession of an enormous ledger, originally intended for very different records, and soon filled the volume
with so-called "skeletons," any one of which he could select
at will, clothe with muscle and nerve, and call into life and
action. Thus, betwixt him and Mr. Lockhart, a preposter-
ously long list was announced of articles already written and
accepted by the editor, many of which, though "putative,"

then, did afterwards appear. As a Lilliputian jest, may be recorded, that being honored in the list with the paternity of a " Sonnet on seeing a spark fall from the Shepherd's pipe," I forthwith wrote the before hypothetical sonnet, and in the next number it was printed, along with a strange figure of a tobacco-smoker from an old wooden block, in good keeping with the grotesque verses.

Of a work so well known, and still flourishing, though in a very different phasis, I need say no more at present. In those early days of its progress, it naturally gave rise to many pleasant meetings, and proved a source of great amusement and hilarity to its supporters, still more, I fancy, than at any time in after years when its character had become firmly established. Mr. Wilson had then a rapidity of executive power in composition, such as I have never seen equaled before nor since. In that way he might be said to realize even the wonders which are ascribed to Lope de Vega. But as he would do nothing but when he liked and how he liked, his productions, whether serious or comic, might all be regarded as mere *jeux d'esprit* and matters of amusement. Mr. Lockhart, I suppose, was more systematic in his pursuits, though his rapidity of pen was also marvelous. I remember he considered thirty-two columns (a whole printed sheet) as an ordinary day's work, which might be accomplished without the slightest fatigue or stress. At this rate he could well have leisure to spare for other divertisements, and, to a superficial observer, might have appeared at all times quite sufficiently occupied with his portfolio of caricatures, and now and then a law paper, not to reckon his never-failing meerschaum and Maracaibo.

LORD JEFFREY.

Among the public characters who were always to be met with at our balls and routs in those days, out of sight and comparison, the most distinguished was Mr. Jeffrey. To every one who appreciated his talents, the wonder was, how he could reconcile his mode of life in this respect with his literary and professional engagements. But that he did so was very cer-

tain. He seemed the gayest of the gay. He was invited everywhere, tried to make his appearance everywhere, and, on all
such occasions his popularity (if possible) increased.

During these records, I have repeatedly pleaded the necessity of retirement and quiet, as indispensably necessary for the
well-being and advancement of the literary character. Mr.
Jeffrey, however, set this rule utterly at defiance. To all appearance he cared not a rush about habits of consecutive application. No one could guess what portion of *his* day was ap-
propriated to literary tasks, nor indeed could have imagined
that he really had any such tasks on hand. In the mornings,
from nine till two, he was on parade, and professionally employed at the Parliament House. Thereafter, till dinner-time,
weather permitting, he walked out or promenaded on horse-
back. Never did it happen for a single day during the season,
that he had not divers invitations both for dinner and evening
parties. Of the former it is needless to say, he could accept
only one *per diem ;* but it was quite possible during the evening, to migrate from one rout to another ; and this he often
did, winding up, of course, where the supper party was the
most attractive and congenial.

Dugald Stewart must have his quiet home, his ample store
of old folios and quartos, and his view of the Calton Hill rocks,
otherwise he was but half a man ! Sir Walter Scott also clung
to the *idéal* of home ; he must have his antiquarian repertories
and his library neatly arranged wherein he could find any volume and consult it at a moment's warning. Never did any fox-
hunter or wild *roué* trample more disdainfully on all such notions than Mr. Jeffrey ! He had third-rate apartments in a
" *land*" situated in Queen Street, where, exclusive of the necessary law books and the very newest publications, his entire
library consisted of a few motley tatterdemalion volumes, for
all the world likest to a set of worn-out school-books, and such
perhaps they really were. Truly there appeared no great
charm in that home to render it an object of attachment and
affection. Its arrangements were not symmetrical nor indicated much attention to comfort. The looking-glass over the

chimney piece remains yet in my remembrance, because within and under its tarnished frame were located a preposterous multitude of visiting cards and notes of invitation, which showered on him from all quarters, "thick as the leaves in Vallambrosa."

From all this and other traits which I might adduce, who could have imagined that the gay young barrister was in truth the most adventurous and successful student in town, the very man of all our Athenian world who was most ready and able to grapple with a difficult question, to torture and twist it by the process of analysis and reasoning, till gleams of light the most unexpected were thrown upon the subject ; and who, when his reader or hearer thought that no more could possibly be done, would start again *de novo*, not merely with unabated but increased vivacity, adding more and more of patient argument and brilliant illustration, till at last a so-styled essay (alias reviewal) came forth, comprising materials that might serve as texts for future volumes.

This was not comprehensible, yet was nevertheless true. *When* did he elaborate his papers ! There was only one way of accounting for it — the old suggestion as applied in the case of Chatterton, that he did not sleep, but could betake himself to work with undiminished zeal when the day's work of the world was done. It would be rather too hypothetical to suppose that he possessed a duality of mind, and could persist in arranging silently a critical argument with one, whilst with the other he managed a nonsensical conversation at the supper table. However, there was one leading peculiarity in Jeffrey's character, which perhaps rendered time of some value in his case, that would otherwise have been lost ; I mean the grace and alacrity wherewith, if opportunity offered, he could turn ordinary conversation to account. If the most commonplace remark were tendered on a subject in itself interesting, he would rapidly reply with an illustration as original as it was unexpected. And if his superficial neighbor luckily ventured to differ from him in opinion, then he would rouse and present the matter in a hundred new lights (if needful) so as to carry his point. And this argument taking its rise, perhaps, from a mere platitude in the course of ordinary table-talk, or during a walk to Corstorphin Hill, might dwell on his remembrance, and if committed afterwards to writing serve for the commencement of a leading article.

REV. CHARLES MATURIN.

One of my favorite and most cherished authors was the Rev. Charles Maturin, author of " Montorio," the " Wild Irish Boy," the " Milesian," " Melmoth the Wanderer," the " Albigenses," " Bertram," a tragedy, the " Universe," a poem, and divers other works. I reckon up their names because I suspect that in this age of iron, even his own name is nearly obliterated. He was indeed like a meteor, whose light passes over a drowsy world, by some few watched and wondered at, but by the majority unappreciated or altogether unnoticed.

Sir Walter Scott and Lord Kinnedder were among the few who watched that light ; in plainer terms, they perceived that Maturin had extraordinary power, which properly disciplined and encouraged might raise him to a high grade in the literary world. For my own part, I thought and felt convinced that his romances were not only something quite new, but in their original strength unequaled. It seemed to me a matter almost of indifference what was the story of Maturin's book, provided only it afforded him situations of anxiety and distress. It was in the pertinacious details, the relentless force with which the author conceived and imparted emotions of gloom, and suffering, and despondency, that his principal merit consisted. Up to the present hour I think that in this department he is unrivaled, unless it be by Godwin in certain portions of "Caleb Williams " and "St. Leon." However, our enlightened public were not over partial to such productions. Maturin, with his wild romances and tragedies, found himself in a sphere where travesties and farces would have succeeded far better, but he had chosen his walk, and excelled in it. Consequently, though he gained no pecuniary profits by " Montorio" and the " Wild Irish Boy," yet Mr. Colburn did at last venture the vast sum

of £80 for the "Milesian," and I suppose somewhat accrued
to him also for " Melmoth" and the " Albigenses."

But in short, Maturin, notwithstanding his extraordinary
powers, scarcely gained by all his productions (" Bertram" excepted) so much as would maintain his family in comfort for a
single year. So true it is that poverty perpetuates poverty,
and that in order to secure favor with the British public, one
must be completely independent of its frowns or smiles.

Sir Walter Scott usually received £8000 at least, instead of
£80 for a single romance ; and even in this age of iron, Sir E.
Bulwer Lytton can draw £1600 for a production, which however meritorious, if brought into the market by a poor man,
would not even find a publisher bold enough to defray the expense of printing.

Not being personally acquainted with Maturin, I have introduced him principally for the sake of reviving once more a
circumstance which at the time made a deep impression on my
mind. All the world of authors in those days aimed at correspondence with Sir Walter Scott, and among the rest Maturin,
by a letter in which he described himself as an " obscure Irish-
man," desirous to learn from the highest authority whether
there might be any chance that booksellers in the " Modern
Athens" would afford him that encouragement and support
which he had vainly sought in his own country and at London.
Is there any *one* eminent author of our present epoch who,
mutatis mutandis, would return a kind and considerate answer
to such a letter ? (I think I do know *one* such, but not more !)
Very certain it is, however, that Walter Scott replied in the
most friendly terms, and as he did not see any immediate way
of driving a bargain with the only publisher at Edinburgh who
had either money or credit, his letter inclosed £50 as a
" trifling " token of his esteem and sympathy, and as a temporary stop-gap till times should grow better.

My reader will hardly suspect me of attaching over importance to a gift of £50. No ; it was the *animus*, the kind and
brotherly sentiment that prompted and accompanied the gift,
which dwelt in my recollection, as an illustrative *trait* of a

character admirable in all the relations of life. The circumstance, trifling in itself, probably never would have been known, had it not been for my anxious wish and earnest request to see the handwriting of Maturin, in compliance with which Scott one day put into my hands the only letters of his which he had then received.

The correspondence thus begun was continued in after years. The original MS. of the once popular tragedy of "Bertram" was transmitted to Sir Walter Scott for consideration, and by him intrusted to me in order that I might return it with a well-pondered decisive opinion ! It was then of great length, and more like a German dramatic poem of the "romantic school" than a tragedy for the English stage. A certain "black knight of the forest" was made to act a very important part, being the manager and instigator of that series of crimes which are perpetrated within a few hours. I delighted in this "black knight," and would rather that the poem should never be tried on the stage at all, than part with him ; a decision which greatly diverted Sir Walter Scott.

"Perhaps you have overlooked," said he, "that our friend in Dublin has neither 'two gowns' to keep him warm, nor any patrimonial acres to rest upon. His object decidedly is to have 'Bertram' brought on the stage, in order that it may succeed there and make money. Now, the 'black knight,' saving your presence, being in plain terms the devil, there is great reason to doubt whether our very wise and respectable public will quietly endure his appearance under any name. They will probably think that his introduction on the boards is taking much too great a liberty either with him or with them, and in either case will feel offended, so that the performance, *malgré* all its merits, will be condemned and lost."

The fate of this production is somewhat remarkable. John Kemble did condescend to read it, and as it violently trangressed what he considered indispensable rules of propriety, he ruthlessly judged that it should be committed to the flames. He was at one and the same time quite in the right and quite in the wrong. Eventually the devil, *alias* "black knight," was cashiered, the drama condensed within moderate bounds, and accepted for the stage ; where, with Kean's help as hero (who cared not a rush about John Kemble's rules of propriety), it had an extraordinary run, and brought £400 or £500 to the author.

In this manner Fortune made a run-away knock at his door, leaving with him, it is true, the aforesaid temporary notice of her favor, whereupon Maturin launched out as if he had at last struck upon the right vein of an inexhaustible mine. He did not precisely think that the sum of £500 was inexhaustible, but felt extremely sure that, before it was all spent, he could prepare another drama quite as good as the former. And he did so, but our wise public would not have it at any price ; it was not condemned, but it failed nevertheless, and during the short remainder of his days Fortune too evidently had forgotten him altogether. I believe she never came to his door again.

SIR BROOKE BOOTHBY.

At Edinburgh, Sir Brooke's habits were insulated and secluded — in his own phrase, he had done with the world, and his best philosophy seemed to consist in forgetting it altogether. He had moved for some part of his life among the gayest of the gay — he now saw no one but the Duke and Duchess of Hamilton, Lord Buchan, and Mr. (now Sir George) Sinclair, who all sought after him in his retirement. According to my peculiar notions, Sir Brooke was the most interesting of all characters whom I had yet met with, seeing that he lived for his literary pursuits alone, perfectly heedless of the world's opinion, or what became of his productions, and might truly say, " *labor ipsa voluptas erat.*" Over and above all this must be remembered his being the author of poems which in a particular department of the art are, for exquisite melody, classical correctness, and pathos, quite unrivaled : I mean the folio collection entitled, " Sorrows sacred to the Memory of Penelope."

Sir Brooke's mode of life was thought eccentric at Edinburgh ; he usually retired to rest at eight or nine o'clock ;

he rose invariably and breakfasted, both summer and winter, betwixt four and five ; he dined at two, and having finished his literary tasks before dinner, usually betook himself thereafter to his water-color drawings. This division of time was the same which he had adopted long ago at Weimar ; where, instead of being eccentric, it was in perfect accordance with general habits in that capital. But when I first knew him, he was not the slave of habit, but at my intercession would occasionally accept an invitation to dinner at six, when his unaffected manners and genial spirit completely triumphed for the moment over that prejudice which his recluse life naturally excited in our enlightened but censorious " modern Athens."

My first acquaintance with Sir Brooke arose from the accidental circumstance that I was called on, at the Speculative Society, to open a debate about the war against the French republic, in 1792, and wished especially to obtain an argumentative pamphlet which he published at the period in question. I applied to him accordingly, but the author could as easily have resuscitated the archives of King Cheops from the pyramids, as any of his own productions. After they were composed and finished they drifted from his grasp, and he thought of them no more. But the pamphlet was eventually found at the Advocates' Library ; and for my behoof at the moment, Sir Brooke, with great readiness and good-humor, noted down the principal arguments against the commencement of that war, which had for twenty years continued to rage ; arguments in the truth of which he had as unalterable confidence in 1811 as he had in 1790.

Sir Brooke was an admirable critic, and cultivated literature in all its branches, those only of the physical and exact sciences excepted. But he now wrote only *pour se distraire*, or as a sedative ; therefore troubled himself little with original composition. After publishing at Edinburgh two volumes of metrical fables, he gave himself *con amore* to a new translation of Horace, in which he made daily unremitting progress. He undertook the task, I suppose, for the sake of its difficulty ;

and as to the question when it would be completed and published (or if ever) felt perfectly indifferent. Indeed, to have reflected on that point would have argued some regard for the goings on of the outward world, which, as already said, he preferred to forget altogether. He seemed to move in it, but kept all the while conveniently aloof and in a sphere of his own.

Sir Brooke's personal memoirs, had he thought of writing them, would doubtless have been interesting, for he had seen much of so-called "life," in its varieties, firstly in his early days at Lausanne and Geneva, where he made acquaintance with the far-famed literati of those romantic regions, but more especially with Rousseau, in whose character he preferred to select all the favorable traits, such as they were, and subdued the bad into shade. This preference, as he owned, had arisen from his having first perused the now-forgotten "Heloise," in the midst of that scenery to which the author so eloquently refers, and been thereby so favorably impressed that he could as little forget the book as the woods, lakes, and mountains of Lausanne. Secondly, during his life in London, after his return from the Continent, at which period his accomplishments and steadfast adherence to the liberal party brought him into *rapport* with the most distinguished members of the literary and political world. At that time, also, he was looked up to and courted by the fantastic literary club at Lichfield, among whom (or rather among their visitors) he failed not to select Dr. Cary, the translator of Dante, as a character of a different stamp and of sterling worth. Thirdly, after his return to the Continent, when he visited divers German courts, sojourning longest at Weimar, where he was in habits of daily intercourse with Goethe, who spoke to me of Sir Brooke with the kindest and liveliest recollection twenty-six years afterwards. Among the various eccentric or eminent characters with whom he had been especially well acquainted abroad and at home, were Queen Caroline, Lord Nelson, and Lady Hamilton. The longest letters I ever happened to meet with in Nelson's own hand-writing were those addressed by him to

Sir Brooke, sometimes followed up by a postscript in a sad scrawling style from "Maria."

Characters which are in themselves the most decided and unaffected are of course the least liable to be changed and deteriorated by advancing age. Sir Brooke had retired from the world without sourness or misanthropy, and in his retreat he was as ready to be attracted by any new literary work, or to shout *vivat* in favor of any modern author as the youngest of his few associates. Accordingly, he had taken great interest in the progress of Sir Walter Scott, and readily accepted my proposal of a meeting *chez moi* at dinner with "our great man," which took place accordingly, and which proved so satisfactory that it led to other meetings of the same convivial character. At my suggestion, too, he accepted an invitation to meet the poet at John Ballantyne's and heartily entered into the humor of the hour, rejoicing specially in the trios and duets which were sung after dinner. No one who knew Sir Walter, will fail to remember his admirable convivial powers, or the quaint good-humor, utterly *sans pretension*, by which these were animated. No sooner had he taken his place at table than by some *naïf* remark, not addressed to any one in particular, he usually effected the utter demolition of "starch," and, without having once in all his life ever *aimed* at saying a "good thing," produced more mirth and joviality than any professional wit or punster ever could. He was so decided an enemy to "starch," or pretension of any kind, that it became invariably decomposed in his presence, and he cared not of what platitudes or "merry-andrada's" he served himself to effect that purpose. Only once, and at his own table, he felt surprised and overthrown. Telling *more suo*, or wishing to tell some brief anecdote from his own stores of recollection, he happened, about mid-way, to interpose the words : "Now whether it occurred from my own stupidity or because " — The break was fatal, and the anecdote to this hour remains untold, for in rushed most unexpectedly- a regular man of starch, a *soi-disant* poet, rejoicing in the euphonious name of ———. "Oh, Sir Walter ! " solemnly exclaimed this worthy, "don't say that ! No one can admit for a moment the plea of *your* stupidity." This was too much. The mighty minstrel changed countenance, drooping his under jaw in a manner that would have done honor to Grimaldi ; but instantly he sought refuge and protection against his literary guest from an honest Leith wine-merchant, who never in his life had perused one page of poetry, earnestly craving from this worthy an opinion as to the merits of a bottle of rare old Madeira, whereupon the critic, applying a Bardolfian nose to the *bouquet,* pronounced favorably, and with great *gusto.* It was easy, then, to begin another yarn, though one story had been strangled, and the man of starch was left alone in his glory.

Of course it was impossible to live at Edinburgh and overlook the genius of Scott ; but not till after the year 1814, except by extracts, did Sir Brooke become acquainted with Wordsworth. During one of our many walks together, he inquired whether I did not think that his poems were often childish, and their subjects very ill-chosen; to which I answered sweepingly that one subject was as good as another in the hands of a veritable poet, and that to resuscitate the feelings and impressions of childhood, and to perpetuate youth, was an important duty. Two or three days thereafter Sir Brooke gave me a MS., entitled "Second Childhood ; or Exercises of a Neophyte in the New School." The said exercises were twofold, first a long poem, in heroic numbers, detailing minutely how the author in a morning ramble met with a juvenile chimney sweeper, who gazed wistfully upon a basket of herrings, whereupon after a train of reflection and inquiries, Sir Brooke produced a penny, and presented three of the best silvercoats to the hungry youth. Secondly, a most laughable ode respecting childhood, which commenced : —

> " Bring, oh bring the cap and bells,
> Stuck with daffodil and daisy;"

and of which I remember only four other lines, as follows : —

> " Namby pamby, dally dilly !
> Never let your thoughts aspire !

> Wisdom lies in being silly ;
> Man was made for nothing higher."

With these travesties, no one was more heartily diverted than the great poet himself, when he found them some years afterwards in an album at my house. I had, and ought *to have*, a large collection of Sir Brooke's MSS., but they have drifted out of my reach, and not through my own neglect, but that of unfaithful custodiars. Among them were two sonnets addressed to my unworthy self, one of which began : —

> " Alas ! good youth, my parts you overrate ;
> Old bosoms glow not with poetic fire ;
> Untuned, neglected hangs my silent lyre,
> Petrarch's sad strains no more to modulate."

But by way of contrast, and in order to prove how truly Sir Brooke deserves to be commemorated and honored among our *very best* poets, I need only refer to the now rare volume already mentioned, namely, " Sorrows Sacred to his Daughter's Memory," printed by Bulmer, 1796, with engravings from designs by Fuseli and Flaxman. I shall quote only two of the sonnets, all of which are eminently beautiful, and excepting that they terminate in couplets are written in strict accordance with the Petrarchan model.

NIGHT THOUGHTS.

> " 'T is midnight. All lies hushed in dread repose.
> Troubled with dreams I leave my restless bed,
> To seek the silent mansions of the dead,
> Sad, soothing scenes, congenial to my woes.
> The moon her melancholy lustre throws
> O'er the dim yews, that darkest shadows spread
> Where Sorrow rests in peace her weary head.
> And the still heart nor joy nor anguish knows.
> — 'T was but the wind that sighed among the leaves ; —
> No plaintive murmur issued from the tomb ;
> There with no pang the tranquil bosom heaves,
> Nor hope, nor love, nor grief, nor memory come.
> Open, O earth, thy hospitable breast ;
> Stretch thy cold arms ; receive another guest !

A RELIQUE.

> " Bright crisped threads of pure translucent gold,
> Ye who were wont with zephyr's breath to play,

O'er the warm cheek and ivory forehead stray,
Or clasp her neck in many an amorous fold,
Now motionless this little shrine must hold,
  No more to wanton in the eye of day
  Or to the breeze your changing hues display,
Forever still, inanimate and cold.
Poor, poor, last relic of an angel face, —
  Sad, setting ray, no more thy orb is seen ;
Oh, beauty's pattern, miracle of grace,
  Must this be all, that tells what thou hast been ?
Come then, cold crystal, on this bosom lie,
Till love, and grief, and fond remembrance die ! "

I believe that in the whole range of English poetry, there could not be found a sonnet more affecting or more musical than this !

THOMAS DE QUINCEY.

During the winter of 1815–16 (or the next) Mr. De Quincey accompanied his friend, the author of the "Isle of Palms," from Westmoreland to Edinburgh. I had then an opportunity of observing the literary character in an entirely new phasis, for up to that time, De Quincey, though he had spent long years in assiduous study, and by his friends was regarded as a powerful author, had not, so far as I know, published a single line. He seemed, indeed, to live for the sake of the labor alone, and fling overboard all considerations either of the *palma* or *pecunia.* His various literary compositions, written in his exemplary hand (the best I ever saw, except Southey's) on little scraps of paper, must have reached to a great extent, but in his own estimation they were by no means "ready for the press ; " like an over-cautious general, he withheld his fire, and remained " *multa et pulchra minans.*" Not only for this reason, but in other respects Mr. De Quincey seemed to me to bring out the literary character in a new light. Very decisively he realized my plan of moving in a separate world (having no doubt realities of its own) ; moreover, he neither spoke nor acted in the every-day world like any one else, for which, of course, I greatly honored him. He was then in the habit of taking opium daily as an article of food, and the drug, though used for years, had scarcely *begun* to tell on his constitution, by those effects which, sooner or later, overtake every one of its persevering votaries ; and which, when they once appear, make quick work in demolishing together the man physical and the man intellectual ; the latter being reduced to the pitiable plight of a musician who essays to play by means of a harp unstrung and broken. But in his case, it had not worked any such evils as yet, and in after years, though not without a long and tough battle, Mr. De Quincey succeeded in vanquishing the narcotic devil.

His voice was extraordinary ; it came as if from dream-land ; but it was the most musical and impressive of voices. In convivial life, what then seemed to me the most remarkable trait of De Quincey's character was the power he possessed of easily changing the tone of ordinary thought and conversation into that of his own dream-land, till his auditors, with wonder, found themselves moving pleasantly along with him in a sphere of which they might have heard and read, perhaps, but which had ever appeared to them inaccessible, and far, far away ! Seeing that he was always good-natured and social, he would take part, at commencement, in any sort of tattle or twaddle. The talk might be of "beeves," and he could grapple with them if expected to do so, but his musical cadences were not in keeping with such work, and in a few minutes (not without some strictly logical sequence) he could escape at will from beeves to butterflies, and thence to the soul's immortality, to Plato, and Kant, and Schelling, and Fichte, to Milton's early years and Shakespeare's sonnets, to Wordsworth and Coleridge, to Homer and Eschylus, to St. Thomas of Aquin, St. Basil, and St. Chrysostom. But he by no means excluded themes from real life, according to his own views of that life, but would recount profound mysteries from his own experiences — visions that had come over him in his loneliest walks among the mountains, and passages within his own personal knowledge, illustrating, if not proving, the doctrines of dreams, of warnings, of second-sight, and mesmerism. And whatsoever the subject might be, every one of his sentences (or of his chapters I might say) was woven into the most perfect logical texture, and uttered in a tone of sustained melody.

Such powers and acquirements could not fail to excite wonder at Edinburgh. He had, indeed, studied " all such books as are never read " in that enlightened capital, and was the first friend I had ever met who could profess to have command over the German language, and who consequently was able (*ex cathedrâ*) to corroborate my notions of the great stores that were contained therein. I flatter myself that he found our house not altogether uncongenial, as he was kind enough to visit there more frequently than in any other.

JOHN KEMBLE.

In praise of Edinburgh as a place of residence, memory affords me an illustration which my reader will probably think more acceptable than such verses, namely, the predilection shown for it by John Kemble, on his retirement from the stage. Instead of living in lodgings as heretofore, he took a good family house, in Heriot Row, and remained with us for six months ; during which time, notwithstanding his hydropathic regimen, he enjoyed the best health and spirits. During my long experience, I have never met with any character more original, decided, and *naïf*, than that of John Kemble. In those respects, assuredly, he might be compared to an old Roman hero of the very best stamp, insomuch that had not accidental circumstances directed his attention to the stage, the same talents and energy of purpose which he manifested there would, doubtless, have raised him to high rank in some other department. Even under adversity he would have been dignified, self-possessed, and distinguished. It was wholly impossible to imagine that under any circumstances, or whatsoever had been his chosen pursuit, he could have subsided into a phasis of mediocrity. Of Garrick it was said, by Goldsmith, —

> " On the stage, always natural, simple, affecting ;
> 'T was never but when he was off he was acting."

This could not with any truth be applied to Kemble. His taciturnity among strangers, his impressive, slow, measured enunciation, his dignity of demeanor were all unaffected and

natural. He was no Proteus like Garrick, consequently the
parts which he enacted willingly and *con amore* were few in
number, and I am sure he could not have laid aside his own
peculiar manner without painful effort, which after all would
not have been successful. Even the Ettrick Shepherd was
not more free from affectation than John Kemble! He had
formed one leading purpose, namely, the study of Shakespeare's heroes, and to this labor of love he found no end ; he
was deepening his own conceptions and striving to improve
his own performance even to the last. The result, as all the
world knows, was indeed admirable and unequaled. Coriola-
nus could not despise the mob of Rome more than the great
actor despised all considerations, excepting that of rendering
justice to his author. Hence his superior and imperturbable
dignity. He was an artist of the highest order, and according
to nature, even as Shakespeare himself had been, and in this
capacity might have riveted attention by his intellectual energy and modulation of voice alone, even if, instead of possess-
ing great personal advantages, he had been comparatively a
dwarf.

I suppose it would have been impossible in all the world to
discover two men, of the same profession, more utterly dissimilar on all points than Kemble and Kean. The Lear and Cor-
iolanus of the former are the parts that dwell indelibly on my
remembrance as unequaled. In both of these Kean signally
failed ; his performance of Lear was in comparison a mere
travestie, whereas in Shylock, or Sir Giles Overreach, he
found a part suitable to him, and unquestionably produced
great effect.

Kemble's intense study of Shakespeare naturally led him to
pursuits of literature and bibliography. He heartily loved old
books for divers reasons, and specially because among such
he could find illustrations of his favorite author. Besides, he
had in early life brought away with him from Douay or St.
Omer a much better education than usually falls to the lot of
Catholic emigrants there ; in other words, he profited more
than his companions by the opportunities offered. And if he

had taken to authorship (luckily for himself he did not!) I feel sure that he would have risen to eminence; but his literary labor, like his acting, would have been confined to some peculiar vein, from which, by indefatigable perseverance, he would have extracted the purest gold. As matters stood he read far more than he wrote, and took to composition only as an amusement. He was a most rigorous and unrelenting critic, sparing himself least of all; for when employed on his little volume of essays, dedicated to the Duke of Northumberland, it seemed as if he never would have allowed it to emerge through the press to the public eye. He weighed every word, accent, and comma. In truth, his fastidiousness seemed then to act as a torpedo on his faculties; and I suppose a popular author of the present day could scribble up a three volume novel with less of care and pains than Kemble bestowed on this little *brochure.*

In ordinary life, ignorant observers of course utterly mistook the great actor's character, and they were allowed, properly enough, to remain in their ignorance; for he was excessively averse to making new acquaintances, and kept himself aloof under the shield of courteous taciturnity. From his apparent formality of manners, they thought that, like Garrick, he was always acting, and from his natural reserve and dignity of demeanor, they supposed that he was on special good terms with himself, and looked on everybody *de haut en bas.* How different was the truth! Contemptuous and disdainful he might be, but there was nothing he held more in contempt than starch and pretension. Even to the last a persevering student, he was his own severe task-master, and could have had but little room left in his mind for arrogance. *Malgré* the convivial enjoyments of his early years, he was a man of domestic habits and the simplest manners. On theatrical days he dined at two, then reclined, perhaps slumbered, till five or six, when Mrs. Kemble awakened him for coffee; thereafter dressed, and wrapt in his cloak, was driven to the stage door. Instead of being an austere formalist, he was one of the quaintest of humorists. Some, who only recollect his foibles, will think that I have said more than enough in praise of our great actor ; but every one who knew him, will agree that on all points he showed decision of character, and that as a friend he might be relied on for sincere kindness of heart and steadfast integrity.

It is very needless to say how much his retirement from the stage was regretted and deprecated at Edinburgh, more especially as his professional powers were unimpaired ; but his plans were already fixed. One morning, when Sir Walter Scott happened to call in Heriot Row, and was received by Mrs. Kemble, the question arose of his composing a few lines to be spoken as a farewell address, to which the poet replied, that though the will was not wanting, it seemed to him inevitable that in writing King John's farewell to the public, he should painfully feel that he also was bidding farewell to an old friend. Such feelings could not be tagged into rhymes ; therefore, he would not even promise to make a trial, being so very sure that he would fail in the undertaking. Within a short time, however, I believe the very next morning, Mrs. Kemble received the address — one of the most appropriate and beautiful compositions of its kind that has ever appeared.

I am naturally led to dwell on this epoch, because it reminds me of many pleasant hours in social circles. Mr. and Mrs. Kemble now and then dined with us, and also accepted invitations from a very few of our near neighbors whom they met, especially from my kind friend Mr. Alexander Gordon, who entertained profusely — and who then possessed the best private collection of pictures at Edinburgh — pictures which had once hung on the walls of the Colonna palace at Rome. In the mornings, if the weather allowed, " King John " often looked in when I was at my desk, and without more than the words, " Don't mind me ; stick to your day's work," helped himself to a change of old books from my confused shelves, and disappeared. He was careful of books to rigidity, and always placed the returned volumes where he had found them. My visits to him in the morning hours were equally short, for I found him always occupied ; sometimes

L Goethe

(*From Maclise Gallery.*)

with a professor of French, from whom he took lessons for practice and improvement, although the language had been familiar to him from early youth. He rightly judged that to obtain a proper command over a foreign language is a purpose that cannot be realized without persevering attention.

JOHN WOLFGANG VON GOETHE.

My short morning's work was to compose three lines of as good German as I could muster, submitting that a humble student from Edinburgh, after a long journey, wished earnestly for the honor of a brief interview with the greatest of German poets.

Provided with this, and accompanied by my brother-in-law, Capt. James Macdonell, I betook myself to the "statesman's" house, a sort of mansion such as a Duke's handsteward, in England, certainly would not have considered very *distingué*. The time was about eleven o'clock, and the valet in attendance intimated that his master was dressing; however, he would present my *billet*. Almost instantly he returned, and with a profound obeisance desired that we should walk into the saloon, where his Excellency would join us after a few minutes.

We had time enough to wonder at the absence of all luxurious or costly appliances in the *salle de reception*. Some few busts and statues there were, it is true, also a grand pianoforte or, as I rather think, it was a harpsichord, from the days of Werther and Charlotte, and of course there were chairs and a table with some few books. But, alas! the dark oak floor was uncarpeted, and if we had a feeling of cold even at midsummer, what must have been the atmosphere of that room in a dreary winter's day, even supposing that the stove had its due supply of wood and turf? Truly, it was evident enough that the poets of Germany were not more fastidious, on the question of "comfort," than were in days of yore the stout heroes of the so-called Reformation.

I have elsewhere recorded the impressions made by an interview with Goethe, and can scarcely do any better than re-

peat my former words, namely, that in figure, contour of features, mode of speech (or penchant to taciturnity), and demeanor,
he bore a certain indefinable resemblance to John Kemble ; I
have said indefinable, because it amounted merely to this —
that one reminded of the other. There were wide discrep-
ancies.   Firstly, Kemble did not live to be old, and besides,
his countenance, even in age, would not have been so deeply
marked by the wear and tear of thought as Goethe's.   No
doubt, a *good* portrait of the latter, if given to Lavater without
any name, would have served as materials for a long chapter.
The forehead, eyes, and eyebrows alone, would have been
enough for several pages.   Now as the door opened from the
farther end of the reception-room, and his Excellency's tall,
gaunt form, wrapped in a long, blue surtout, which hung
loosely on him, slowly advanced, he had veritably the air and
aspect of a *revenant.*   His was not an appearance, but an
apparition.   Evidently and unmistakably he had belonged
to another world which had long since passed away ; but
malgré attenuation, and some traces of impaired health (such
as a yellow suffusion of the eyeballs) there were, nevertheless,
indications that the smouldering fire of youth yet lingered in
that gaunt frame, and that though he had belonged to a past
world, he was yet perfectly able to sustain a part in the present.

This was at first rather a perplexing interview, a vehement
contrast to that with Hofrath Müllner, who took his place at
the supper-table and chatted away from the moment of his
entrance.   On the contrary, Goethe advanced in profound
silence, in a mood, seemingly, of utter abstraction, and after
the manner of ghosts in general, he waited to be spoken to !
The spirit had been evoked from his other world, had condescended to appear, and now the question was, what sort of
conversation ought to be, or might be without impropriety, addressed to him ?   The plain truth was, that I had set my heart
on seeing Goethe, but did not for a moment imagine that my
communications could have any interest for him, and in sheer
desperation I contrived to tell him this much, then fortunately

made allusions again to our long journey, and of my great wish to settle somewhere, at Weimar, for example.

As it happened, the best of diplomatists could not have managed better. This was a practical point to which (with a half smile at my broken German) he answered readily, that nothing could be more easy ; Weimar was not over-populous, and he believed that Hoffmann, the court bookseller, was at that moment charged to dispose of a house and garden at a very low rent. To this he added : " In days of yore, there were Englishmen here, who passed their time pleasantly enough, and some of whom I remember with esteem and regret." I ventured to inquire whether Sir Brooke Boothby had been among the chosen few ? This question was a lucky hit, for he immediately fixed his eyes with searching expression, and spoke with animation : —

" I saw more of him," said he, " than of any other English resident, and regretted his departure the most. You know him perhaps ? "

" Very intimately."

" Is he still alive ? "

" I believe so. But he left Scotland in 1815, and since then I have not received any letters from him."

" Sir Brooke was a pleasant neighbor, and friend of mine. *Was hat er bey Ihnen gemacht ?* " (What was he about in Scotland ?)

" He filled up his time after his own fashion — wrote a good deal, especially in verse, dined early, and in the afternoon painted in water-colors."

" Has he ever spoken to you about Weimar ? "

" He told me about his having obtained a commission in the Duke's cavalry, in order to have the privilege of appearing at court in boots instead of silk stockings."

" *Ganz richtig* (very true). His health was not good : he complained of our cold winters, disliked silk stockings, and could ride better than he danced."

This important fact disposed of, I mentioned that Sir Brooke always had beside him a first edition of " Werther,"

20

and a few other German books, from which he had made some translations, and that one of these, the "Genius and the Bayadere," was, at my suggestion, published in the "Edinburgh Annual Register."

"I gave him those books," said his Excellency, "but there was one point of difference betwixt us. He was a good French scholar, but never would take the trouble of studying our language so as to comprehend our best authors. He began zealously — *allein es mangelte ihm an Ausdaur.* (He was wanting in perseverance.) Another of your countrymen, Mr. Mellish, was in that respect more praiseworthy."

I tried to introduce other literary characters, but could only bring him thus far, that he desired to be particularly informed whether Sir Walter Scott had quite recovered his health, to which I replied, that not only had he recovered, but seemed stouter than before ; and that his industry was unequaled and indomitable. I then endeavored to speak of the singular influence that "Faust" and "Wilhelm Meister" had exercised on English authors ; of Lord Byron's debt to the former in "Manfred," and so forth ; but to this his answers were in a tone of perfect indifference. He cared not a staw about praise, and was inaccessible to flattery. About twenty minutes sufficed for our audience ; but he was very courteous at parting, and said he should rejoice to hear that I could meet with an abode at Weimar suitable to my finances and views.

Truly there is little enough in the conversation as recorded above : but I had forgotten to mention that his Excellency was then said to be slowly recovering from a serious illness, and from what we heard afterwards, I had more reason to wonder that he condescended to speak so much than that he said little, for upon such occasions of strangers desiring to see the lion, he was usually very reserved, *nonchalant*, and taciturn.

My own notions of Goethe's character are, perhaps, both erroneous and peculiar ; for it seems to me that in his case, not only was the poet subservient to the man of the world, but that as a poet he has frequently been overrated. For example,

I am unable to think of the "Helena" otherwise than as a *bizarre* mystification ; yet we have heard it called a "philosophy of literature set in poetry" and an "encyclopædia of erudition !" It is not impossible that he may have laughed in his sleeve at the profound views imputed to him, where none such had been intended. As a literary artist and man of various talent, Goethe perhaps is unequaled. If he had enthusiasm, he held it under prudent subjection ; it never became fitful or too fervid. During his long life he seems to have taken especial care that no one faculty or pursuit should gain undue preëminence, and thereby wear out his physical strength. In this respect, of how different a temperament was Schiller ! With a share of Goethe's caution and worldly wisdom he probably would have enjoyed thirty years more of life, and completed the noble plans which he left in embryo. In his ordinary goings-on, it is clear enough that Goethe was very real, very workmanlike, yet very quiet and natural, consequently very wise. He did not forget that the brightest flowers may spring out of the darkest earth, and therefore set considerable store by that earth. He reflected that the dross had its value as well as the ore. With his romance was ever blended not only a due proportion of life's rudest realities, but also a strong spice of the sarcastic and contemptuous. There is not one among all his characters in which he speaks with such entire consistency, with so much *onction* and *verve* as in "Mephistopheles." One might suppose that Byron, as the poet of "Don Juan," was acting a part, perhaps a distasteful one, and that he had recourse to schiedam-and-water at midnight to keep him up under the self-imposed task ; but Goethe plays the devil with all his heart and *con gusto*.

The *platitudes*, the coarseness of "Wilhelm Meister," also of the "Dichtung und Wahrheït," of parts even in the "Tasso," are such as a half-witted critic might turn from with real or pretended wrath and disgust ; but in German phrase, all this *wurde mit fleiss gethan*, was done intentionally. It was the black setting from which sprang the brightest flowers, the heavy dross out of which the pure ore and indestructible gems

emerged, and shone resplendent. Jeffrey seems to have puzzled sadly over Mr. Carlyle's translation of "Wilhelm Meister," till he came to the author's analysis of the character of
"Hamlet." Then all at once his eyes were opened, and he
acknowledged the light of a master mind. In his every-day
manners, Goethe, according to my fancy, was perfectly simple
and *naïf;* his abstraction and taciturnity were not assumed
out of *hauteur,* for this would have implied an alloy of self-
conceit, moreover, a lurking deference for the opinions of Mrs.
Grundy; than which nothing could be more out of keeping
with that sort of contemptuous indifference with which, possibly enough, Goethe regarded all the world (himself, perhaps,
not excepted).

I know not how I have been led into these remarks, my object in these volumes having been to record events and impressions, not to enter into criticism. I began these critical
paragraphs by saying that Goethe, as a poet, had frequently
been overrated, and yet have already opposed my own assertion. Perhaps it is the leading characteristic of a truly original genius, that in the words of Oehlenschläger's "Correg-
gio," he is a riddle to all the world, and no less so to himself!
If the Danish Shakespeare, according to Sir T. Lawrence's
opinion, embodied in a drama the best illustrations that have
been given of the artist character, Goethe, in his "Tasso," had
previously aimed at doing the same thing by the poet, as con-
trasted with the man of the world; but in this instance, as it
appears to me, he has given too much of the dross and black-
setting; in plainer terms, he has ascribed too much of wildness and weakness to Tasso: so that on the whole the poet
becomes more an object of pity than of respect. But in this
way it is true that the lustre of particular passages comes out
with more effect, and their beauty dwells on remembrance indelibly.

As I have said elsewhere, this notable drama presents
Goethe's conceptions of a single day spent at Belriguardo, the
country-house of Alphonso, Duke of Ferrara, with no other
dramatis personæ but the said duke, Torquato Tasso, a state

secretary named Antonio, and two young ladies, namely Leonora d'Este, the Duke's sister, and her friend the Countess Leonora Sanvitale. Technically speaking, there is little or no dramatic action. The interest chiefly hinges on, we cannot say the adventures, but rather the psychological phenomena arising within a space of about twelve hours in the irritable mind of Tasso; who placed amidst the most amiable, kind, and accomplished society, yet contrives to render himself miserable, and to torment or disappoint all those by whom he is surrounded, more especially the amiable, sensitive, learned, and romantic Princess Leonora, who has been led to take the liveliest interest in his behalf, and to whom he is fervently but insanely attached. It is, in short, an illustration of the poetical character with all its eccentricities, as Goethe supposed it to exist in this justly celebrated author yet most capricious and unhappy of beings. That such eccentricities are *inevitable*, it would be too much to say, because at least their indulgence may be kept under control; but that such are the natural concomitants of poetic genius, I suppose must be admitted as an undeniable proposition. Byron, who pretended to sneer at morbid sensibility, has himself observed —

> "'T is to create, and in creating live
> A being more intense, that we endow
> With form our fancies, gaining as we give
> The life we image."

And to what does this creative propensity owe its origin, except to more acute intuitions and more vivid conceptions than fall to the lot of other men? If one must look at all times through the same *lens* or Claude Lorraine glass, will it not equally exercise the same magnifying or coloring power on all objects? And is not the poet thus naturally inclined to view every event or situation in a light different from that in which it appears to less excitable and colder-blooded mortals?

The first passage which occurs to me as memorable, is the Countess Sanvitale's eulogy of Tasso, in answer to her friend, who has rallied her on the poet's attentions.

> " I must endure thy jest.   It strikes indeed,
> But wounds me not.   I judge of every man
> By his deserts, and only render Tasso
> The praise he merits.   Evermore awake
> To heavenly unison, he scarcely seems
> To fix his eyes on this our common earth.
> What history or experience can afford,
> He grasps in fragments ; yet from them brings forth
> A grand symmetric whole, by his own fervor
> Enlivening that which else were cold and dead.
> What others treat with scorn he oft ennobles,
> Or from some object of our special favor
> Tears off its wonted garniture.   So moves
> This man within his orb like an enchanter ;
> Yet to his magic circle are we drawn
> By bonds invisible.   *He seems to greet us,*
> *Yet is in spirit far remote.   His looks*
> *Are fixed on us, but in our place perchance,*
> *He sees unearthly forms !* "

The next, I think, is eminently beautiful : it is from a dialogue betwixt the Countess and the poet, when the former visits him in his confinement : —

> " *Leonora.*   Tasso, what means this ?
> All are astonished.   Whither now have fled
> Thy wonted mildness, caution, penetration ?
> Thy judgment unto each awarding rightly
> What unto each belongs ?   Thy prudent sway
> O'er lips and tongue ?   Scarce can I recognize thee !
>   *Tasso.*   And if those virtues were forever lost ?
> If in the friend once affluent, thou found'st
> A groveling beggar ?   Thou art in the right ;
> I am no more myself, and yet remain
> Even what I was.   A paradox it seems,
> And yet is none.   *The beauteous moon whose light*
> *So pensive and so pure, by night attracts thee —*
> *That self-same moon glides through the skies by day,*
> *A pale and rayless cloud.*   I am obscured
> By noon-tide glare.   You know me not, and from
> Myself I feel estranged ! "

I shall venture on two more brief extracts.   The next shall be from one of Tasso's long soliloquies in prison : —

> " Yes ; all forsake me now !   Even thou, Leonora !
> In those dark hours, no token has she sent,
> Of her remembrance.   Have I then deserved this,
> Whose heart so naturally did adore her,

With deep emotions to her slightest voice
Responding? By her presence, in mine eyes,
The sunbeams were outshone, and as I caught
The fascination of her look or smile,
Resistless seemed the impulse to fall prostrate,
And worship such perfections!   But no more
Of this delusion!   *By the clear cold light
Of merciless truth,* I must perceive and own
The change that I so gladly would conceal! —
I *will* not, and yet *must* believe the change.
Leonora too! — Accuse her not, but yet,
No longer be deceived; like all the rest,
Leonora, too, forsakes thee!
These dread words,
Whose import, long as in my heart remained
One lingering gleam of hope, I should have questioned,
Those words are now with iron pen engraved
On the full tablet of my miseries,
Indelibly, like Fate's eternal doom! —
Now first, mine enemies are unconquerable,
And I indeed am powerless! If she, too,
Must in the ranks appear, how shall I combat,
Or how endure mine injuries, if from her
Nor look nor gesture cheers the supplicant?
The words are spoken; thou hast dared to frame them,
And they were true, while no suspicion crossed thee.
Naught then remains, but with the expiring force
Of consciousness and reason to lament,
And in thy lamentations to repeat
The direful truth — *Leonora too forsakes thee!* "

My last extract shall be from the final colloquy of Tasso
with Antonio (the " man of the world "), in which the poet's
comparison of himself to the storm-driven wave, appears to
me equally fine with the passage already quoted in allusion to
the moon as a pale rayless cloud.

> " *Tasso.*   And am I so deeply fallen,
> So weak as in thy sight I have appeared?
> Has pain o'erthrown the fabric of the mind,
> Leaving a heap of ruins, whence no fragment
> Of intellect, once powerful, can be drawn
> For my support and guidance?   Is all fervor
> Quenched and extinguished in this heart? Aye, truly,
> The world surrounds me, but *I am no more!*
> The soul's identity is lost.
>   *Antonio.*   And yet,
> Thou liv'st.   Then summon fortitude, and learn
> To know thyself even as thou art.

> *Tasso.* I thank thee
> For such admonishment.   In lore historic,
> Might I not find again some proud example,
> Some hero that had suffered more.than I,
> And with his fate compare mine own, thus gaining
> The fortitude that I have lost ?   But no, —
> 'T is vain and hopeless all.   If man's affliction
> Exceeds endurance, Nature has provided
> One only solace, — tears and lamentations.
> But to the POET, in his grief is given
> The power to weave into melodious numbers
> His fiercest of emotions, and this power
> Has Heaven vouchsafed me."

With an expression of friendly interest and compassion, Antonio here takes him by the hand, and Tasso resumes : —

> " In thy wisdom thou
> Stand'st like the rock, so firmly and exalted,
> Whilst I am like the wave by tempests driven !
> But of thy strength be not too proud.   Those laws
> Omnipotent that fixed the rigid rock
> Gave also to the wave its quivering motion.
> The storm awakes ; the helpless wave is borne
> In headlong furious course, revolving, foaming !
> But on its bosom once, *ere thus assailed,*
> How beauteously the sunlight and the moon
> With all her bright attendants were reflected !
> That bosom is of peace bereft ; the light
> Of Heaven *no longer* finds therein a mirror !

> Amid the tempest's rage, I can no more
> Even recognize myself.   The helm is broken,
> The ship in every timber cracks ; the floor
> Is rent beneath my steps.   I cling to thee,
> With both arms thus, as to the rugged cliff
> Whereon his vessel struck, the mariner
> At last cleaves for protection."

I had not intended to transcribe more, but, by way of variety and contrast, feel inclined to add from the same old repertory, an epigram containing Goethe's notions of a reviewer.   I translated it from recollection of an engraving in an old *taschenbuch*, accompanied by the verses ; but I believe my version is sufficiently accurate : —

"You make a feast, you spread the hoard
With all your larder can afford —
Fish, fowl, and flesh ; then comes a guest,
Who eats as if he were possessed,
Tears up and hacks your savory roasts,
And of his gluttonous prowess boasts.
Thereafter, through the town he goes,
Resolved your folly to expose,
In throwing pearls before a swine.
'Your soup was thin ; austere your wine ;
Your venison was not larded well ;
You had not truffle nor morel,
For sauce to capons tough, that looked
As if with soot and cinders cooked.
In short, 't is true as he 's a sinner,
You know not how to give a dinner.'
So croaks the cormorant, and repeats
His obloquy to all he meets.
Who could such insolence endure ?
Go, hang the dog ! HE'S A REVIEWER ! "

WILLIAM TENNENT.

I must not overlook Dr. Willam Tennent, who for some years resided most contentedly at Lasswade, as parish school-master of that humble village, and who, I presume, is living still as a dignified professor at the secluded college of Dollar. The village itself would warrant some especial notice, were it for no more than that it most probably afforded the prototype for Sir Walter Scott's "Gandercleugh." It was an easy mat-ter for the poet's imagination to convert the ruins of the de-serted old church and gloomy church-yard into the remains of an old monastery or abbey, and besides this, it was only need-ful to suppose that Lasswade was fifty miles distant from Ed-inburgh, in order to establish the resemblance and analogy. The learned and astute Dr. Tennent, it is true, could not so well have been lowered down and degenerated into " Jede-diah," but he happened not to assume his functions until after the " Tales of my Landlord " were commenced.

Strangely enough, in a labored article of the " Edinburgh Review," William Tennent and James Hogg were classed to-gether, though the only point of analogy betwixt them was, that they both emerged from the lowest grades of poverty. I recollect well the first demonstrations of the former as an author, when, under the *anonyme* of "William Ready-to-halt" (in allusion both to the "Pilgrim's Progress" and his own excessive lameness), he sent the first manuscript of "Anster Fair" to Doctor Robert Anderson, who gave it me to read. The Doctor was puzzled, and so was I. Not perceiving and not being informed that the humorous and utterly unknown author had already studied the Italian writers of *ottava rima*, and had found among them examples of buffoonery and extravaganza, which by precedent warranted the dance of Maggie Lauder's mustard-pot, we could not imagine in what school he had *noviciated*, nor what he was driving at. I suppose the public understood him no better, but Dr. Tennent troubled himself very little about their decisions, being in truth far more inclined to turn into ridicule the criticisms of *soi-disant* judges, who in their luxurious elbow-chairs and surrounded by books, were not half so learned and laborious as he was in his loneliness and poverty. Truly, if a new series of that popular work, "The Pursuit of Knowledge under Difficulties," were attempted, Dr. Tennent ought to hold in it a distinguished place.

Of all the self-educated poets that I have ever known or heard of, Tennent and Hogg were in their views of literary duty the most incongruous and dissimilar. The former went even beyond my old ally, John Pinkerton, in his notions of the necessity for book-learning. He looked upon facility and rapidity of composition with a mixture of wrath and scorn, insisting that such work was no better than twisting ropes of sand, or building without a foundation. Notwithstanding his lameness and inability to move without crutches, he had marvelous strength of constitution and unconquerable spirits. Whilst at Lasswade, he rose, summer and winter, at five o'clock, in order that he might have time for his private studies before his irksome duties as pedagogue began. In the evenings he did not flag, but unless a neighbor came to partake of a jug of toddy, resumed his labors. Tennent's leading crotchet was, that, by dint of lonely application, without any collaborator or any help but that of books, he would gradually command all languages, but more especially the Oriental. I have heard him complain of want of time, but never of weariness or want of power. Difficulties with him were always conquerable. He would teach himself and teach others ; but his soul disdained the notion of *being taught*. One result of all this was a very dictatorial and pompous manner of speech which I did not admire, and which our mutual friend, James Hogg, could not tolerate. But notwithstanding the peculiarities of our world, merit like his could not be suffered to remain over-clouded in the school-room at Lasswade. I lost sight of him after he went to the college at Dollar.

MRS. SIDDONS.

I remember, like a dream, that Mrs. Siddons came to Edinburgh that winter, — I think it was in the month of February, and probably it was her last appearance among us. She played all her best parts, but did not stay to repeat any of them. As might be expected, the greatest rush and pressure was to see her unequaled Lady Macbeth. I remember meeting in the lobby Mr. Dugald Stewart, who was quite as much puzzled how to find a place as I was, the box to which he had been specially invited, being already over-crammed. I know not what became of him in the crowd, but I clambered to the "slips," and made the most of my station there. Imagination, it has been said, transcends reality, and sometimes no doubt this is true ; but I believe no one ever imagined of Mrs. Siddons that which she did not more than realize. The same might be said of Miss O'Neill, great as was, in other respects, the contrast betwixt them. According to my humble notions, however, the natural and unequaled dignity of Mrs. Siddons was not *wholly* in keeping with the real character of Macbeth's atrocious wife. In the demon conceived by the poet, there is a passionate fierceness, an anxiety visible through the disguise of calmness which are not reconcilable with that sustained dignity or solemnity of which Mrs. Siddons could not, upon any occasion, not even in ordinary life, divest herself.

JAMES GRAY.

Gray was one of the masters of the High School at Edinburgh, and in that capacity was most attentive to his duties and highly respected. He was an excellent Greek scholar, a veritable enthusiast in all his undertakings, and a man of original genius. He married Miss Peacock, a poetess and voluminous letter-writer, who had, I think, been acquainted with Burns. Gray himself had that honor, and among poor Burns's associates was perhaps the only man surviving who had any pretensions to literary talent. Hence, Mr. Wordsworth addressed to him his letter on the character of our national poet, which was published in the year 1815 or 1816. For genius, or even the semblance of genius in every phasis, James Gray felt the most sincere and ardent sympathy. He seemed always on the watch for its demonstrations, and his humble abode at St. Leonards, especially at the dinner-hour, became a sort of rendezvous or club-house for *soi-disant* poets, some of whom little deserved his patronage. Greatly to his honor, James Hogg often remonstrated, but in vain, against the expense and inconvenience of such hospitality, by which he himself would not profit except sparingly, and which he too truly predicted would one day lead to serious embarrassment. There was another point of difference betwixt them, which sometimes led to ridiculous disputes. Truly zealous for the honor and fame of the Shepherd, Gray wished him to read and study, as well as to write, and directed his attention to the fact that Shakespeare, though risen from the station of a link-boy, and self-educated, became possessed of extensive acquirements and learning. But James Hogg was obdurate in his contempt for books, whether old or new. Not even the example of Shakespeare nor the exaggeration of the implied compliment, could propitiate him. He would work out his own reveries upon the "sclate," after his own fashion, and this was all. Nevertheless, he took up by rote divers of Gray's Latin phrases, and in his prose writings used to table them at hap-hazard.

Worthy James Gray ! He rose early and studied late. He

was generous and high-spirited; "obscurely wise and coarsely kind." His greatest luxury or happiness was when, during the long vacations, he could set out, accompanied by his wife, in long pedestrian excursions through the remote Highlands. But he had a family, as well as a squad of parasitical genii to provide for. Embarrassments thickened at last, as Hogg had predicted ; and, as usual in such cases, he found in the hour of adversity that he was "no prophet in his own land." He gave up his appointments, and with strong testimonials in his pocket, as to learning and moral worth, came to London, where, by some means or another, he succeeded in obtaining a clerical employment in the East Indies ; after which I heard no more of him, except that he and his wife soon died there.

WILLIAM SCOTT IRVING.

He wrote and published a long poem, with notes, entitled "Fair Helen of Kirkconnel," dedicated to Sir John Heron Maxwell; from whom, doubtless, he expected patronage ; but I suppose that worthy baronet worshipped more steadily at the shrine of Plutus than of Apollo ; for I did not hear of any wealth flowing from his coffers into the empty purse of the poet. Irving covered reams of paper with his various productions, in prose and verse ; yet all that he wrote bore the fatal stamp, not of plagiarism, but of undeniable imitatorship. Almost invariably he labored to make a ballad or a book in the style of Scott or Byron, but *haud passibus equis*. Supposing, however, that he had come nearer to his models, his reception would not have been any better. Our wise public were contented with Scott and Byron, and by no means wanted to see a reduplication or double of either in the person of Mr. Irving. He had a wife and family, this poor man, and thought to support them by serving pertinaciously at the Muses' shrine. But, seemingly, neither the Muses nor any one else cared a straw about his services. At length he sank into the most abject poverty ; yet, if on any day he found some one ready to do him the " God-like favor " (his own phrase) of administering a "pound note," he would instantly set himself at his desk

again, and work night and day for the next week. Over and
over I tried, as Gray and others did, to get him regular employment as a teacher of writing, arithmetic, book-keeping,
and geometry, for which he was not unqualified ; but though
we succeeded in finding him pupils, his poetical propensity
was a monomania that came betwixt him and every rational
pursuit. Again and again he applied by letters to his friends
for pecuniary aid, till the notion of his real miseries was obliterated, and they thought of him only as a persevering mendi-
cant. I cannot accuse myself of having ever in any instance
repulsed his applications ; as little did Sir Walter Scott or
James Gray, but others did, especially those who were best
able to help. The end was, that one morning he wound up
his reckonings for this world, precisely in the same method,
and with the same sort of instrument, which Lord Prime Minister Castlereagh adopted about the same epoch. Rather sarcastically James Hogg observed, that for once in his life William Irving had shown good sense, inasmuch as the act of
suicide was the only effectual step he could take in order to
please the world, whom for years past he had striven in vain
to propitiate. Of this poor victim Sir W. Scott once remarked,
that in his opinion, " Irving had come the nearest to being a
poet of any man who ever missed."

JOHN GALT.

Among Blackwood's new allies, John Galt held a distinguished place ; having, doubtless, exhibited a notable vein of
originality, inasmuch as he contrived, by a quaint style of eccentric *naïveté*, to render even the merest platitudes diverting.
I suspect such productions would not *tell* equally nowadays,
but at that time, his " Ayrshire Legatees," and other works of
the same class, were very popular. For once the old maxim
was reversed ; for with him easy writing made easy and pleasant reading. He might, therefore, well suppose, as he too
rashly did, that the road to fame and wealth by literature was
open and smooth before him ; for he could have scribbled such
things, *ad infinitum*, and found no end to the ridiculous exhi-

bitions of Scottish character and phraseology in which he delighted.

I have already remarked, rather querulously, how few in number are the characters one meets with during a long life, that deserve any special commemoration. Galt's career was the more remarkable, as he took to literature under circumstances which, though not strictly analogous to those of the Ettrick Shepherd, might be considered almost equally unfavorable, for he was educated exclusively for pursuits of trade and commerce — was, in his literary capacity, self-educated, and to scholastic acquirements made no pretension ; yet, having once commenced as an author, he showed no little *verve* and perseverance. He cared not for obstacles nor failures, and one of his favorite maxims was, that book-making being at best a kind of lottery chance, he could by merely keeping the pen in hand, begin and end a work in less time than a fastidious author would consume in laying his plans and debating *how* the thing was to be done. But in the various works published for him by Blackwood, he could by no means be stigmatized as a mere book-maker, for in all of them were traces of observation on real life and manners ; and they were attractive accordingly. Some years later, and for other publishers, he carried his principles of composition *à l'outrance*, by finishing no less than three romances, or novels, of three volumes each, in little more than six months. For the first of that mechanical series I believe he received £500, and he reckoned on an equal sum for the second and third. When, with the freedom of friendship, I remonstrated against this fatal facility, he answered briskly, "Where's the harm ? It answers a temporary purpose both of author and publisher. As to reputation, posthumous fame, and all that sort of thing, you little suspect how much I shall accomplish within two or three years more ! " At that date (about 1824), he seemed to indite books as readily and pertinaciously as he would have scribbled mercantile letters, and often averred to me that his literary resources were far greater in extent than those of Sir Walter Scott or any other contemporary ; moreover, and on the faith of these plans, he had bargained for, or actually purchased, a small property on the sea-shore, I forget in what county. And there, for his home and *studio*, his *pied à terre*, he intended building a veritable fortress, a petty stronghold, exactly in the fashion of the oldest times of rude warfare. It was to be a miniature edition, or single tower of Dunstaffnage, or Dunnottar, I believe, and was to stand upon a rock, near enough to be washed by the sea spray, where in safety he could contemplate from his windows the grandeur of the storm. He had arranged even the details of his future *ménage*, even to the stock of wines wherewith he would open his cellar, and the number of select friends who were to be welcomed !

I do not doubt that all this would have been realized, had not Galt's disposition, strange to say, been as versatile as it was obstinate. *Malgré* the attention which he bestowed on novels and magazines, he was always revolving questions political and statistical. He had parliamentary friends, whom he well knew how to retain. He appeared always at his ease and independent, kept lodgings constantly in Downing Street, had great placidity and amenity of manners, and looked and talked very wisely. All of a sudden, when he appeared settled, *en famille*, at Eskgrove, (once the home of a judge who bore that title), he disappeared from our literary circles, having obtained from government a good appointment (a commissionership of some sort or another) in Canada. The next I heard of Galt was, that, from causes which are detailed in his autobiography, he had got into disputes with authorities at head-quarters. Regardless of his immediate pecuniary interests, he quitted his post, and, in order to have his grievances redressed, he came back to London, where, shortly after his arrival, he was arrested for a debt of eighty pounds, claimed (as Dr. Maginn informed me) either by the Rev. Dr. ——, or by some one of the Doctor's learned and amiable family.

Doubtless, had the worthy creditor been cross-questioned, he would have disclaimed the slightest shade of animosity or hostility towards Galt, whose character for probity and fair dealing was unimpeachable, and would have pleaded that he desired nothing more nor less than strict justice, and the assertion of his rights according to law. I was in London then, and I remember how differently Galt viewed the question. In his opinion legal power was one thing, but right or justice another. The result of this proceeding was, that, in *dour* silence and with imperturbable stoicism, he suffered a long confinement, during which, in solitude, he wrote "Laurie Todd," in three volumes. The learned and reverend creditor did not receive one sixpence, and Galt was irretrievably injured in mind, body, and estate. Stoicism may teach to bear, but cannot blunt painful feelings. His constitution that had appeared invulnerable, suffered irreparably from the restraint to which he had been so little accustomed. The end was repeated attacks of paralysis, with which he contended for the short remainder of his life, and for which he endured the most painful treatment in vain. Return to his official duties became out of the question, but he wrote or dictated even to his last moments.

William Maginn.

Up to the year 1827, and for some years afterwards, Dr. Maginn retained all that buoyancy and elasticity of spirit for which, naturally, he was so remarkable, and which it *then* seemed as if no trials or pressure could subdue. So little had his habits, either of daily task work or conviviality, injured his nerves, that he enjoyed our excursion with all the zest of a school-boy broke loose for a holiday. The only darkening trace left by his intercourse with the world and its ways were betrayed by his disposition to make sarcastic remarks on leading characters of the day, sparing neither Tory nor Whig. Yet his was ever a playful kind of sarcasm, entirely free from any bitter alloy of misanthropy and rancor : to such feelings, indeed, he was of all men I ever knew the most impassive ; insomuch that if his worst enemy had fallen into a state of suffering and distress, on hearing of the circumstances he would have hurried away at his most rapid pace, to find out whether he could render any assistance.

At this distance of time, to attempt recapitulating our conversation during a two miles'.walk would be absurd ; wild and desultory it was no doubt, a very perfect example of the style which the French call *abandon*. And yet I remember that some part of our talk turned on subjects which, it might have been supposed, were very much out of his way. The discussion, however, arose naturally enough, because as editor then of a new Quarterly Review, I had received some elaborate papers on metaphysical subjects, by the contents of which I felt puzzled. If deep, they were not clear, either in matter or style ; and on this occasion I felt astounded, as many of his friends must at other times have been, at the extent and variety of his reading, and the accuracy and readiness with which he could bring it to bear on any analogous topic of the moment. Not only mediæval logicians, but fathers of the church, folios of St. Gregory, St. Basil, and St. Thomas of Aquino, which, judging by his usual occupations and disposition, he never could have opened, were even familiar to him. He could cite their decisions on intricate questions, and undertake to point out the identical passages if needful.

In Dr. Maginn's literary character there was one leading trait, which, during the course of a long life, I have always found to be of most rare occurrence, namely, that to great vivacity and quickness of apprehension and feelings, he united patience, perseverance, and amenity of temper. For this virtue of perseverance, indeed, as applicable to any separate and exclusive line of study, his life in London, from its commencement to its untimely close, allowed him no opportunities whatsoever. In Ireland, as I believe, his position had been such, that by continuing his employment there he might have enjoyed a competent income, and yet have had some hours daily at his command for literary undertakings ; but London allured him, as it has allured hundreds of others, into its fatal vortex. The well-intentioned, but not so well-judged, advice and invitations of friends conspired to rivet his destiny. That perfect command which he seemed to exercise over his own faculties, the almost unexampled facility and readiness with which he could write in verse or prose on any given subject, rendered his aid of preëminent value in periodical literature, but especially in productions of the daily and weekly press. The result naturally was, that engagements in this department were proffered to him, nay, crowded on his attention from the first week of his arrival in town. He accepted such as a matter of course, and never afterwards, until disabled by adversity and illness, was allowed to pause in his desultory career, — a career indeed unworthy of his high talents, and uncongenial to the real bent of his mind, which I suspect was, even among his professing friends, but little understood and appreciated.

At our first meeting in Edinburgh, when I earnestly pressed on his attention the plan of sojourning there, he designated himself as a mere "scrap-writer," for which occupation London, as he said, afforded the best field. The term jarred on my ears then, as it does now. Too true it was, that in consequence of his daily engagements to the organs of a party, he had become a scrap-writer, and not having any independent fortune, he never could emancipate himself from the yoke. By talents, by acquirements, by unconquerable patience and equanimity, Maginn was qualified for works of long laborious research, and the nicest critical investigations. Nor was he less capable of romantic and poetical invention. But a family depended on his exertions ; the wants of the day and of the week must be supplied. He must write, although *invitâ Minervâ*, on the topics of last night's debate, evanescent and paltry as their interest might be. The longest and most sustained efforts which circumstances allowed him to make, were only fugitive chapters for magazines and reviews.

Patience and good-humor might and did render this kind of life supportable ; the burden was borne with such apparent ease that by-standers did not suspect its weight ; but by no possibility could such broken and desultory application prove sanative, cheering, or in the long run prosperous. His contributions to magazines had, no doubt, a liveliness and *verve*, joined with a command of language which few have equaled. And yet, these essays were for the most part written so hastily, and under such pressure, that I have heard him avow again and again, with transient bitterness, that he scarcely ever sent such papers to the printer without feeling an almost irrepressible impulse to throw them into the fire. It argued, indeed, but little presumption on the part of Maginn's nearest friends and relatives if they sometimes entertained hopes that, after his long services and steadfast adherence to the Tory party, he should be protected against such pressure. But neither place nor pension, rarely even a well-filled purse to meet an emergency, fell in his way. It is true enough that excuses can easily be made for the wealthy leaders of that party ; for his own conduct was such as to leave them in ignorance of his real situation. His constant habit of suppressing all notions of *self*, his cheerfulness and willingness to be occupied with engagements which did bring remuneration, however vacillating and inadequate, were enough to deceive lookers-on, and lead them to believe that he had sufficient resources. During his *last* days of suffering, Sir Robert Peel, as on some former occasions, stood preëminent in his kindness and liberality to this man of learning and genius. I do not forget that towards the same melancholy epoch the King of Hanover and Lord G. Somerset manifested their sympathy.

But the relief came too late. The same funds which were then applied might, if obtained twelve months earlier, have saved his life.

During long experience I have scarcely ever met with any one better fitted than he was to live happily and economically in a quiet country home, where in applying his excellent talents to literary tasks not of an ephemeral character, he might have secured both income and fame. But he had no such quiet home ; he had no sufficient capital whereon to fall back even *for a single year* until any regular work was completed. I have seldom or never known any one more affectionately attached to his family, yet by the force of external circumstances he was from them too often (though not in heart), disunited and dissevered. Provident he certainly was — for their sakes anxiously and conscientiously provident — having his plans well arranged and working daily at the top of his speed. Notwithstanding the temptations of life in London, of all places that where an author is most easily misled into reckless expenditure, and where he is most mercilessly treated if he falls into arrear, — notwithstanding such temptation, I firmly believe that up to the year 1830, or, I might say, 1833, Dr. Maginn had not contracted any obligations which his literary income, if continued, would not have enabled him to meet and to fulfill.

Gradually and steadily, despite of obstacles, he had risen in public estimation. His personal friends (among whom he reckoned many of high rank and ample fortune) were numerous, and by them he was *fêted* and flattered, having frequent invitations to assist at their jovial banquets. He had accepted regular employment as editor of the " Standard," a paper which, under his management, throve rapidly. Thus far and no farther he was over sanguine and improvident, namely, in cherishing the belief that he would be allowed to continue his occupations and to work his way up in the world. Already this newspaper afforded him £600 per annum, and by time and perseverance the profits might have been doubled. In his case, however, it must be allowed there were some arrears to be met. A proletarian or professional man in London, especially if he be of a generous disposition, cannot entirely escape such. Their liquidation, of course, depended on his continued industry and uninterrupted discharge of his editorial functions. But a literary man thus placed is, in London, watched with lynx eyes ; his steps are dogged wherever he wends his way. No sooner was it known that Maginn held a responsible and profitable situation, than his creditors, with that peculiar sagacity which belongs to the English creditor, aided by so-called English law, endeavored to dispossess him of it, by rendering him wholly incompetent to its duties. Against circumstances like these, patience and fortitude are evidently no protection. To bear with adversity and to conquer it, notwithstanding the poetical *dictum* on this matter, are widely different. He was injured and molested, of course, but contrived to rebut these wise proceedings for some time, and retain his usual place, but this could be done only by transactions which our clear-sighted world would call "reckless improvidence," by forestalling his income, and becoming more deeply involved. This mode of defense, this parrying of attacks could not last long. At last there came an *ultra* sagacious claimant, a man of decisive measures, who "would not be trifled with, no, not he!" and by this good creature, Maginn's *regular* course of employment was effectually cut short.

Not a murmur escaped him on that score, *c'était la fortune de guerre.* He was removed from his editorial desk, on which his income then principally depended, and for a time, consequently, debarred from intercourse with his family and friends. To these beneficial and prudent arrangements he submitted cheerfully and as a matter of course; although we read in Lockhart's "Memoirs" that the mere menace, the *imagined* possibility of such treatment, unhinged, paralyzed, and upset the strong mind of Sir Walter Scott for more than a week! But this first act of molestation and annoyance by no means disunited Maginn from his editorial duties — it only compromised his interests by cutting off his personal and regular attendance, and by increasing the amount of his embarrassments. After some time he resumed possession of the editor's room; but the sagacious example set by one creditor was soon followed by others. The next interruption was of longer duration, the third still worse, and at last he was forced to remain a year or more in the so-called "Liberty of the Rules," a pitiable resource; which, as being too great an indulgence, has of late been abolished. By repetition these wise proceedings absolutely broke up all his plans, carefully as they had been framed, and zealously as he would have carried them out. It is true enough, that to superficial and ordinary observers, Maginn seemed to meet such annoyances with perfect indifference; he could continue to write under any circumstances and in any place; but the superintendence and care which he had bestowed on the daily papers were, of course, at an end, and regularity of habits in regard to it or any other employment, became more and more hopeless and impossible.

From all this the question might naturally arise, had Dr. Maginn no real friends, or was he like the " hare with many friends ? " I should be a very unfair and indiscreet annalist, either as regards justice to his own memory or the reputation of others, if I allowed this question to remain unanswered. On one occasion a plan was suggested and organized by an intimate and sincere friend in order to buy off all his embarrassments, and it was munificently supported by Sir Robert Peel and others. But unluckily this kind adviser was not much experienced, if at all, in the beautiful workings of our so-called legal system. It had not been sufficiently taken into consideration, that the worshipful class of gentlemen attorneys in London (four or five thousand in number !) derived great part of their income from costs ; and that in almost every instance of Dr. Maginn's engagements, the original amount was thereby doubled. Friends were not wanting nor slow to manifest their good-will or liberality, but the original claims, and the rapacity of attorneys, *together* proved too much. The aggregate had not been duly reckoned, and enough was left unadjusted to embitter the remainder of his days. *Me ipso teste,* during the last seven years of his life, Dr. Maginn had constant pecuniary troubles ; but like his *ci-devant* friend and ally, Theodore Hook, he would allow no one, except his men of business or some very special confidant, to know or suspect this. In society he might have appeared the same as ever, only that his engagements being painfully multiplied, and his application more than ever broken and desultory, his manner also became more abrupt, his habits more irregular, and his nervous system too evidently shaken.

Sir Egerton Brydges.

But Sir Egerton — that model of an English gentleman, whose memory is most dear to all who knew him — that noblest of hearts, and bravest of spirits — to whom the relation in which I stood was that of worthless dross to the pure and brilliant diamond — had he himself escaped free from the effects of chance and change ? Alas, no ! The clouds that

impended at Abbotsford during my brief visit there, hung
darkly on the gothic halls and beautiful grounds at Lee. At
one and the same time, pecuniary embarrassments weighed
heavily both on Sir Egerton Brydges and Sir Walter Scott,
and dissimilar as the two cases were in many points, upon one
they were alike, namely, that both had been wronged and ca-
lumniated, also that both cherished under adversity a noble
courage and uniformity of purpose.

The points of difference were marked and obvious, for Sir
Egerton's literary pursuits had never in any instance been carried on with the remotest view to pecuniary gain. Sir Walter
Scott, on the contrary, avowed himself to be " born and bred
a man of business." Sir Egerton, though educated for the
bar, had never practiced ; and I fear he held the character of
a mere man of business in contempt. He had succeeded to
old family estates ; he claimed, with right, an ancient peerage ;
his property was extensive ; for many years he represented
Maidstone in Parliament, and his eldest son had inherited Mr.
Barrett's beautiful estate of Lee. Sir Egerton had not suffered, like Scott, by the bankruptcy of a speculative and deceptive bookseller ; but in the management of his estates he
had been scandalously wronged by rapacious attorneys and
dishonest receivers ; and of the embarrassments gradually
thence arising, there were not wanting individuals who ascribed
the whole blame to himself alone, although the entire tenor of
his life, being devoted to constant intellectual exertions, was
the very antithesis of luxury or vanity.

After several years' residence abroad, Sir Egerton had returned to Lee Priory, intending, I believe, to remain there, to
continue his literary employments, and perhaps to resume his
station in Parliament. But in England, if the plague-spot of
a mortgage once exists on the family acres, it festers and
spreads ; with the help of " clever and respectable " men of
business in the inns of court, one evil engenders another, till
at last the very air seems empoisoned. The woods and fields
appear tranquil, as of yore ; but, alas ! they are so, only for
the disengaged mind of a casual spectator. Their owner is

forced to view them through a darkening medium. The subjects which demanded Sir Egerton's attention after his return from the Continent, were such as to render his wonted pursuits impracticable. His disposition remained unchanged, his will was unalterable, but to give up his attention to literature became impossible. I presume he felt too keenly his sense of wrong, and the difference of his situation then from what it formerly had been. He declared that he felt his literary powers quite suspended, and seemed without hope of their reanimation. I feel convinced that had he not been persuaded by the late amiable and exemplary Colonel Barrett to return to the Continent, there could have been no such hope.

There has been no stage of these memoirs, at which I have more regretted being obliged to write in haste, than now. My recollections of Sir Egerton during a literary intercourse of twenty-five years, would require a separate volume, and I cannot at present write more than another page. But my remembrance is fresh and vivid of his kind and hospitable reception ; how many times in the course of that short evening, when " hours were thought down to moments," he reverted to the question, " Do not leave us, — do not go to-morrow ; " and, when I urged dire necessity, added, " But, at all events, fix your day for coming again," — and with what kind earnestness Lady Brydges proposed that my family would make Lee Priory their country quarters for next summer, "as at least there was room enough, and Sir Egerton would be so glad." These memoranda may seem too minute, too personal and particular, but, on the contrary, I think they should remain, not merely as feeble expressions of my own gratitude, but as evidence, to the honor of those deeply respected friends, that their kindness did not abate, though they well knew that, from being what is called "a man of substance," I had declined into dark, dreary Shadowism.

INDEX.

1. Three volumes may be taken at a time, and only three on one Share.

2. Books may be kept out 14 days, and, at request, may be renewed once. New books, bearing the " not renewable" label, cannot be renewed or transferred.

3. Books overdue are subject to a fine of one cent a day for fourteen days, *and five cents a day for each day thereafter.*

4. Neglect to pay the fine will debar from the use of the Library.

5. No book is to be lent out of the house of the person to whom it is charged.

6. Any person who shall soil (deface), or damage or lose a book belonging to the Library shall be liable to such fine as the Directors may impose; or shall pay the value of the book or of the set, if it be part of a set, as the Directors may elect. All scribbling or any marking or writing whatever, folding or turning down the leaves, as well as cutting or tearing any matter from a book belonging to the Library, will be considered defacement and damage.

7. No books shall be taken from the shelves by any person not employed in the Library, except such as are deposited in the Reading Room for reference, unless with the permission of the Librarian or a Director.

January, 1888.